IN CONTEXT

Teresa of Ávila, John of the Cross, and Their World

In Context

Teresa of Ávila, John of the Cross, and Their World

Mark O'Keefe, O.S.B.

ICS Publications
Institute of Carmelite Studies
Washington, D.C.

ICS Publications
2131 Lincoln Road NE
Washington, DC 20002-1199

www.icspublications.org

© Saint Meinrad Archabbey, 2020
Published with Ecclesiastical Approval

All rights reserved. No part of this book may be reproduced or transmitted in any form or by any means, electronic or mechanical, including photocopying, recording, or by any information, storage or retrieval system without prior written permission from the publisher.

Cover and text design and pagination by Rose Design
Printed in the United States of America

Cover image (center): Convent church of Santa Teresa de Jesus, UNESCO World Heritage Site. Avila city. Castilla León, Spain Europe. Contributor: Jerónimo Alba / Alamy Stock Photo.

Cover image (bottom): City view of Cordoba: John and Mary Osman Braun and Hogenberg Collection, Irvin Department of Rare Books and Special Collections, University of South Carolina Libraries, Columbia, S.C.

Library of Congress Cataloging-in-Publication Data

Names: O'Keefe, Mark, 1956- author.
Title: In context : Teresa of Ávila, John of the Cross, and their world / Mark O'Keefe, O.S.B.
Description: Washington, D.C. : ICS Publications, Institute of Carmelite Studies, [2019] | Includes bibliographical references and index.
Identifiers: LCCN 2019043103 | ISBN 9781939272850 (trade paperback) | ISBN 9781939272867 (ebook)
Subjects: LCSH: Catholic Church--Spain--History--16th century. | Spain--Church history--16th century. | Carmelites--Spain--History--16th century. | Teresa, of Avila, Saint, 1515-1582. | John of the Cross, Saint, 1542-1591. | Mysticism--Spain--History--16th century. | Monasticism and religious orders--Spain--History--16th century. | Inquisition--Spain. | Avila (Spain)--Social conditions--16th century.
Classification: LCC BX1584 .O54 2019 | DDC 282.092/246--dc23
LC record available at https://lccn.loc.gov/2019043103

ISBN: 978-1-939272-85-0

CONTENTS

A Word of Thanks vii
Foreword ix
Translations and Abbreviations xiii
Introduction xv

1 The Spanish World of the Sixteenth Century 1
2 The City of Ávila 24
3 Honor, Social Class, and Poverty 34
4 Reform of the Church and Religious Orders 60
5 The Carmelites 75
6 The Monastery of the Incarnation 100
7 Spiritual Antecedents 113
8 Alumbrados 151
9 Jews, Conversos, and the Spanish Inquisition ... 172
10 Teresa of Jesus: A Woman in
   Sixteenth-Century Spain 213

Conclusion 233
General Bibliography 237
Index 251
Other Books by Mark O'Keefe, o.s.b. 273

A WORD OF THANKS

I want to express my thanks to my faculty colleagues at Saint Meinrad Seminary and School of Theology who awarded me a research grant from the school's Adrian Fuerst Faculty Development Endowment. I also wish to offer my thanks to the successive abbots who have enabled and encouraged my study of Teresa and John (a Benedictine studying Carmelite mystics!): Lambert Reilly, O.S.B.; Justin DuVall, O.S.B.; and most recently Kurt Stasiak, O.S.B.

Again, as with the two previous books that I have been privileged to publish with ICS Publications, I want to express my sincere thanks to and admiration for its editorial director, Patricia Lynn Morrison, who ably shepherded and skillfully improved my texts. Her professional expertise and her knowledge of and love for Teresa of Jesus and John of the Cross have proven invaluable to my work.

I did the majority of the Spanish-language research for this project in the fine library of the Centro Internacional Teresiano Sanjuanista in Ávila. The staff there provided important professional and personal support for my work, and I remain grateful for their congeniality and friendship. I found many useful resources at the Herman B. Wells Library at Indiana University in Bloomington and in the Archabbey Library of Saint Meinrad Seminary and School of Theology. Although small and less scholarly by comparison to those already mentioned, the library of the Carmel of Saint Joseph in Terre Haute, Indiana, yielded a number of classics, especially concerning the Carmelites, their history and spirituality. It is for the nuns of that community that I am privileged to serve as chaplain, and it is with great love and respect that I dedicate this book to them.

FOREWORD

The Second Vatican Council (1962–1965) ended over a half century ago. Yet, graces and blessings from that historic event continue to enrich Christianity even while various interpretations of the council's teachings have evolved. For religious orders the council's impact on the study of their spiritual traditions has been momentous. Thus the Carmelite Order has been significantly blessed with a spirit of *ressourcement* (back to the classics). This movement, fostered by distinguished figures like the Dominican Yves Congar and the Jesuit Henri de Lubac, not only molded the work of the council, but it inspired the subsequent retrieval of various schools of spirituality in the church. Happily the spirit of *ressourcement* was already in place before the council at the Teresianum (Discalced Carmelites) and at the Institutum Carmelitanum (Carmelites of the Ancient Observance), both institutions are situated in Rome.

Father Mark O'Keefe, a monk of Saint Meinrad Archabbey, has published, in a spirit of *ressourcement*, *In Context: Teresa of Ávila, John of the Cross, and Their World*. The word "context" in the title of this book signals the author's intention: to explore the various situations that influenced the life and times of Teresa and John, two Carmelites who have been recognized as two of the best known and most influential Christian mystics. For too long readers had to read mystical texts without a knowledge of the historical, theological and other contexts of the Christian mystics. Too often mystics came across as disembodied spirits.

But, truth be told, a mystic's path is a pilgrimage through the everyday pain and joys of being human. They were not spared the tribulations that occur in the lives of humans the world over. An authentic mystic is on a journey in which she grows in love, the love that makes her resemble God and that shapes her into the person God created her to be yet without exempting her from the struggles humanity must endure. Mark O'Keefe's book overcomes the temptation of hagiography to paint the saints and mystics as flawless and even super human. That kind of hagiography is no favor to today's Christians who seek spiritual paths to God.

Jesuit theologian Bernard Lonergan, an expert in method, can help one understand what Fr. O'Keefe does as he explores contexts in the texts of Teresa and John. Such contexts form ". . . a nest of interlocked or interwoven questions and answers . . ."[1] that unearth the reality that make the mystics more approachable and understandable. For too long the study of mysticism was left exclusively in the hands of the experts. O'Keefe takes his readers behind the scenes of factual history to give his readers access to the backstories of Teresa and John. In this way O'Keefe enables readers to become more fully informed interpreters of the classical texts of the two Spanish Carmelite mystics. Experts have established reliable texts; translators like Father Kieran Kavanaugh have produced readable texts in English. Now Father Mark O'Keefe puts "flesh" on Teresian and sanjuanist texts, offering readers an opportunity to enlarge their horizons and so deepen their grasp of the wisdom of these two Doctors of the Church.

---

1. Bernard J. F. Lonergan, *Method in Theology* (New York: Herder and Herder, 1972), 163.

Father Mark O'Keefe brings impressive credentials to his research on the contexts of Teresa and John. With a doctorate in theology from the Catholic University of America, he has served as president-rector of Saint Meinrad School of Theology. He has published a five-book series on the priesthood besides four other books. Of special Carmelite interest are two books authored by O'Keefe: *Love Awakened by Love: The Liberating Ascent of Saint John of the Cross* (2014), and *The Way of Transformation: Saint Teresa of Ávila and the Foundation and Fruit of Prayer* (2016). Both of these books have been published by ICS Publications in Washington, D.C.

Readers of the texts on Teresa and John, O'Keefe's own and others, will find in his contextual study much helpful information, e.g., he has investigated Spain at the time of Teresa and John as well as cultural issues like the place of *honra* in Spanish society, the reforms of the church and of religious orders, the status at that time of the Carmelite Order, the Monastery of the Incarnation where Teresa spent many years, the Inquisition, Jews and *conversos*, Teresa as a woman of her time and much more. O'Keefe has produced a wide ranging exploration of the backstories of these two Carmelites who have made large imprints on the tapestry that is Carmelite spirituality and mysticism. The horizons of these two mystics seems endless as one gets to know their writings, their backgrounds and their significance for contemporary Christianity.

Saints Teresa of Jesus and John of the Cross have found their way into the spiritual literature of countless modern languages, but the books and articles written about them in Spanish is truly overwhelming. O'Keefe could never have explored all the vast Spanish literature on Teresa and John, but his command and exploration of Spanish Carmelite literature is a truly remarkable feat.

Readers of O'Keefe's books will find them to have a clarity and even an elegance not easy to achieve when one is dealing with complex issues. In addition each chapter is followed by pertinent bibliography with a general bibliography at the end of the book. Carmelite libraries as well as others will surely profit by including the Carmelite texts of Mark O'Keefe. My hope is that other authors who write in English will take his example by publishing contextual studies of other Carmelite saints and mystics.

KEITH J. EGAN, T. O. CARM.

Guest Professor of Theology,
University of Notre Dame

Joyce Hank Aquinas Chair in Catholic
Theology Emeritus, Saint Mary's College

TRANSLATIONS AND ABBREVIATIONS

Scripture quotations are from the *New Revised Standard Version Bible: Catholic Edition, Anglicized Text*, copyright ©1999, 1995, 1989, Division of Christian Education of the National Council of Churches of Christ of the United States of America. Used with permission. All rights reserved.

Teresa of Avila

All quotations from the works of Teresa of Avila are taken from *The Collected Works of St. Teresa of Avila*, trans. Kieran Kavanaugh, O.C.D., and Otilio Rodriguez, O.C.D., 3 vols. (Washington, D.C.: ICS Publications, 1976–1985, 1987, 2012).

The following abbreviations will be used in references to Teresa's works:

- Con   *The Constitutions*
- F   *The Book of the Foundations*
- IC   *The Interior Castle*
- L   *The Book of Her Life*
- Ltr   *Letters*
- SS   *Meditations on the Song of Songs*
- ST   *The Spiritual Testimonies*
- W   *The Way of Perfection*

In general, when cited in abbreviated form, the abbreviation of the work is given. The first number refers to the chapter, and the second number refers to the paragraph. Thus, W 3.5 refers to *The Way of Perfection*, chapter 3, paragraph 5. Regarding *The Interior Castle*, the first number refers to the dwelling place, the second number refers to the chapter, and the third number refers to the paragraph. Thus, IC 3.4.2 refers to the third dwelling place, chapter 4, paragraph 2.

John of the Cross

All quotations from the works of John of the Cross are taken from *The Collected Works of St. John of the Cross*, translated by Kieran Kavanaugh, O.C.D., and Otilio Rodriguez, O.C.D., rev. ed. (Washington, D.C.: ICS Publications, 1991).

Abbreviations for these works, as they appear in this book, are as follows:

- A   *The Ascent of Mount Carmel*
- C   *The Spiritual Canticle*
- F   *The Living Flame of Love*
- N   *The Dark Night*

References to particular texts within these works are indicated in the following way: For *The Ascent of Mount Carmel* and *The Dark Night*, the first number indicates the book, the second number refers to the chapter, and the third number indicates the paragraph. For example, A 2.3.4 would refer to *The Ascent*, book two, chapter 3, and paragraph 4. In a similar manner, for *The Spiritual Canticle* and *The Living Flame of Love*, the first number refers to the stanza and the second number to the paragraph. Thus, C 3.4 is a reference to the commentary on stanza 3, paragraph 4 of *The Spiritual Canticle*.

INTRODUCTION

Teresa of Ávila (1515–1582) and John of the Cross (1542–1591) are two of the most influential and well-known mystical writers in the Christian tradition. Their works are available in every major language, published in new editions and translations since shortly after their deaths.[1] Virtually every serious subsequent Christian reflection on advanced prayer, contemplation, and mysticism has referenced and even depended on their distinctive insights. It is no wonder that their perennial spiritual insights and teaching resulted in both of them being named Doctors of the Church—John of the Cross in 1926 and Teresa in 1970 (the first woman so honored, together with Catherine of Siena). Countless Christians and other spiritual searchers have read Teresa's *Life* (sometimes inaccurately called her "autobiography"), *The Way of Perfection*, or *The Interior Castle*. Although reading John of the Cross's works are often considered more daunting, many have dived into his *Dark Night* or *Ascent of Mt. Carmel* with great profit. Biographies abound,

---

1. The contemporary English translations of the complete works of both authors are available from ICS Publications (the Institute of Carmelite Studies) in Washington, D.C., translated by Kieran Kavanaugh, O.C.D., and Otilio Rodriguez, O.C.D. See the select bibliography at the end of this introduction for the full references. In addition, ICS Publications has also released study editions of these texts, including commentary. Earlier English translations by E. Allison Peers are also widely available and remain highly respected.

both scholarly and popular, especially of Teresa. There is a vast literature on their lives, writings, and thought.[2]

Even without drawing upon available commentaries, simply reading the works and biographies of Teresa and John have proven fruitful to countless numbers of men and women. And yet, like reading biblical texts, we know that a more profound understanding of these mystics requires deeper knowledge of the context in which they lived, were formed, and wrote. We can gain great benefit from simply reading the Gospels and the letters of St. Paul with attention and faith, but a deeper grasp of these texts requires knowing as much as we can about the presumed authors, their historical and cultural contexts, and their original audiences/readers. This is no less true of the writings of saints and mystical writers throughout the Christian tradition. Every text is more completely grasped in its context. And every life is understood more thoroughly when it is seen within its surrounding culture and time.

The need to examine this context—historical, cultural, intellectual, ecclesiastical, and spiritual—became apparent to me as I began my previous work in preparation for studies of John of the Cross and Teresa of Jesus.[3] I found that many authors,

---

2. A comprehensive bibliography of works about John of the Cross published in the year 2000 contains 6,328 entries, spread over 725 pages. See Miguel Diego Sánchez, *Bibliografía sistemática de San Juan de la Cruz* (Madrid: Editorial de Espiritualidad, 2000). A comprehensive bibliography of works about Teresa of Jesus published in 2008 contains 12,647 entries, spread over 1,246 pages—and this is prior to the explosion of articles and books on Teresa around the five hundredth anniversary of her birth in 2015! See Miguel Diego Sánchez, *Bibliografía sistemática de Santa Teresa de Jesús* (Madrid: Editorial de Espiritualidad, 2008).

3. Mark O'Keefe, *Love Awakened by Love: The Liberating Ascent of Saint John of the Cross* (Washington, D.C.: ICS Publications, 2014); Mark O'Keefe, *The Way of Transformation: Saint Teresa of Avila on the Foundation and Fruit of Prayer* (Washington, D.C.: ICS Publications, 2016).

recognizing the need for this contextual background (especially biographical studies), did provide the basic information critical to their own particular focus. But it was difficult to find in English—and in one place—what is much more abundant in Spanish (as the bibliography will show): studies that focus broadly on the frame of reference for a deeper reading of Teresa of Jesus and John of the Cross.[4] And thus I decided to take up this work in order to benefit people like myself who are interested in delving more deeply into their lives and work but who may lack the time or resources to access the available materials.

As might be expected, there is an abundance of studies in Spanish that examine the background for a more profound reading of Teresa and John—that is, on the topics covered in this book. But these works might be difficult to locate or to read for many English speakers and especially for nonscholars. It is my purpose to make some of the principal insights from contextual studies available to a wider audience and, through footnotes and bibliographies, to direct interested readers to further resources. In doing so, I have tried to be thorough in examining the many books noted in my bibliography—without claiming to be exhaustive. In the end, I am not a Carmelite, a historian, or a professor of spirituality, nor am I truly expert in the many other disciplines that might take up the topics to be found here. Because of both the need to narrow my research and my own

---

4. Two notable exceptions are Federico Ruiz Salvador, ed., *God Speaks in the Night: The Life, Times, and Teaching of St. John of the Cross*, trans. Kieran Kavanaugh (Washington, D.C.: ICS Publications, 1991, 2000); and Tomás Álvarez, *St. Teresa of Ávila: 100 Themes on Her Life and Work* (Washington, D.C.: ICS Publications, 2011). The companion piece to the latter, on John of the Cross, is not yet available in English: José Vicente Rodríguez, *100 fichas sobre San Juan de la Cruz: Para aprender y enseñar* (Burgos, Spain: Editorial Monte Carmelo, 2008).

linguistic limitations, I have restricted my research to English and Spanish sources. Many more valuable works can be found in other languages—especially in French, Italian, and German—but I have judged that the majority of the foundational insights for understanding the context of these two Spanish mystics can be found in Spanish sources.

The book opens with a brief overview in chapter 1 of some major events and cultural factors present in the sixteenth-century Spain in which Teresa and John lived—the so-called Golden Century (*Siglo de Oro*). It is followed in chapter 2 by a closer look at the city of Ávila in which Teresa was born, grew up, entered religious life, and began her Discalced Reform. John of the Cross, born within the same province, spent several years there as confessor to the nuns of the Monastery of the Incarnation. Chapter 3 looks at the sixteenth-century Spanish obsession concerning honor and social class as well as the reality of poverty, setting up a contrast between the social concerns and reality of Teresa's well-to-do family and that of John's poverty-stricken family. In chapter 4, we focus our attention on the reform movements in the church and within religious orders that marked the sixteenth century and those that preceded it. Both the Discalced Reform and the distinctive spirituality of Teresa and John are a special piece of the fabric of these wider developments. A brief history of the Carmelite Order in chapter 5 sets the stage to understand the tangle and conflict surrounding the Discalced Reform in which both Teresa and John found themselves engulfed. A look, in chapter 6, at the Monastery of the Incarnation in which Teresa was professed, but that she ultimately left, helps us to understand more clearly the actual focus of Teresa's reform. Chapter 7 provides an overview of the spiritual antecedents of the thought and writings of these two Carmelite mystics.

While distinctively insightful and, in different ways, uniquely effective in communicating the unfolding of contemplative and mystical realities, the spirituality of Teresa and John exists in and builds on a tradition that, in part, helps to explain their work. Chapter 8 examines the so-called Alumbrados ("illuminated ones"), contemporaries of Teresa and John, whose mystical teaching slipped into heresy. Because they sprouted from the same spiritual ground that flowered in the work of Teresa and John, the errors of this misguided group (or, really, groups) help to reveal more clearly, by contrast, the authentic teaching of the two Spanish Carmelite Doctors. Chapter 9 looks at the Spanish Inquisition, which focused much of its attention in the sixteenth century on the Alumbrados and other suspected false mystics, on converted Jewish Christians who were feared to have reverted secretly to their former religion, and later on the perceived encroachment of Reformation thinking into Catholic Spain. Teresa and John wrote with an active awareness of the Inquisition's concerns—and at least Teresa herself (and perhaps to some degree John) had brushes with the tribunal. Finally, chapter 10 looks at the situation of women in the culture of the time, focusing on Teresa both as clearly formed by her times and as transcending its prejudices.

The chapters are meant to build on each other. To some degree, one chapter may depend on something examined in a previous one. But in general, the chapters can be read independently and in any order, according to the reader's interest. Each chapter ends with a select bibliography of works relevant to that section—first, those available in English, followed by those available in Spanish. Footnotes serve for even more focused references. A general bibliography at the end of the book identifies all of the works used in preparing this book.

In the course of my own studies, I discovered the wide range of people interested in and studying the lives and works of John of the Cross and especially of Teresa of Jesus. This includes, of course, people seeking to deepen their faith and prayer. But these two Carmelite doctors are of interest as well to students of the academic disciplines of theology and spirituality, of Spanish religious and ecclesiastical history, of Spanish language and literature, and of women's studies (as well as many others, I am sure). It is my hope that all of them might benefit from the present work. Every serious reader must understand Teresa and John in their context in order to ensure that we are not reading our own cultural and religious views into their lives and works.

SELECT BIBLIOGRAPHY

English

Álvarez, Tomás. *St. Teresa of Avila: 100 Themes on Her Life and Work*. Translated by Kieran Kavanaugh. Washington, D.C.: ICS Publications, 2011. (From the Spanish original: *100 fichas sobre Teresa de Jesús*. Para Aprender y Enseñar [To Learn and to Teach]. Burgos, Spain: Editorial Monte Carmelo, 2007.)

Carrera, Elena. *Teresa of Avila's Autobiography: Authority, Power and the Self in Mid-Sixteenth Century Spain*. London: Legenda/Modern Humanities Research Association and Maney Publishing, 2005.

The Collected Letters of St. Teresa of Avila. Translated by Kieran Kavanaugh. 2 vols. Washington, D.C.: ICS Publications, 2001, 2007.

The Collected Works of St. John of the Cross. Translated by Kieran Kavanaugh and Otilio Rodriguez. Rev. ed. Washington, D.C.: ICS Publications, 1991.

The Collected Works of St. Teresa of Avila. Translated by Kieran Kavanaugh and Otilio Rodriguez. 3 vols. Washington, D.C.: ICS Publications, 1976–1985.

Edwards, John. *The Spain of the Catholic Monarchs, 1474–1520*. Oxford, England: Blackwell, 2000.

Egido, Teófanes. "The Economic Concerns of Madre Teresa." In *Carmelite Studies IV: Edith Stein Symposium, Teresian Culture*, edited by John Sullivan, translated by Michael Dodd and Steven Payne, 151–72. Washington, D.C.: ICS Publications, 1987.

———. "The Historical Setting of St. Teresa's Life." In *Spiritual Direction*, edited by John Sullivan, translated by Michael Dodd and Steven Payne, 122–82. Vol. 1 of *Carmelite Studies*. Washington, D.C.: ICS Publications, 1980. (Both Egido works are taken from the Spanish original: "Ambiente histórico." In *Introducción a la lectura de Santa Teresa*, edited by Alberto Barrientos, 43–103. Madrid: Editorial de Espiritualidad, 1978. (A 2002 revised edition of the Spanish original includes an extended version of this "Ambiente histórico.")

McGinn, Bernard. *Mysticism in the Golden Age of Spain (1500–1650)*. Vol. 6, part 2 of *The Presence of God: A History of Western Christian Mysticism*. New York: Herder and Herder, 2017.

Payne, Stanley G. *Spanish Catholicism: An Historical Overview*. Madison, Wisc.: University of Wisconsin Press, 1984.

Ruiz Salvador, Federico, ed. *God Speaks in the Night: The Life, Times, and Teaching of St. John of the Cross*. Translated by Kieran Kavanaugh. Washington, D.C.: ICS Publications, 1991, 2000.

Spanish

Álvarez Vázquez, José Antonio. *Trabajos, dineros, y negocios: Teresa de Jesús y la economía del siglo XVI (1562–1582)*. Madrid: Editorial Trotta, 2000.

Barrientos, Alberto, ed. *Introducción a la lectura de Santa Teresa*. 2nd ed. Madrid: Editorial de Espiritualidad, 2002.

Egido, Teófanes, ed. *Aspectos históricos de San Juan de la Cruz*. Ávila, Spain: Institución Gran Duque de Alba de la Diputación Provincial de Ávila, 1990. (See pp. 99–115.)

———, ed. *Perfil histórico de Santa Teresa*. 3rd ed. Madrid: Editorial de Espiritualidad, 2012.

[Montalva], Efrén de la Madre de Dios, and Otger Steggink. *Tiempo y vida de San Juan de la Cruz*. Madrid: Biblioteca de Autores Cristianos (BAC), 1992.

———. *Tiempo y vida de Santa Teresa*. 3rd ed. Madrid: Biblioteca de Autores Cristianos (BAC), 1996.

Pérez, Joseph. *Teresa de Ávila y la España de su tiempo*. 3rd ed. Madrid: Editorial EDAF, 2015.

Rodríguez, José Vicente, ed. *Aspectos históricos de San Juan de la Cruz*. Ávila, Spain: Institución Gran Duque de Alba de la Diputación Provincial de Ávila, 1990.

———. *100 fichas sobre San Juan de la Cruz*. Para aprender y enseñar [To Learn and to Teach]. Burgos, Spain: Editorial Monte Carmelo, 2008.

Ros García, Salvados, ed. *Introducción a la lectura de San Juan de la Cruz*. Salamanca, Spain: Junta de Castilla y León, Consejería de Cultura y Turismo, 1993.

Velasco Bayón, Balbino. *San Juan de la Cruz: A las raíces del hombre y del carmelita*. Madrid: Editorial de Espiritualidad, 2009.

See also, in the general bibliography, the proceedings of a number of congresses/conferences on Teresa of Ávila and John of the Cross that have been held in Spain in recent decades. Individual contributions to these proceedings are cited in footnotes and sometimes in the select bibliographies that conclude individual chapters of this book.

Chapter 1

The Spanish World of the Sixteenth Century

Teresa of Jesus and John of the Cross lived, were formed, and contributed significantly to the so-called Golden Age or Century of Gold (*Siglo de Oro*) that was sixteenth-century Spain. The convergence of vibrant movements, both secular and ecclesial, as well as significant historic events shaped the spirit of the time and culture in which Teresa and John lived and pursued their mature reforming, spiritual, and literary work. In later chapters, we will look more closely at reform movements in the church and in religious orders as well as the spiritual antecedents and formative influences on the spirituality of these two Doctors of the Church. Here, in broad strokes, we will examine some important elements of the political and social reality of the time. Of course, any attempt to present a full picture of sixteenth-century Spain would be well beyond the scope of the present book. We will begin instead by examining some key historical events and a few more particular aspects of life at that time in order to better understand the context of Teresa and John's lives and work.

The Year 1492

The year 1492 was a critical gateway to the developments of the next century. In that year, as every American schoolchild knows, Christopher Columbus "discovered" America (or at least he "discovered" its existence for his Spanish patrons, Queen Isabella and King Ferdinand). Less well known but equally important for Spanish history, this was also the year that the last Muslim kingdom on the Iberian Peninsula, centered in Granada in southern Spain, was defeated. This brought to a conclusion a seven-century effort to bring the whole peninsula once again under Christian rule. Finally—and tragically—1492 was also the year that the Jews were expelled from Spain (or forced into conversion to Christianity).

The "discovery" in 1492 and subsequent colonization of what would become Latin America had a massive impact on sixteenth-century Spain. Soon, silver and gold as well as other resources began to pour into Spain. In the short term, this brought great wealth to many in Spanish society. And the grand churches, religious houses, and palaces of the period that today serve as a marvel to tourists to Spain give some tangible evidence to some of the economic rewards of the American expansion. At the same time, this wealth fueled the broader European ambitions and entanglements of the Spanish crown—ultimately to its own detriment, as we will see when we look more closely at the economy of the time. The promise of wealth and fame sent hordes of young Spaniards to the Americas, including Teresa's own brothers. To the church, for its part, the Americas presented a vast field for evangelizing, and Teresa reports how the visit of the Franciscan missionary, Alonso Maldonado, and his report on the American mission fired her own support for that work

(F 1.7–8). We recall too that, in 1591, toward the end of his life, John of the Cross was briefly slated to join a Discalced mission to Mexico. We cannot of course mention the Spanish involvement in the Americas without acknowledging the huge cost to the indigenous peoples—their virtual enslavement, the suppression of their cultures and languages, and the ravages of the diseases brought by the colonizers. In fact, Teresa heard of this maltreatment firsthand from Maldonado, and she expressed her concern in a letter dated January 17, 1570, to her brother, Lorenzo, who was in modern-day Ecuador (Ltr 24.13). It in no way excuses the abuses of the "conquistadors," but the arousal of consciences like that of Teresa at least resulted in some of the first significant Christian reflections on the nature of human dignity and rights in Spanish universities and religious orders of the time.

The surrender of the last Muslim kingdom on the peninsula in 1492 represented the culmination of a centuries-long effort. Islamic forces had crossed over to the Iberian Peninsula from North Africa in the early eighth century, and they rather quickly controlled almost its entirety, except for a small Christian enclave along Spain's northern coast. In the next seven centuries the armies of the many small Christian kingdoms of the peninsula slowly pushed the Muslims southward. The very name of the kingdom of Castile is a reflection of this history, since it is dotted by castles (*castillos*) and fortified cities that date from this period. The grand walls of the city of Ávila in which Teresa grew up are an especially impressive extant example of this history. Over these centuries, the effort at "reconquest" (*Reconquista*) had taken on the character of a kind of Spanish Crusade, and the final victory in 1492 was not only a Christian victory but also seen as a completion of the divine will and a sign of special divine mission and blessing for the unified Spain. It resulted in a distinctively robust, militant, and missionary sense of the faith. But while Muslim forces were finally driven out, the impact of the long-standing presence of the cultured Islamic presence remained—on such things as the Spanish language, architecture, and (some would say) its spirituality and mysticism.

The expulsion or the forced conversion of Spanish Jews also in 1492, as we see it today, is a sad moment in Spanish history—the culmination of a history of sporadic, localized Jewish persecutions over the decades. At its time, it was seen as an effort to further consolidate the unity of Spain through a more focused unity of its Catholic faith. We will see its deeper impact on Spanish society and church when we examine such varied topics of "purity of blood," Teresa and John's social status, and suspicions of the Inquisition about the unfolding of the Spanish mysticism of the time.

These three events of 1492 are important foundations—or at least key moments in the development—of the distinctive attitudes and worldview of the Spanish society of the sixteenth century: a sense of expansion, destiny, and even divine mission.

A "Unified" Spain Engaged in the Old and the New Worlds

Even today, Spain is a country with very distinct regions, with different dialects and even distinct languages, and differing local cultures. Both John and Teresa speak, for example, of what they perceived to be the very different outlook of the people of Andalusia, in the south of Spain, which they contrasted—largely unfavorably—with that of their native region of Castile. The reform of the Carmelites, as we shall see, before the Discalced reform, proceeded unevenly throughout the peninsula, depending on the province and the regions they encompassed.

The marriage of Queen Isabella of Castile and King Ferdinand of Aragon in 1469 united the two major Christian kingdoms of the peninsula that would form modern Spain. The kingdom of Granada would be added in 1492 and the northern kingdom of Navarre in the early sixteenth century. But this unity was certainly not complete, and each region often retained laws and practices that would be more typical of neighboring independent states. This is one reason that the reform of the church and the religious orders as well as the functioning of the Inquisition developed unevenly in Spain. In the same way, the Spanish ventures in the Americas were largely the work of the kingdom of Castile, which received its profits but also principally bore the costs of the Spanish crown's European wars.

Although not a fully centralized state in a modern sense, the unity of Spain allowed it, for the first time, to begin to direct its attention to the rest of Europe. The kingdom of Aragon, on the east coast of the peninsula, was already an economic player in the Mediterranean and a maritime power politically involved in Italy. In fact, King Ferdinand of Aragon was also king of Sicily. And this Italian involvement would facilitate the inflow of reform and renaissance ideas and movements into Spain. With their new international outlook, Ferdinand and Isabella married their daughter, the ill-fated Catherine of Aragon, to Henry VIII of England as well as another daughter, Juana, to the heir to the Holy Roman Emperor. This latter marriage meant that the grandson of Ferdinand and Isabella would rule Spain and its territories as well as the largely German-Austrian Holy Roman Empire and notably its territories in the Low Countries (modern-day Netherlands and Belgium). By the end of the fifteenth century, Spain had arrived on the European stage in a grand way, making the sixteenth century, politically speaking, a true Golden Age for Spain—though the subsequent international entanglements and conflicts would cost Spain dearly in the decades ahead.

When the grandson of Isabella and Ferdinand, Charles V,[1] inherited the Spanish throne in 1516, he arrived from the Low Countries without being able to speak Spanish (or "Castilian," to distinguish it from other dialects and languages of the peninsula, although it was certainly the predominant language of the unified Spain). His arrival, along with courtiers and scholars from northern Europe, advanced the inflow of humanistic and reform ideas into the country, notably the works of Erasmus. Books of all sorts and on varied topics, art, and new ways of thinking flooded into the newly more outwardly looking Spain. Included, as we will see, was the more rapid introduction and availability of foreign spiritual and mystical works.

The Economy: Wealth and Bankruptcy

In a later chapter, we will explore the social classes and structures of sixteenth-century Spain, contrasting the early formation and experience of Teresa of Jesus with her upwardly mobile and financially comfortable family with that of John who grew up in abject poverty. But we cannot understand their experience or the challenges of Teresa's work of founding monasteries

---

1. He was Charles V of the Holy Roman Empire. In Spain, he was actually Charles I of Spain—though, even during his own lifetime, he was often referred to as Carlos V even in Spain.

without a sense of the economic realities of the time.[2] In fact, Teresa, who was the daughter of a mercantile family (at least until their rise into the lower nobility), demonstrated herself to be quite astute in the financial practicalities of her times and quite adept at dealing with merchants and financiers of various types. The success of her work of founding monasteries of the reform is a testimony to her abilities at this practical level as well as to the background from which she came (though she herself complains to her brother, Lorenzo, of all of the time that she had to spend on "money and business affairs" [Ltr 24.12; January 17, 1570]).

Spain, as we noted above, was not an entirely unified economic and political reality in the sixteenth century, and each of the constituent kingdoms (principally Castile and Aragon) retained a good deal of institutional identity including fiscal policies, import duties, and even monetary systems. Furthermore, the distances and difficulties of travel, slow means of communication, and the widely spread nature of the Spanish territories made the work of developing a national economic policy and planning very difficult. Central to all of it was the economy of the kingdom of Castile, the largest and wealthiest as well as the principal beneficiary of the gold and silver coming from the New World—but also principal in bearing the cost of foreign wars on multiple international fronts against Christian and Turkish forces.[3]

---

2. For a more in-depth look at the sixteenth-century Spanish economy, see José Antonio Álvarez Vázquez, *Trabajos, dineros, y negocios: Teresa de Jesús y la economía del siglo XVI (1562–1582)* (Madrid: Editorial Trotta, 2000); and Valentín Vázquez de Prada, "La economía castellana en la época de Santa Teresa," in *Congreso Internacional Teresiano (4–7 octubre, 1982)*, vol. 1, ed. Teófanes Egido et al., 229–46 (Salamanca, Spain: Universidad de Salamanca, 1983).

3. Vázquez de Prada, "La economía castellana," 229.

While the gold and silver of the New World often paid for international involvements, the mainstay of the Spanish economy of the time was agriculture and livestock.[4] Artisans and industry were largely concentrated in the production of fine wool (and secondarily with production of silk). Teresa's family had, among other enterprises, been involved in the sale of cloth, as had the father of John of the Cross until his marriage to a humble weaver reduced him to the low end of cloth production. Until the middle of the sixteenth century, cloth production in Spain was largely a "domestic" industry in which small-time, home-based operations sold directly to merchants—as was the case with the parents of John of the Cross. But beginning in cities like Segovia, production gradually became more concentrated in a "factory system," bringing the resources and production together. This was a decidedly more efficient system, better suited to compete with similar industries in Italy, England, and the Low Countries. Unfortunately, these competitors were already more "industrialized" and efficient, and the Spanish cloth industry found it increasingly difficult to compete.[5] Added to these realities were the difficulties of transporting goods even within the country, due to the often poor road system except between large cities and a lack of navigable rivers and internal waterways. Moreover, transporting goods from one Spanish kingdom through another could require the payment of duties—resulting in increased costs of production.

A general trend toward urbanization brought a flow of potential workers into the cities. But the middle of the sixteenth century also saw a series of bad harvests—notably between 1540 and 1545 in addition to a locust scourge in 1542—which

---

4. Vázquez de Prada, 229.
5. Vázquez de Prada, 234–39.

dramatically increased the flow of the unemployed into cities. Theoretically at least, this phenomenon might have meant increased capacity for industrial production. But existing industries were largely tied to traditional guilds that held a monopoly on jobs and required higher wages. The result was again higher prices. The poverty of John of the Cross's family—workers on the low end of cloth production—can be understood in light of all of these larger, economic realities.

The introduction of Spain into the mainstream of Europe and into the larger, international reality of the Holy Roman Empire did open up trade opportunities for Spanish industries, but at the same time, it also placed these native commercial activities into a more competitive environment. Southern Germany, the Low Countries, and northern Italy generally had more advanced industries, more efficient forms of production, and well-developed banking systems. Simply in regard to its principal industry of cloth production, Spain soon became simply a producer of raw cloth products that were exported elsewhere to produce final products that would in turn be imported to Spain at a higher price. The result was a consistent annual trade deficit.

The Americas were not only a source of gold and silver (and later, other products such as other metals, chocolate, and sugar). They also represented a vast market for Castilian products. But tied together with other countries in the empire, Spanish goods had to compete with products from other imperial countries whose companies won trading rights in exchange for the loans made to the cash-strapped Spanish crown. Ultimately, trade with the Americas came largely into the hands and for the profit of foreigners.[6]

---

6. Vázquez de Prada, 245.

The Inflow of Precious Metals and Economic Decline

Between 1503 and 1555, about one million kilos (2.2 million pounds) of silver came to Spain from America. Another eight million kilos (17.6 million pounds) followed in the decades from 1555 to the end of the century. In the course of the entire century, about 200,000 kilos (440,000 pounds) of gold also entered Spain. This meant of course, for some, great wealth—evident in the building of palaces, churches, monasteries, and government buildings, and the patronizing of the arts. New money was available, especially among the upwardly mobile, for building and for supporting new religious orders such as the Discalced Carmelites.

But for reasons like those outlined above, the Castilian economy was ill equipped to deal with the influx of wealth, most of which went to foreign wars (which was taking up an increasing part of the national budget and resources). Meanwhile, virtually none of it went to strengthen the native industries of agriculture and cloth production (already hit hard by foreign competition), and so, for the average citizen, the chief result of the influx of American wealth was inflation.[7] One estimate is that the cost of living in Spain increased by 400 percent between 1571 and 1581.[8] In the end, the gold and silver from the Americas never amounted to more than a quarter of the annual government income. The rest came from taxes of various sorts—a burden felt especially by the middle class and poor (since nobility and clergy did not pay many of the normal

---

7. Vázquez de Prada, 239.

8. Sonya A. Quitslund, "Elements of a Feminist Spirituality in St. Teresa," in *Centenary of St. Teresa*, ed. John Sullivan, 19–50, vol. 3 of *Carmelite Studies* (Washington, D.C.: ICS Publications, 1984).

taxes of the lower classes—one of the reasons that a family like Teresa's would have sought noble status). The Spanish crown began to borrow heavily from foreign lenders (Germans, Genovese, and Flemish), and these loans then became increasingly difficult to repay as there was no respite from foreign wars.

The Spanish economy reached its height between about 1540 and 1550, but its decline began soon thereafter. This would have been noticeable by 1580–1590.[9] The steady rise in prices and inflation between 1560 and 1590 meant less disposable income among Teresa's donors to support her monasteries—which was one reason she accepted the need to found monasteries with fixed sources of income.[10]

The decline of the city of Medina del Campo in which John of the Cross's poor family finally settled gives a window into this broader downturn. Once an international center in Castile for the cloth trade with a large marketplace for the exchange of goods from around Europe, in 1570 it had a population of 20,000. By the end of the century, it had dwindled to 9,000. The economic factors described above and, more specifically, the extended years of rebellion against Spanish rule in the Low Countries disrupted trade while at the same time the bankruptcies of the Spanish crown eroded financial trust that is at the heart of a viable modern economic system.[11]

The result of the systemic economic problems was the rapid increase of widespread poverty throughout the sixteenth century. It was the poor and lower working classes that were hardest hit by inflation, epidemics, and hunger. Given the unfavorable economic

---

9. Vázquez de Prada, "La economía castellana," 241.

10. Álvarez Vázquez, *Trabajos, dineros, y negocios*, 2.

11. Federico Ruiz Salvador, ed., *God Speaks in the Night: The Life, Times, and Teaching of St. John of the Cross* (Washington, D.C.: ICS Publications, 1991), 347.

conditions generally, it became easy for working-class families to fall into abject poverty. It was reported that cities and roads teemed with the wandering poor and beggars. Major Castilian cities such as Salamanca, Valladolid, Zamora, and Toledo passed ordinances to try to prevent the influx and to address the needs of the poor already resident.[12] We will examine this phenomenon more closely in the next chapter. The lack of solid economic prospects forced the sons of even wealthier families to seek a livelihood with the dream of wealth in foreign wars and especially in the New World. This seriously depleted the number of available marriageable men and contributed the influx of women into religious communities such as the Monastery of the Incarnation at the time of Teresa.

The Castilian Language, Literacy, and Literature

The year 1492 is significant for yet another reason. It was the year in which the first full-scale grammar text of the Castilian language was published—in fact, it appears that Castilian was the first European vernacular to have its own published grammar. The sixteenth century saw the maturing of the language and a flowering of vernacular literature and poetry. In the 1530s, two members of the international court of Charles V, Juan Boscán and Garcilaso de la Vega wrote the first secular masterpieces of Renaissance Castilian poetry and prose. Their influence on the poetry of John of the Cross is evident, and it appears that he studied their works while a student in the Jesuit school in Medina del Campo. John's own poetry went on to become among the most celebrated in the Spanish language.

---

12. Ruiz Salvador, 27.

The increasing use of the vernacular made books more available to the average person who was not trained in Latin. Still, it is estimated that some 80 to 85 percent of the general Castilian population was illiterate—and this rate was higher among women.[13] But literacy was much higher among the nobility—perhaps as high as 90 percent for men, certainly less for women. Also, conversos—that is, Christians from a Jewish background—also seem to have had significantly higher rate of literacy—perhaps, among the men, as high as 75 percent.[14] But of those who could read, it is not clear that they could do so well enough to read an entire book.[15]

The father of Teresa de Ahumada y Cepeda had insisted that his daughters be able to read, and Teresa was an avid reader of books in the vernacular.[16] Her written style is both vernacular

---

13. Tomás Álvarez, *St. Teresa of Avila: 100 Themes on Her Life and Work*, trans. Kieran Kavanaugh (Washington, D.C.: ICS Publications, 2011), 21. See also Serafín de Tapia, "La alfabetización de la población urbana castellana en el Siglo de Oro," *Historia de la Educación* 12–13 (1993–94), 275–307; Tomás Álvarez, *Cultura de mujer en el siglo XVI: El caso de Santa Teresa* (Burgos, Spain: Editorial Monte Carmelo, 2006), 26.

14. Daniel de Pablo Maroto, *Teresa en oración: Historia-experiencia-doctrina* (Madrid: Editorial de Espiritualidad, 2004), 82.

15. Maxime Chevalier, *Lectura y lectores en la España de los siglos XVI y XVII* (Madrid: Ediciones Turner, 1976), 19.

16. For a man of his times, Teresa's father maintained a respectable library. An inventory of his books at the time of the death of his first wife in 1507 is extant. See Álvarez, *Cultura de mujer en el siglo XVI*, 28. As a youth, Teresa shared her mother's passion for tales of knightly romance, a genre called *cabellerías*. For a list of such books published in Spain during the first twenty years of Teresa's life, see Álvarez, 49n71. Since Teresa's father disapproved of such books, it is possible that Teresa and her mother borrowed them from friends and family—a common practice due to the relative expense of books. See: Luis Enrique Rodríguez-San Pedro Bezares, "Libros y lecturas para el hogar de don Alonso Sánchez de Cepeda," *Salmaticensis* 34 (1987), 181.

and oral, that is, she writes as one would speak in an informal conversation. Her vocabulary, images, spelling, and syntax are indicative of this style, which can be both more engaging and more difficult to read. This manner of expression was noted already by the first compiler of her collected works, the Augustinian Luis de León, in the dedicatory letter on its publication. Her readers get the sense that she is speaking to them—often in great excitement and sometimes just having descended from mystical heights. This makes her works feel more accessible and personal—certainly more than when reading the more academic and conceptual style of John of the Cross—and its use is probably not by accident. Certainly, as Teresa says, she was often writing spontaneously as if in conversation with her nuns, but even without formal academic training, she had read many books in a more formal style. At least nominally, she was writing some of her works explicitly for her academically trained confessors. Her oral style, then, seems at least to be an effort to make her work more accessible to ordinary readers. At the same time, it may have been a strategy not to seem to be claiming the authority to offer formal academic spiritual teaching—which many at her time would have considered grossly inappropriate and even suspect for a woman.

The printing press was invented around 1450, not a hundred years before Teresa's birth. But as we noted above, books were pouring into Spain during the sixteenth century, and printing presses were being set up throughout the country. We will look more closely at the work of publishing during the sixteenth century in a later chapter. Here, we note the phenomenon as part of the linguistic and literary flowering of the century. It must be said that books were very expensive, and print runs tended to be very small—perhaps as few as two thousand copies of a book printed at publication.[17] But books were often shared, and reading books aloud was common before the modern era, making books accessible even to the illiterate and to those who could not afford their purchase. Books were typically read aloud in convents of women as well as in groups of more well-to-do women. We know that the translated works of Augustine, Gregory the Great, Ludolph of Saxony, Bonaventure, and others were commonly read aloud in convents throughout Spain.[18] Less direct access to theological and spiritual books was also provided by other avenues such as preaching, and we know that Teresa was fond of listening to good sermons (L 8.12).

Education and Universities

In 1450, there were six universities in Spain. By 1600, there were thirty-three.[19] John of the Cross himself studied at the University of Salamanca, founded in 1218. During his time, it was at its height, with 6,000 students and with professors of the highest caliber. Rivaling it was the University of Alcalá, founded in 1499 by Cardinal Francisco Jiménez de Cisneros, a leading figure in ecclesiastical reform and in the promotion of publishing (in part, to promote a more contemplative spirituality). Salamanca's focus

---

17. Joseph Pérez, "Mística y realidad histórica en la Castilla del siglo XVI," in *Vivir en Ávila cuando Santa Teresa escribe el libro de su "Vida,"* ed. Rómulo Cuartas Lodoño and Francisco Javier Sancho Fermín, 39–68 (Burgos, Spain: Editorial Monte Carmelo, 2011), 43.

18. Ronald Surtz, *Writing Women in Late Medieval and Early Modern Spain: The Mothers of Saint Teresa of Avila* (Philadelphia: University of Pennsylvania Press, 1995), 13.

19. Stanley G. Payne, *Spanish Catholicism: An Historical Overview* (Madison, Wisc.: University of Wisconsin Press, 1984), 30; Ruiz Salvador, *God Speaks*, 28.

was more classical, emphasizing a return to the sources such as Sacred Scripture, the church fathers, and a renewed attention to St. Thomas Aquinas. It was at Salamanca that Dominican theologians reflected on such questions as the rights of indigenous peoples and the meaning of economic rights and justice in early capitalism. Alcalá was more imbued with the spirit of humanism and of Renaissance thought. But it was a time of theological and intellectual richness throughout the universities of Spain as professors sought to break out of the dry scholasticism that had descended on Catholic theology shortly after Aquinas. While John himself had studied at Salamanca, he also spent time in Discalced houses of study connected with the universities of both Alcalá and of Baeza in southern Spain where it seems that he interacted actively with their professors.

In addition to university education, the Jesuits in particular founded first-class secondary schools throughout Spain—including the one in which the young John of the Cross studied in Medina del Campo before joining the Carmelites. The Jesuits had been formally established in 1540—just two years before John's birth—and their members very soon began work in Spain. By 1563, the Jesuits had thirty-eight schools in Spain and Portugal. Their school in Medina was founded in 1551, was installed in a new building in 1558, and offered a good education focused on Latin and the humanities. Teresa too would benefit from many Jesuit confessors and counselors.

Traveling and Road Conditions

Both Teresa of Jesus and John of the Cross traveled extensively within Spain—Teresa in the work of the foundations, and John in making visitations and in assisting Discalced communities of both men and women.[20] Many factors had to be considered in making a foundation (e.g., donors and availability of recruits), but surely accessibility by road had to be among them in order to ensure communication and exchange.[21] It is estimated that John of the Cross traveled somewhere between 16,000 and 17,000 miles between his birth and death.[22] Teresa is estimated to have traveled almost 5,000 miles in the course of making her foundations—surprising especially considering her age in those years (between 52 and 67—not young in that era).[23]

In order to understand how extraordinary such estimates are, we must recall that travel in sixteenth-century Spain was a challenge. Of course, this was a time before any modern forms of transportation, but also the condition of roads was generally bad. Spain has few navigable rivers that might have served for travel and transport. Plus, the country lacked any form of a planned network of roads, nor was there any regular maintenance. Upkeep often depended on local municipalities—with very mixed results. The better roads involved major trade routes and connected cities between which the royal court might move regularly. Seville, for example, a port city in the south of Spain, was the principal arrival point for gold, silver, and other goods from the New World. Medina del Campo and Burgos were major trading centers. Roads connecting such cities with other

---

20. Ruiz Salvador, *God Speaks*, 282–84. See also Joseph Pérez, *Teresa de Ávila y la España de su tiempo*, 3rd ed. (Madrid: Editorial EDAF, 2015), 74–79.

21. Teófanes Egido, "Ambiente histórico," in *Introducción a la lectura de Santa Teresa*, ed. Alberto Barrientos, 63–155, 2nd ed. (Madrid: Editorial de Espiritualidad, 2002), 69.

22. Ruiz Salvador, *God Speaks*, 283, 303.

23. Daniel de Pablo Maroto, *Santa Teresa de Jesús: Nueva biografía* (*escritora, fundadora, maestra*) (Madrid: Editorial de Espiritualidad, 2014), 23.

major points were certainly the best maintained, and Teresa and John would certainly have taken advantage of them when possible.

Spain has a varied terrain—including mountains and semi-arid plains—difficult at times to traverse. Many rivers lacked bridges and became difficult to cross when they were swollen by rain. The planned building of bridges often failed because of corruption in the administration of funds. A year after John of the Cross's death, it appears that of the three hundred bridges that had been slated to be built, only one was. Besides the terrain, the weather could vary from the extreme heat of summer to winter snows—plus rains that could turn dirt roads into pools of mud. There were few inns along roads, except the most traveled, which could make finding food difficult. Punishment for robberies was severe, which made roads generally safe, but such crimes remained a cause for concern.[24]

Roads typically lacked signage to indicate directions, and so it was not unusual for travelers to get lost. The first guide for travelers appears to have been published in Medina del Campo in 1546. A more thorough guide was published in 1576 and included distances between cities, the location of inns, and even the rough value of coinage in different parts of the country. Inns, although supposedly regulated by law, were often crowded, dirty, and unruly. Many were havens for prostitutes, drunkenness, violence, and brawls.

The Discalced constitutions of 1581 required friars to walk. Or if it was necessary to ride, to use a donkey. If the travel was both urgent and necessary, using a mule or even a horse might be permitted. In any case, the norms specified that the harness was to be of rope rather than leather, and the saddle was to

---

24. Ruiz Salvador, *God Speaks*, 282–84.

be the most basic, without a padded seat. On the other hand, people of means could travel by coaches or carriages drawn by horses or mules. Huge covered wagons drawn by many animals for transport of goods could also be used to transport people. There were also smaller wagons, covered with awning and driven by muleteers. This was a common form of transport for Teresa and her nuns on their way to found a new monastery—though, on occasion, wealthy patrons also sent carriages for her comfort and speed. Ox-drawn wagons could travel about nineteen miles a day; drawn by mules, they could cover about twenty-five miles.

Letters and Mail

Letter writing was an important form of communication in the sixteenth century, and we know that Teresa of Jesus was a prolific writer of letters.[25] Four hundred and fifty of these are extant, but it is variously estimated that she may have written 1,200, 5,000, or even 15,000 of them in her lifetime—addressed to nuns, family, friends, counselors, and benefactors—many concerning the reform and the spreading and maintenance of her many foundations.[26] (By contrast, only thirty-four letters of John of the Cross are extant. Many were destroyed during John's final years by their recipients who wanted to protect him from some malicious confreres looking to discredit him.)

---

25. On postal service in sixteenth-century Spain, see especially Carmen Rodríguez, "Infraestructura del epistolario de Santa Teresa: Los correos del siglo XVI," in *Congreso Internacional Teresiano (4–7 octubre, 1982)*, ed. Teófanes Egido et al., 1:65–90 (Salamanca, Spain: Universidad de Salamanca, 1983).

26. Bárbara Mujica, *Teresa de Ávila: Lettered Woman* (Nashville, Tenn.: Vanderbilt University Press, 2009), 8–9. Others have placed the number at between 10,220 and 25,550. See Rodríguez, "Infraestructura del epistolario," 65.

Writing letters is one thing; getting them delivered in a reliable and timely manner is another. Something approaching a modern postal service had its roots late in the fifteenth century but began in earnest in the sixteenth especially as the government's national and international correspondence increased to sometimes far-off places. In the middle of the century, an ordinary mail service was established, largely contracted out to private enterprises and consisting of regularly scheduled transport of mail between fixed points (which did not generally include smaller cities or rural areas). This service consisted of a series of different carriers and transfer points. It could be slow and unreliable—better and faster between larger cities on roads on which royal business and major enterprise passed. Teresa certainly used this service in her work of promoting the reform and in founding monasteries. There was also an "extraordinary" service for royal business. Theoretically, it was available to others, but its cost was usually prohibitive.

In addition to public mail services, it was also possible to hire special, private couriers who were quick, reliable, and secure—but quite expensive. Teresa also depended on known travelers to deliver letters on her behalf. These could be friends or acquaintances known to be traveling in the right direction but, more regularly, drivers of commercial carts pulled by either mules or oxen carrying merchandise or goods along established routes. This method was actually more reliable and secure than the ordinary postal service, as it did not involve using multiple carriers and transfer points. But even this service was limited and slowed by the state of the roads on which such carts could pass and depending on the season. Rain and snow could make travel along dirt roads treacherous. Even summer presented the problem of adequate water for the animals who were, after all, pulling heavy carts loaded with goods. In the end, March through October was the most reliable time to be on the roads. Mule-driven carts were usually smaller and lighter and thus better able to maneuver small or bad roads.

A letter traveling by ordinary post would ordinarily take about eight days between Madrid and Valladolid (a distance of about 120 miles); eleven days between Madrid and Burgos (about 150 miles); and fifteen days between Madrid and Seville in the south of Spain (about 330 miles). Of course, Teresa did found monasteries in smaller cities, and mail to those locations would have been more complicated and slow. International postal service was considerably slower. Thinking, for example, of correspondence between Teresa and the Carmelite general, Rubeo (Giovanni Battista Rossi), a letter to Italy could take a month, but the official, ordinary service only set out twice a month between Italy and Spain. But again there was also an extraordinary service that could make a round trip in about thirty days. Rubeo reported to Teresa that on June 17, 1575, he had received two letters from her—one dating from January of that year (five months earlier) and another from the previous October (about eight months earlier). It is clear to see why misunderstandings and hard feelings could fester in these long delays. Mail from the New World (where Teresa's brothers had gone) usually took about fifty days, though it could take as few as 35 or as many as 111. This required, of course, catching the fleet making a regular trip between the New World and Spain—and getting the correspondence to its departure point. Thus a letter from Teresa to one of her brothers would have to get to Seville first, await the next departure of the fleet, and make its way to the actual location of the recipient in the Americas.

Conclusion

The present chapter has examined some elements for better understanding what will follow. In a later chapter, we will look more closely at social class and poverty in Spanish society of the sixteenth century, contrasting the experience and formation of Teresa of Jesus and John of the Cross.

SELECT BIBLIOGRAPHY

English

Egido, Teófanes. "The Economic Concerns of Madre Teresa." In *Carmelite Studies IV: Edith Stein Symposium, Teresian Culture*, edited by John Sullivan, translated by Michael Dodd and Steven Payne, 151–72. Washington, D.C.: ICS Publications, 1987.

———. "The Historical Setting of St. Teresa's Life." In *Spiritual Direction*, edited by John Sullivan, translated by Michael Dodd and Steven Payne, 122–82. Vol. 1 of *Carmelite Studies*. Washington, D.C.: ICS Publications, 1980. (Both Egido works are taken from the Spanish original: "Ambiente histórico." In *Introducción a la lectura de Santa Teresa*, edited by Alberto Barrientos, 43–103. Madrid: Editorial de Espiritualidad, 1978. A 2002 revised edition of the Spanish original includes an extended version of this "Ambiente histórico.").

Lovett, A. W. *Early Habsburg Spain, 1517–1598*. Oxford: Oxford University Press, 1986.

Spanish

Álvarez Vázquez, José Antonio. *Trabajos, dineros, y negocios: Teresa de Jesús y la economía del siglo XVI (1562–1582)*. Madrid: Editorial Trotta, 2000.

Chevalier, Maxime. *Lectura y lectores en la España de los siglos XVI y XVII*. Madrid: Ediciones Turner, 1976.

Rodríguez, Carmen. "Infraestructura del epistolario de Santa Teresa: Los correos del siglo XVI." In *Congreso Internacional Teresiano (4–7 octubre, 1982)*, edited by Teófanes Egido et al. 65–90. Vol. 1. Salamanca, Spain: Universidad de Salamanca, 1983.

Vázquez de Prada, Valentín. "La economía castellana en la época de Santa Teresa." In *Congreso Internacional Teresiano (4–7 octubre, 1982)*, edited by Teófanes Egido et al., 229–46. Vol. 1. Salamanca, Spain: Universidad de Salamanca, 1983.

Chapter 2

The City of Ávila

St. Teresa *of Ávila*. Teresa of Jesus is forever associated with the city of her birth, her childhood, her entrance into the monastery, and her first foundation of the reform. John of the Cross was born within the province of Ávila, and he spent important years of his life as a resident confessor at the Monastery of the Incarnation in the city. Thus, to understand Ávila's history and its life in the sixteenth century is to gain a better understanding of John and especially Teresa.[1]

History

Ávila is a city that dates to pre-Roman times. It was conquered by the advancing Muslims in the eighth century and recaptured by Christian forces in the eleventh. From Roman times on, the

---

1. The essential study of this topic is provided by Jodi Bilinkoff, *The Avila of Saint Teresa: Religious Reform in a Sixteenth Century City* (Ithaca, N.Y.: Cornell University Press, 1989); and in greatly abbreviated form in Jodi Bilinkoff, "St. Teresa of Avila and the Avila of St. Teresa," in *Centenary of St. Teresa*, ed. John Sullivan, 53–68, vol. 3 of *Carmelite Studies* (Washington, D.C.: ICS Publications, 1984). See also: María Cátedra, *Un santo para una ciudad: ensayo de antropología urbana* (Barcelona, Spain: Editorial Ariel, 1997). Cátedra's book is a social scientific study of Ávila. The *"santo"* of the title refers to San Segundo, the mythical first bishop of the city and co-patron (with St. Teresa) of the city of Ávila.

city was surrounded by fortifications. The current walls—which would have been known to Teresa and are still an impressive sight—were built in the twelfth century on the foundations of previous fortifications as a continued defense in the back-and-forth wars with Muslims forces. It was a city proud of its military history, popularly known as "Ávila of the Knights" (Ávila de los Cabelleros). Perhaps it is no wonder that military images—such as the interior "castle"—were often used by Teresa to describe spiritual realities.

One of the most famous stories of the city's fabled history is the legend of Jimena Blázquez. In the time of ongoing battles between Christian and Muslims, she was the wife of the Christian governor of the city. When Muslim forces advanced on the city while he and the majority of his soldiers were away, she organized the city's women. Dressed in the military garb of their husbands, they fooled their would-be invaders into retreating from what appeared to be a well-armed city. In a medieval culture in which women were supposed to play a silent and submissive role, she was a bold example of determination and shrewdness. It is not hard to suppose that the celebrated legend of this courageous woman would stir the imagination of a bright girl like the young Teresa.[2]

By the early sixteenth century, Ávila was one of the most prosperous cities of Castile. Queen Isabella and King Ferdinand built a palace for themselves there, adjacent to the Dominican monastery of Santo Tomás that Teresa knew in her youth and that remains an impressive sight to this day. Their male heir whose death predated theirs, Prince Juan, is entombed in the monastery church. Santo Tomás was an early headquarters of the Inquisition.

The prominence of the city suffered a serious setback when it ended up on the wrong side of the *Comuneros* revolt that

---

2. Bilinkoff, *Avila of Saint Teresa*, 2–3.

opposed the rule of the foreign-born grandson of Ferdinand and Isabella, Charles V, and the influence of his Flemish courtiers. The rebels correctly foresaw the entanglement of Castile and its resources in the international politics of the soon-to-be Holy Roman Emperor. As a result of the war, the city fell out of royal favor, and its nobility lost some of their ancient privileges. But the city benefited with the rest of Spain from the economic growth brought about by the influx of wealth from the New World and by increased international trade (though this also contained the roots of its later decline). As the sixteenth century unfolded, the city grew prosperous. During Teresa's lifetime, there was a flurry of building—palaces of the wealthy, government buildings, and (supported especially by the rising merchant classes) churches and religious houses.

A perpetual problem for the city was ensuring an adequate water supply, especially as its population grew. Castile itself is generally rocky and dry. The city of Ávila sits high on a hill, but it stretches down to the small Adaja River. In the city center, the problem was to bring and distribute water across the burgeoning city. Down near the river, seasonal flooding could be a problem. All of this led to continual disputes about water rights, its use and its flow. Perhaps it is no wonder that, as a daughter of a city in which water was a precious commodity, Teresa would be so drawn to water images to describe religious experience. We recall too that one of the early objections to the foundation of San José was a question of access to water in the neighborhood.

The People

In 1561 (around the time that Teresa founded the first monastery of her reform), early in his reign, King Philip II ordered a report on the major cities of Castile, including population and the professions of their citizens.[3] Toward the end of the fifteenth century, Ávila had a population of about 8,000 people. But because of the expulsion (or forced conversion) of the Jews in 1492 and of the Moors in 1503, as well as epidemics and economic downturns, numbers had dropped to about 5,000 at the birth of Teresa in 1515. The city's numbers rebounded in the sixteenth century so that by 1560–1570 there were as many as 13,000 or even 15,000 people. This made it one of the ten largest cities in Castile and one of the fifteen largest in all of Spain.

Like the rest of Spain, Ávila's population was divided along clear class lines: the high nobility, hidalgos, well-to-do merchants and attorneys, artisans and city officials, laborers, servants, and the poor. The nobility of all ranks constituted 11.4 percent of the population; 5.5 percent were clergy—neither of which paid regular taxes.[4] To modern sensibilities, it is ironic that the tax-exempt old nobility traditionally controlled the city government, high church office, and local patronage of religious communities. But the balance of power was shifting as the rising class of merchants, artisans, and professionals such as physicians and lawyers began to challenge the nobility's monopoly on power and influence in the city.

---

3. Juan Bosco de Jesús, "Ávila, cuidad de," in *Diccionario de Santa Teresa: Doctrina e historia*, ed. Tomás Álvarez, 712–15, 2nd ed. (Burgos, Spain: Editorial Monte Carmelo, 2006).

4. Serafín de Tapia offers slightly different percentages: in 1591, 7.2 percent noble and 4.8 percent clerics. See Tapia, ""La sociedad abulense en el siglo XVI," in *Vivir en Ávila cuando Santa Teresa escribe el libro de su "Vida,"* ed. Rómulo Cuartas Lodoño and Francisco Javier Sancho Fermín, 69–133 (Burgos, Spain: Editorial Monte Carmelo, 2011), 92.

Sixteenth-century Spain was plagued by epidemics and bad harvests. The poor typically bear a disproportionate share of the weight of such calamities, but the state of medicine did not provide immunity to the wealthy. In 1507, widespread disease took the lives of Teresa's paternal grandfather, an uncle, and her father's first wife. A serious plague afflicted the city in 1523–1524, followed in the next decades by disastrous harvests. Still, the population of Ávila continued to grow until the end of the century. Crowding in the city, as people came in from the countryside looking for work and the poor for assistance, undoubtedly contributed to the easy spread of disease.

The city's population generally lived in neighborhoods according to social status, occupation, and ethnic background. Teresa's family home was located in a patrician part of the city, near the center and near the family's parish church of St. John the Baptist where she was baptized. Even in prosperous times, probably at least 10 percent of the city's population lived in serious poverty. Following the trend throughout Castile at the time, about 20 percent of its population consisted of widows and their children. This does not include women who were listed officially as "abandoned" (that is, their husbands had taken off for the New World or some other adventuring); theirs was a very precarious economic existence. Like the major cities of the realm, Ávila had a school of doctrine for poor boys, such as the one in which the young John went to school in Medina del Campo about fifty miles to the north.

Economy

Like Castile in general, Ávila's economy was heavily dependent on the textile industry, especially the production of wool and wool products.[5] The city itself was on one of the chief routes of the massive annual winter migration of sheep from northern Spain to pasturing in the warmer south. At the beginning of the century, about 20 percent of the city's population was involved in the cloth industry. This grew to about 30 percent by the 1560s. Unfortunately, various factors—such as increased competition and more efficient production in other parts of Europe—led to the decline of the Spanish cloth industry in the latter half of the century (and the fortunes of Ávila with it).

It is the prominence of the textile industry that most probably led Teresa's paternal grandfather, Juan Sánchez, to move his family there from Toledo after his unfortunate encounter with the Inquisition in that city. This was the principal source of the family's wealth. But like all of Spain, agriculture in general was important to the local economy. The city's nobility maintained country estates from which they collected rents. In fact, Teresa's family possessed lands outside the city, brought into the marriage by Teresa's mother. Teresa may have actually been born at the family estate at Gotarrendura.

The Church

Economic prosperity in the first half of the sixteenth century meant sufficient wealth to support a large number of religious communities and institutions in the city of Ávila. In addition to the cathedral, there were as many as twelve churches served

---

5. See, especially, Serafín de Tapia, "La sociedad abulense en el siglo XVI," 80–90; Serafín de Tapia, "Estructura ocupacional de Ávila en el siglo XVI," in *El pasado histórico de Castilla y León* (Burgos, Spain: Junta de Castilla y León, 1983), 2:201–23; Vázquez de Prada, "La economía castellana"; and Álvarez Vázquez, *Trabajos, dineros, y negocios*, esp. 57–115.

by diocesan clergy, fifteen charitable hospitals (which would include what we today would call homeless shelters), and a number of lay confraternities with an outreach to the poor. There were seven monasteries of men: Benedictines, Premonstratensians, Franciscans (both Observants and Conventuals), Carmelites, Dominicans, and Jesuits (the last arrived only in 1553 but quickly became a prominent group within the city)—for a total of about 180 religious men. There were also seven religious houses of women: Cistercians, Dominicans, Carmelites, Clarisas (Poor Clares), Franciscan Conceptionists, Augustinians (Nuestra Señora de Gracia where the young Teresa was briefly a boarding student), and finally the Discalced—for total of about 335 nuns. The Clarisas were early supporters of the nuns of Teresa's first foundation of San José (L 33.13).[6] Despite the long-standing presence of these feminine communities, it is a sign of the low esteem in which women were held that when twenty-five people (city officials, scholars, and male religious superiors) were gathered in a special city meeting to consider the "problem" of the new foundation of San José, not one of the women superiors was present or apparently seriously consulted.[7]

Many of these religious houses, like the Monastery of the Incarnation in which Teresa was professed, reflected the social structures of the society and were subject to varying degrees of interference by their wealthy donors.[8] But it was a time of social change, and rising merchant classes wanted to join in expressing their faith and seeking heavenly favors by funding religious communities. Teresa herself came from this class, and her reform would

---

6. Maroto, *Teresa en oración*, 81–82.

7. Tapia, "La sociedad abulense," 98.

8. Bilinkoff devotes a chapter to the relationship between religious houses and founding families and benefactors. See Bilinkoff, *Avila of Saint Teresa*, 15–52.

benefit from the generosity of members of this social group. But the entanglement of monasteries with the social structures and interests outside these religious communities did not necessarily prevent the religious from being serious in living the demands of their religious vows. One of the reasons that the young Teresa did not enter the Augustinian monastery of Nuestra Señora de Gracia, where she had been a boarding student, was because it appeared to her to be too strict. Jodi Bilinkoff notes the irony that Teresa would later seek the austerity and strict enclosure that characterized the Augustinian house that she had rejected.[9]

As in all of sixteenth-century Spain, in Ávila there was an active spirit of reform of ecclesiastical institutions and personal spirituality. This would have been promoted especially by both Franciscans and Jesuits, both of whom were very influential on Teresa's own formation. But also of particular importance in Teresa's life was the local reform group influenced by the followers of John of Ávila (1499[?]–1569). John, declared a Doctor of the Church in 2012, was not actually from Ávila (and certainly not to be confused with that other Doctor of the Church, John of the Cross, who was from the province of Ávila). A diocesan priest, John of Ávila was a popular preacher, confessor, and spiritual director in southern Spain. He founded schools and promoted reform of religious education and of the life and spirituality of the clergy. John, influenced by the early Jesuits (and vice versa), was an advocate of interior mental prayer. His thought was in turn influential on the layman Francisco de Salcedo (Teresa's "holy gentleman") and the diocesan priest Gaspar Daza, leaders of this local reform group in Ávila also with strong ties to the Jesuits. They played an early and important role in

---

9. Bilinkoff, 112.

support of Teresa's reform and in the mystical unfolding of her spirituality (though not always in the most helpful way). In the same way, Julían de Ávila—who was a chaplain, companion, and early biographer of Teresa—probably had come into actual contact with John of Ávila. And it was to John of Ávila that Teresa sent the manuscript of the *Life* so he might review its spiritual teaching.

Maridíaz (whose full name was apparently María Díaz), whom Teresa met at the home of her friend and benefactor, Doña Guiomar de Ulloa, was a well-known and influential person in Ávila in the middle of the sixteenth century. Illiterate, she became a *beata*, widely known for her deep spiritual experience and for her spirit of asceticism. Like Teresa, she turned to the Jesuits for directors and confessors. And it was through them that she became friends with Doña Guiomar and then to members of the aristocracy of Ávila. Shortly after Teresa founded San José, Maridíaz became a recluse in a hermitage attached to a local church where she offered spiritual advice and prayer for those who came to her.

Conclusion

Teresa of Jesus never referred to herself as Teresa "of Ávila." But in fact this is the title by which she is most popularly known. While she subsequently made the city famous around the world, at the same time it played an important role in her own early formation. Recipient of mystical knowledge, she was nonetheless profoundly human, formed by her environment and experiences. Ávila provided the sights and sounds from which she drew the imagery to describe her most profound spiritual encounters with God, her experience of social and cultural realities that would form her worldview, her sense of the state of religious life, and her first encounters with the spirit of reform—all of these and more formed the Teresa that we encounter in her writings and learn of her through the reform that she initiated and inspired.

SELECT BIBLIOGRAPHY

English

Álvarez, Tomás. *St. Teresa of Avila: 100 Themes on Her Life and Work*. Translated by Kieran Kavanaugh. Washington, D.C.: ICS Publications, 2011.

Bilinkoff, Jodi. *The Avila of Saint Teresa: Religious Reform in a Sixteenth Century City*. Ithaca, N.Y.: Cornell University Press, 1989.

———. "St. Teresa of Avila and the Avila of St. Teresa." In *Centenary of St. Teresa*, edited by John Sullivan, 53–68. Vol. 3 of *Carmelite Studies*. Washington, D.C.: ICS Publications, 1984.

Spanish

Cátedra, María. *Un santo para una ciudad: ensayo de antropología urbana*. Barcelona, Spain: Editorial Ariel, 1997.

Cuartas Lodoño, Rómulo, and Francisco Javier Sancho Fermín, eds. *Vivir en Ávila cuando Santa Teresa escribe el libro de su "Vida."* Burgos, Spain: Editorial Monte Carmelo, 2011.

Egido, Teófanes, ed. *Perfil histórico de Santa Teresa*. 3rd ed. Madrid: Editorial de Espiritualidad, 2012.

Fernández Álvarez, Manuel. "El entorno social de Santa Teresa." In *Congreso Internacional Teresiano (4–7 octubre, 1982)*, edited by Teófanes Egido et al., 91–101. Vol. 1. Salamanca, Spain: Universidad de Salamanca, 1983.

Juan Bosco de Jesús. "Ávila, cuidad de." In *Diccionario de Santa Teresa: Doctrina e historia*, edited by Tomás Álvarez, 712–15. 2nd ed. Burgos, Spain: Editorial Monte Carmelo, 2006.

Tapia, Serafín de. "Estructura ocupacional de Ávila en el siglo XVI." In *El pasado histórico de Castilla y León*, 2:201–23. 3 vols. Burgos, Spain: Junta de Castilla y León, 1983.

Chapter 3

Honor, Social Class, and Poverty

The family backgrounds of Teresa of Jesus and of John of the Cross present a significant contrast. Born only about thirty years apart and in the same province of Ávila, their childhood experiences of the state of sixteenth-century Spanish society could hardly have been more different. A brief examination of these backgrounds will shed light both on their subsequent lives and work as well as broader trends in Spanish society of the time.

Teresa was born in a well-to-do family of the very lower rungs of nobility with all of its advantages. While it is true that the shadow of a converso (converted Jewish) background hung over the family, her early years in both her home and in the monastery provided for her a level of comfort, education, and opportunity that would have been completely foreign to the young John of the Cross. At the same time, it brought for her the burden of social expectations that she came to despise under the title of "honor" (*honra*).

John of the Cross grew up among the poorest of the poor. According to John's early biographers, his father gave up a life probably in many ways similar to that of the young Teresa in order to marry for love "beneath his station." He died young, leaving his wife poverty stricken with three young sons—one of whom would soon die, probably of complications from malnutrition. John's father too may well have had a converso background. His mother's origins are unknown, but some have conjectured even a Morisco (i.e., converted Muslim) background. But at their level of the social strata, this hardly mattered. Concerns for adequate food and shelter would have ruled out any concern about "honor" that so plagued noble families of the time.

The practical differences in their childhood circumstances are evident in the reality of infant mortality. The poor always bear more immediately and heavily the burden of rising prices, food shortages, and disease. Of the twelve children born from the two marriages of Teresa's father, eleven lived into adulthood. Meanwhile, the deaths of both John's father and infant middle brother were probably related to malnutrition and disease. Of the seven or eight children born to John's oldest brother and his wife, only one survived to adulthood.[1]

To adequately grasp the lives of these two saints, we must understand their social and economic status in their formative years. Just a few examples will suffice to make this point evident. Only in this wider context can we appreciate Teresa's often-repeated criticism of concerns for honor and precise rules of social etiquette, not only as a spiritual concern for humility but also as a form of social critique. The testimony about John's later compassionate concern for the poor and the sick makes greater sense in the context of the struggles of his own childhood. The embrace of religious poverty by these two early Carmelite

---

[1]. Ruiz Salvador, *God Speaks*, 28.

reformers takes on a different perspective in light of their very different economic backgrounds. To look at the socioeconomic backgrounds of each is to get glimpse into the society of the time—just as a study of the time gives us a context to understand them.

The Hagiographic Lives of the Saints

The real social reality of the early lives and backgrounds of both Teresa and John has only truly come to light in recent decades.[2] Their first biographers in the seventeenth century could hardly imagine that a saint would not be the descendant of a noble and even wealthy lineage. Any apparent blemish in their family background would have to be ignored, explained away, or softened. In fact, as the sixteenth century progressed, Spanish religious orders insisted on "purity of blood" for admission—and, after Teresa's death, this included the Discalced Carmelites—so that technically she would not have been admitted to the order that she founded. And so, Teresa's Jewish/converso background was forgotten, and her family depicted as of long-standing nobility rather than having basically bought their way into its lower rungs. The extreme poverty of John's family could not be ignored, but it became important to highlight that his father

---

2. On the hagiographic nature of these first biographies, see Teófanes Egido, "El tratamiento historiográfico de Santa Teresa: Inercias y revisiones," in *Perfil histórico de Santa Teresa*, ed. Teófanes Egido, 13–31, 3rd ed. (Madrid: Editorial de Espiritualidad, 2012); and Eulogio Pacho, "Hagiografías y biografías de San Juan de la Cruz," in *Estudios sanjuanistas: "Historia, textos, hermenéutica,"* 1:27–52 (Burgos, Spain: Editorial Monte Carmelo, 1997). See also José Vicente Rodríguez, *San Juan de la Cruz: La biografía* (Madrid: San Pablo, 2012), 30–38.

was of a noble family who was disowned by his relatives for marrying for love beneath his status. Poverty was seen to fit somehow into God's plan for John's subsequent holiness and an opportunity to display his heroic virtues. As we will see, today there are divergent opinions on how accurate such paternal lineage might be.

It must also be recalled that the first written accounts of the saints' lives were prepared by those who were supporting their beatification and canonization—both to display their undoubted sanctity and for the reputation of the Discalced Carmelite Order and in support of its foundation myths. This gave these earliest works almost an apologetic character. Further, these biographies conformed to the culture's expectation that the lives of saints must involve miracles and other extraordinary experiences linked with multiple examples of superhuman virtues. Those witnesses who provided testimony for the processes of beatification and canonization—and from which later biographers drew much of their source material—also shared the cultural focus on the extraordinary and the supernatural. This is not to suggest that either these witnesses or biographers set out to deceive. It was simply a different time with a different sense of what constituted both good biographical and historical writing as well as Christian sanctity. And besides, such works with their emphasis on the extraordinary and the heroic undoubtedly served as a comfort to their readers amid the poverty, decay, and disease prevalent in much of seventeenth-century Spain.[3]

---

3. Egido, "El tratamiento historiográfico," 15–17.

The Socioeconomic Context of Teresa's Early Years

Teresa de Cepeda y Ahumada (daughter of Alonso Sánchez de Cepeda and Doña Beatriz Dávila de Ahumada) was born into a family with Jewish roots that had gained its wealth in commerce but that had managed to rise to the rank of the lower nobility. This status brought both advantages and burdens that would impact the formation and the unfolding of the lives of Teresa and of her entire family.

A Strictly Hierarchical Society

The society of sixteenth-century Spain was divided rather sharply among various classes in a strict hierarchy.[4] At the top were the nobility—within which there were further clear demarcations. Then there were clerics in their various levels from archbishops of major cities down through bishops, canons of cathedrals, and rural parish priests. The nuns too—as was evident in the Monastery of the Incarnation that Teresa first joined—had social levels, based largely on family lineages. Some monasteries of women catered in particular to women of the nobility. Then came artisans, merchants, and tax-paying workers. Beneath them were servants, the profoundly poor, slaves, and beggars. It was simply assumed that such stratification was part of the divine plan and thus largely unchangeable.

In the middle of the sixteenth century, Castile had about 180 noble families. The highest, called "grandees," were treated

---

4. Eulogio Pacho, "Escenario histórico de Juan de la Cruz," in *Historia, textos, hermenéutica*, 53–99, vol. 1 of *Estudios sanjuanistas* (Burgos, Spain: Editorial Monte Carmelo, 1997), 61–62.

formally as if they were all close relatives ("cousins") of the king, usually possessing enormous estates and the income produced from them. In the biography of St. Teresa, the princess of Eboli and the duchess of Alba are two examples of such nobles. At the lowest end of the nobility were hidalgos—the status attained by Teresa's father. This was a kind of knightly class. Officially, nobility of any rank could only be attained by birth into a family of noble lineage, but in the sixteenth century an upwardly mobile family could attain the status by the manipulation of the legal system and by bribery. But regardless of the level of nobility, all of them were obsessed with their honor, family prestige, and good name. And all of them were also exempt from most taxes.[5]

The ranks of the clergy increased through the course of the century. When John was born in 1541/1542, it is estimated that there were 51,225 members of the clergy—about 23,700 diocesan and nearly 28,000 religious. When he died in 1591, the numbers are estimated to have risen to 74,153 with 33,000 diocesan and 41,000 religious. Again, there was a strict hierarchy among them: archbishops and bishops of major dioceses, usually from high noble families, and were the equivalent of great lords—and down the ranks to nearly illiterate rural parish priests.

Major cities would have counted dozens of religious houses of men and women. The houses of men grew in the sixteenth century, as the numbers above make clear. The houses of women saw less growth, and they were more susceptible to the economic hardships of the times. All of the religious were, like the clergy and nobility, tax exempt.

---

5. Pacho, 60.

An Obsession with Honor and Lineage

Sixteenth-century Spain was a society obsessed with honor—the honor of one's family name and one's own personal honor.[6] To some degree, this was simply a remnant of feudalism and medieval knightly honor. Grounded in that background, families of the nobility typically looked with disdain on the rising merchant classes in a time of developing capitalism. In this, Spain was typical of the other European cultures of the time. Nonetheless, European visitors to Spain wrote home, expressing their surprise at the particular Spanish obsession with honor.[7]

In Spain, added to the remnant of feudal sensibilities, was a layer of concern about so-called purity of blood (*pureza de sangre*)—the ability to claim freedom from the mixture of Jewish or Muslim blood. The Iberian Peninsula had seen the intermingling of the people of the three great Western religions since the eighth century. Even if frowned upon, intermarriage among them over the centuries was a fact. But the question of purity became heightened after Isabella and Ferdinand decreed the expulsion or forced conversion of the Jews in 1492, followed only about ten years later by the same fate for Muslims. It became a mark of honor and ultimately an obsession for Christian families to claim adherence to the Christian faith for generations (so-called Old Christians) and for noble families especially to claim the lack of any drop of Jewish or Muslim blood. Increasingly, purity of blood became not only a point of honor but also essential for advancement

---

6. Teófanes Egido, "The Historical Setting of St. Teresa's Life," in *Spiritual Direction*, ed. John Sullivan, trans. Michael Dodd and Steven Payne, 122–82, vol. 1 of *Carmelite Studies* (Washington, D.C.: ICS Publications, 1980).

7. Egido, "Ambiente histórico," 97.

in virtually every Spanish institution—including admission to religious orders.[8] It was generally felt that it was more honorable to be a commoner with true purity of blood than a noble without it.[9]

Teresa of Jesus was notable in her ability to interact with people of every social class.[10] She seemed most comfortable with hidalgos and with merchants (many of them conversos) who reflected her own background and who were principal supporters of her reform. But she moved easily among the highest nobility who often called on her for personal and spiritual support and whose gifts and patronage were also important for her work. Likewise, she counted many high prelates—themselves of noble backgrounds—as friends and supporters. (We lack much information about any regular interaction that Teresa had with the poor and lower classes. John of the Cross evidently engaged more freely with them in the course of his preaching and work as a local superior in various places.)

And yet, despite her easy interaction with members of the nobility, Teresa was adamant in her criticism of the society's

---

8. Throughout the late fifteenth and into the sixteenth century, one religious community after another instituted these statutes of *limpieza de sangre* (purity of blood): the Dominicans and Jeronimites in the last decades of the fifteenth century and Franciscans, Calced Carmelites, the Jesuits, and even the Discalced in the sixteenth. See Gillian T. W. Ahlgren, *Enkindling Love: The Legacy of Teresa of Avila and John of the Cross*, Mapping the Tradition (Minneapolis: Fortress Press, 2016), 4–5; and Alistair Hamilton, *Heresy and Mysticism in Sixteenth-Century Spain: The Alumbrados* (Cambridge: James Clarke and Co., 1992), 66–67.

9. Daniel de Pablo Maroto, "Resonancias históricos del *Camino de Perfección*," in *Congreso Internacional Teresiano (4–7 octubre, 1982)*, ed. Teófanes Egido et al., 1:50 (Salamanca, Spain: Universidad de Salamanca, 1983).

10. Álvarez devotes a brief chapter to Teresa's interactions with the social classes of her time. Álvarez, *St. Teresa of Avila*, 17–20.

obsession with honor and with all of the intricate social etiquette required of the nobility (see, for example, L 37.5–6, 9; W 27.5). Such concerns were present in the Monastery of the Incarnation in which she was among the nuns entitled to be addressed as "Doña" ("Dame" or "Lady") and where nuns from noble families were deeply concerned with status, forms of address, and apparent slights and offenses. Teresa's teaching on the central place of humility as a foundation of any authentic spiritual growth made her critique of such things inevitable. Her own spiritual maturity made her see the utter ridiculousness of such concerns in light of the divine realities increasingly and more deeply revealed to her. Moreover, the petty concerns of social status and purity of blood could affect her work very practically—as it did in her effort to found a monastery of the reform in the city of Toledo with the help of a donor of the merchant class but with stipulations contrary to the sensibilities of the city's nobility (F 15–16). In that particular case, it appears that God made clear to her the ridiculousness of such concerns (ST 5).

But it seems likely as well that her own converso background and her own family's struggle to attain and maintain its status as hidalgos contributed to the depth and vigor of her social critique.[11] Trying to hide their Jewish roots and the financial burdens of maintaining a lifestyle in keeping with their hard-won status as hidalgos may have weighed heavily on Teresa's father—likely evident even to a bright and sensitive girl like the young Teresa. At the same time, the reader can sense her compassion for the members

---

11. Pérez argues that Teresa's critique of the culture's obsession with *honra* was related not directly to her own status as a converso but rather to having watched her father financially ruined by his effort to maintain it. Pérez, *Teresa de Ávila*, 31. Maroto concludes that both her own converso status and her spiritual priorities led to her aversion to *honra*. Maroto, "Resonancias históricos," 58.

of the nobility—especially the women—made virtually slaves of the concerns and demands of their status (L 34.4).

Pleito de Hidalguía

Teresa's family on her father's side was of Jewish origins (*judeoconversos* or simply *conversos*).[12] To us today, this may seem simply an interesting fact, like saying that someone has an Irish or German background. But even a few decades ago, it was a bombshell when, in 1946, a seemingly obscure file in government archival offices in the city of Valladolid made evident that her grandfather had been disciplined by the Inquisition for reverting to practices of Judaism. It was revealed that her father and his brothers, being of Jewish origins, had sought (to some degree, bought) and obtained recognition of noble status rather than being born into it. In part, it was an obvious attempt to cover over their Jewish background that at the time was a serious social stigma. This fact had remained hidden for centuries, unmentioned since her earliest biographies. And shortly after the records of the legal process initiated by her father and uncles were discovered, they were mysteriously "lost"—only to be "rediscovered" three decades later.[13]

---

12. The extant petitions, letters, and testimony from the legal process by which Teresa's family obtained its patent of nobility are provided, after an introduction that lays out the chronology of the process, by Teófanes Egido, *El linaje judeoconverso de Santa Teresa: Pleito de hidalguía de los Cepeda* (Madrid: Editorial de Espiritualidad, 1986). The process is thoroughly discussed in Tomás Álvarez, *Estudios Teresianos I: Biografía e historia* (Burgos, Spain: Editorial Monte Carmelo, 1995), 65–139. For a brief discussion in English, see Bilinkoff, *Avila of Saint Teresa*, 64–67; and Álvarez, *St. Teresa of Avila*, 67–70.

13. Peter Tyler, *Teresa of Avila: Doctor of the Soul* (New York: Continuum, 2014), 30–32; and Pérez, *Teresa de Ávila*, 17–18.

The legal process (*pleito*) by which Teresa's father, Alonso de Cepeda, and his brothers Pedro, Ruy, and Francisco had obtained their status as hidalgos (*hidalguía*)—that is, as lower members of the noble class—is itself a window into the social structures, legal processes, and corruption of the time. And the process pursued by the Cepeda brothers is both a perfect example of the phenomenon and a window into their own family history. The very fact that there were government offices and officials whose sole function was to review requests to obtain (or technically to prove or have recognized) a family's noble lineage and status indicates how common such attempts were at the time. The attainment of the *hidalguía* would both exempt a person from major forms of taxation in an age of ever-increasing taxation to pay for foreign wars (which only commoners paid) and free one, at least formally, from any perceived taint of Jewish or Moorish blood. The willingness of the government to permit the virtual buying of such status and exemption reveals how cash-strapped it was—even more since this immediate inflow of cash through fees (and bribes) would come at the long-term cost of losing the well-to-do family's tax revenues. Meanwhile, the family obtained a considerable bump in social status that could, in turn, have financial advantages—as Teresa notes when she tells us that concern for social status (*honra*) almost always goes with concern for wealth (W 2.6). While families of authentic noble lineage might look down on the process and its beneficiaries in the short run, more humble backgrounds could easily be forgotten or overlooked as sometimes cash-strapped old noble families could now marry their offspring to newly noble and more financially comfortable hidalgos without shame.

The process for Teresa's father and uncles began on August 6, 1519, when Teresa was four years old. It was a protracted undertaking, though a favorable decision was granted in November

1520, reiterated though slightly restricted in August 1522. Although Teresa never mentions it in her writings, it is difficult to imagine that she was not aware of it—though perhaps only later. It began with the imposition of a tax that the four Cepeda brothers (Alonso, Pedro, Ruy, and Francisco) refused to pay, claiming that, as hidalgos already, they were exempt and their names should be dropped from the taxpayer rolls. And this set into motion the process to prove their status and have it legally and publicly acknowledged by the court.

Technically, commoners could not buy their way into the nobility. It was supposed to be a matter of lineage and blood. The successful *pleito de hidalguía* was the effort to demonstrate the immemorial possession of such a background—concretely by demonstrating that it had been held for at least three generations. But at the time, testimony such as "I have heard . . ."; "it is widely known . . ."; and "it is commonly held . . ." could be considered admissible evidence—as could evidence of long living in a manner consistent with noble status as perceived at the time. At the same time, supportive testimony had to avoid any recollection that the family had amassed wealth by commerce or mercantile activity, which was believed to be beneath the nobility.

Teresa's grandfather, the converso Juan Sánchez, married Inés de Cepeda (and thus the family name of Teresa's father) and had accumulated considerable wealth. After the public shame of having been "reconciled" by the Inquisition, the family moved from Toledo to Ávila where they were not known.[14] It appears

---

14. It is possible that Juan Sánchez had obtained a *pleito de hidalguía* for himself. See Mujica, *Teresa de Ávila*, 20. But such a document has never been found, and it is noteworthy that his sons did not produce it or use it as basis for their own claim. See Egido, "Ambiente histórico," 89.

that his sons had successfully used the family wealth to live a lifestyle consistent with a higher social status and to marry into the *hidalguía* of Ávila.[15] One of the principal functions of the nobility, for example, since medieval times was to maintain horses and arms at the disposition of the king in time of military need. We know that Teresa's father did so at some point in the process of the conquest of the kingdom of Navarre (the same wars in which St. Ignatius of Loyola was wounded in 1521), though we don't know his exact role. He also, in keeping with his status, maintained hunting birds and donated the hunted meat to the poor. The family had the exclusive services of wet nurses to breastfeed their infants, services which families of lower rank would not have been able to obtain. And since it was a society obsessed with external appearances and display, both the marriages and the lifestyle of Teresa's father and uncles were used as further evidence that they were already in fact hidalgos.

Unfortunately, seeking noble status required abandoning the very trade or mercantile activities by which a family had likely amassed sufficient wealth to give evidence of a higher social status. What was left to them were the rents received from landed estates and ownership of some types of business operations. But maintaining the facade of nobility could itself be an expensive undertaking, and without previously lucrative income streams, it could slowly wipe out a family's financial resources. This was the case with Teresa's father who, by the time of his death, was deeply in debt. Her brothers were among the many young men of noble families required by financial realities to seek their fortunes in

---

15. Such marriages would make subsequent children hidalgos but technically not the parent who had not been born into noble status.

the New World.[16] It would have been an afront to their "honor" to return to the commercial enterprises that had been the source of their family wealth, and the Cepeda family lacked the connections with the royal court and higher nobility which might have served as an avenue for advancement. Freedom from taxation did not come without a price.

The process began well for the Cepeda brothers, but it dragged on with the presentation of evidence, witnesses, and letters by both the brothers and the city seeking its taxes—all of it undoubtedly at significant cost to the Cepedas. While most of the proceedings were held away from the city of Ávila where one of the brothers owned taxable land, some were held in the city itself. Both the prolongation of the proceedings and the activity in Ávila itself likely caused some public embarrassment to the family. But most distressing to the family was the submission as evidence of the official record of the public "reconciliation" of the men's father, Juan Sánchez, by the Inquisition of Toledo. The fact that the clear evidence of Jewish background did not derail their efforts makes it almost impossible that the brothers did not resort to bribery to achieve their goal. In any case, it was the discovery of this record in the proceedings for *hidalguía* that finally revealed Teresa's own converso background.

---

16. Álvarez (*St. Teresa of Avila*, 59–66) provides a chapter that briefly reviews the chronology, fortunes, and fates of Teresa's brothers in the Americas. See also Mercedes de Lara Marcano, "Hermanos de Santa Teresa de Jesús en el nuevo mundo," in *Santa Teresa y la literatura mística hispánica*, Actas del I congreso internacional sobre Santa Teresa y la mística hispánica, ed. Manuel Criado de Val, 245–51 (Madrid: EDI-6, 1984); Tomás Álvarez, ed., *Diccionario de Santa Teresa: Doctrina e historia*, 2nd ed. (Burgos, Spain: Editorial Monte Carmelo, 2006), 664–67; 682–88; and Pedro Tomé Martín, *Los Hermanos de Teresa de Ávila en América* (Ávila, Spain: Institución Gran Duque de Alba de la Disputación Provincial de Ávila, 2015).

The Socioeconomic Context of John's Early Years

Teresa of Jesus was not of the highest nobility of Spain, nor was her family among the wealthiest by any means. Still, her early life and the concerns of her family were vastly different from those of the young John of the Cross. To look at his childhood situation is to show the stark contrasts of sixteenth-century Spain.

John de Yepes was born in 1541/1542 in the town of Fontiveros in the province of Ávila, about twenty-nine miles from the city of Ávila, in the midst of a largely agricultural area. At the time, there were 439 heads of households listed in the city tax rolls—and thus all of them commoners. In addition, there were the nobles, clerics, and nuns who did not pay taxes. This leads to an estimated population of about 2,000 inhabitants. A few years later, in 1553, the number had grown to 573 tax-paying households and about 111 hidalgos (tax-exempt lower nobility). This leads to an estimate of a total population of about 3,000 people at the middle of the sixteenth century—not a major city but not tiny in a country with a population of only about seven million.[17]

The decade of the 1540s was difficult economically with poor harvests, disease, and hunger. An official visitation of Fontiveros by a representative of the bishop of Ávila in 1546 reported severe poverty in the town, with both of its former "hospitals" (probably more like homeless shelters or refuges) closed. It was probably for this reason that John's family moved to the far more prosperous Medina del Campo, which in 1530 had a population of somewhere between 15,000 and 20,000. It was a center

---

17. Efrén de la Madre de Dios [Montalva] and Otger Steggink, *Tiempo y vida de San Juan de la Cruz* (Madrid: Biblioteca de Autores Cristianos [BAC], 1992), 49.

for the cloth trade, and its markets and fairs drew people from all over Spain and even other parts of Europe. The young John spent his adolescence there.

John's Family Background

The early biographers of John of the Cross tell us that his father, Gonzalo de Yepes, was of noble lineage, his family having been engaged in the production and sale of cloth.[18] He was disowned by his family when he married the poor Catalina Alvarez and was forced to take up her humble craft as a weaver. In 1624, some thirty years after John's death, a cousin produced an elaborate family tree—swearing before a notary to its authenticity—showing the noble lineage of his paternal family going back at least to 1448 to a "Francisco García de Yepes," a "man of arms" who fought for the Castilian king Juan II. In recent years, however, notable scholars have expressed doubts about the authenticity of such claims, arguing that the claim of nobility for John's paternal family was a construct of seventeenth-century Baroque biographers who couldn't imagine sanctity without nobility and who were implicitly advocating for John's beatification and canonization.[19] This is not to suggest, as we saw above, that the authors were intentionally deceptive or insincere, but they

---

18. For a brief study of the history of the Yepes family, see Ruiz Salvador, *God Speaks*, 106. For recent critical studies of the early life of John of the Cross within the context of the times, see, especially, Rodríguez, *San Juan de la Cruz*; and Balbino Velasco Bayón, *San Juan de la Cruz: A las raíces del hombre y del carmelita* (Madrid: Editorial de Espiritualidad, 2009).

19. This point has been made especially by Teófanes Egido. See, for example, "Claves históricos para la comprensión de San Juan de la Cruz," in *Introducción a le lectura de San Juan de la Cruz*, ed. Salvador Ros García, 59–124 (Salamanca, Spain: Junta de Castilla y León, Consejería de Cultura y Turismo, 1993);

certainly possessed a different view of writing biographies. Others have argued strenuously for the authenticity of the claims.[20] In the end, the author of a recent massive biography of the saint argues, at least tentatively, for the authenticity of the claims of nobility, based on the factual nature of the names and dates that appear on the genealogy as well as the fact that John's brother, Francisco de Yepes, reports it as fact.[21]

Secure details of John's family background and early years are sparse. Although perhaps from a wealthy merchant family, some conjecture that Gonzalo de Yepes was from a converso background. This is likely given the number of conversos in the merchant class, but the evidence is not conclusive.[22] As it was for Teresa, "purity of blood" would have been important for early biographers of John of the Cross to maintain.

The background of John's mother, Catalina Alvarez, is even more vague. Again, some have conjectured that because Gonzalo's rejection by his family was so total and enduring, the issue must have been more than the simple difference of class and financial status (though those sorts of things mattered a great deal in that culture). And so, some have theorized that she was a converso or even a Morisco (from a Muslim background) of

---

"La infancia de un santo del barocco," *San Juan de la Cruz* 47, no. 1 (2013–2014): 43–84; and "Los Yepes, una familia de pobres," in *Aspectos históricos de San Juan de la Cruz*, ed. Teófanes Egido, 25–41 (Ávila, Spain: Institución Gran Duque de Alba de la Disputación Provincial de Ávila, 1990).

20. For a copy of the Baroque "family tree" of the Yepes family, see Elizabeth Christina Wilhelmsen, *San Juan de la Cruz y su identidad histórica: Los telos del León Yepesino* (Madrid: Fundación Universitaria Española, 2010), 377–84.

21. Rodríguez, *San Juan de la Cruz*, 68–70. The Rodríguez biography is a book of nearly 1,000 pages in forty chapters and with six appendices! See also Velasco Bayón, *San Juan de la Cruz*, 55–78.

22. Rodríguez, *San Juan de la Cruz*, 72–74.

more recent conversion or perhaps had even been guilty of crime. In the end, beyond her poverty and her low social status (which even Baroque hagiographies generally could not deny), all of the rest is conjecture. But guesswork can go both ways: one earlier biographer noted that "Alvarez" was a well-known family name, including some among the nobility, so that perhaps Catalina was related to a branch of one of those families. In sum, we can say that John's father may well have grown up in circumstances not unlike those of Teresa, but at John's birth the family was living in extreme poverty and at nearly the lowest social level possible. In addition to her sometime work as a weaver, Catalina was a wet nurse for the infants of wealthy families. And extant parish baptismal records list her as wet nurse and as godmother of abandoned infants whom she had presumably tried to assist.

Poverty in Sixteenth-Century Spain

John of the Cross lived in a century of widespread poverty in Spain,[23] born in a decade of particularly bad harvests that inevitably increased food prices and lessened purchases of nonessential items like the cruder cloth produced by weavers like John's mother.[24] In the five years between 1541 and 1546, the price of wheat more than doubled.[25] Many common people lived on the edge of falling into poverty. One bad crop or the death of a head of the household (as in the case of John's family) could

---

23. See, especially, Alberto Marcos Martín, "San Juan de la Cruz y su ambiente de pobreza," in *Historia*, ed. Teófanes Egido, 143–84, vol. 2 of *Actas del Congreso Internaticional Sanjuanista* (Valladolid, Spain: Junta de Castilla y León. Consejería de Cultura y Turismo, 1993).

24. Marcos Martín, 146–48.

25. Marcos Martín, 151.

easily push a family into abject poverty and homelessness with its accompanying hunger, susceptibility to disease, and premature death (as seems to have been the case with John's middle brother, Luis, who died in childhood).[26] John's short stature as an adult may well have been related to malnutrition as a child.

Larger cities were populated by widows and their children who, like John's little family, sought survival. Throughout the sixteenth century, 15 percent of the population of the twenty-five cities around Valladolid were widows and their children. The percentage was often even higher in larger cities to which poor widows, like the mother of John of the Cross, migrated in order to seek more available assistance. A staggering 23 percent of the population of Medina del Campo consisted of widows and their children. Likewise, in Ávila, between 20 and 27 percent lived in households headed by widows.[27] This phenomenon as well as the seeming omnipresence of wandering beggars on the highways and in the cities was very concerning both to the central government and to local municipalities who struggled to address the needs of the poor, to quell their influx, and to prevent crime and delinquency. The bad harvests and epidemics at midcentury created a veritable avalanche of people in need, stretching the resources of cities, private philanthropists, confraternities, and religious communities. Throughout the century, larger Castilian cities developed ordinances to exclude wandering beggars and to restrict public assistance to their "own" poor—even as they made efforts to distinguish the "truly needy" from those who could work and from charlatans and "professional" panhandlers.[28]

---

26. Egido, "Los Yepes," 34–37.
27. Marcos Martín, "San Juan de la Cruz y su ambiente de pobreza," 153–54.
28. Marcos Martín, 160.

Such efforts to address the presence of larger numbers of the poor coincided with a gradual change of attitude throughout Europe toward the poor and responsibility for them.[29] Care of the poor in the Middle Ages had been largely viewed as a pious duty of Christian charity for those who wished to attain heaven. It was accepted that the presence of the poor was part of the mysterious divine ordering of society that served as an opportunity for those with abundance to share God's bounty. The presence of an abundance of charitable voluntary organizations called confraternities is one sign of this social attitude in the culture of the time. (In Medina del Campo at the time of John's childhood, there were perhaps sixty of such pious associations—all of them with some form of charitable outreach.) But gradually this sacralized perspective gave way to a more secular and bourgeois view of poverty as a social problem with a need to try to distinguish the "deserving" from the "undeserving" poor. Care of the poor took on more the character of the prudent prevention of social unrest and crime.

Even the nobility could fall into poverty—called *"pobres vergonzantes"* (shamefaced or embarrassed poor). In their case, "honor" would prevent them from publicly seeking available means of support and certainly from begging. We know that later in life John would reach out discreetly to such families while he was a superior in Granada. The Carmelites, like other religious houses of the time, also understood it as their responsibility to reach out to the needy with what we today might call soup kitchens.

Various laws and city ordinances codified assistance (*privilegios*) for the poor. And it is clear that John's family were

---

29. Marcos Martín, 159–64.

profoundly poor (*pobreza de solemnidad*, in the terms of the time). But this status, recognized by local governments, afforded them the assistance of established charities and social assistance provided by cities, confraternities, and wealthy benefactors. Medina del Campo was a particularly good choice for the family to settle in since, in the mid-1500s, its prosperous market and fairs provided abundant wealth to be shared by wealthy donors in support of the poor. This included the "school of doctrine" (*colegio de los doctrinos*) for the poor that the young John was able to attend and thus learn to read and write as a prelude to his admission to a secondary school run by the Jesuits. John's older brother, Francisco, on the other hand, later renowned for his sanctity and dearly beloved by John, appears to have spent his youth in a way sadly not unusual in systemically poor families. He learned to "work the system," moving from job to job and accustomed to seeking alms. Later in life, he attained some financial stability due to the reputation and admirers of his brother.[30]

Major cities in Spain in the sixteenth century sought to establish, through private donors, these "schools of doctrine" for poor children, especially for orphans. In 1553, this practice was mandated by royal decree. The children could learn basic arithmetic, reading and writing, catechism,[31] and a useful trade to help them rise out of abject poverty (though the young John did not seem adept at any that he tried—except the academic). At the same time, such institutions served the practical benefit to the municipality of keeping bands of poor children

---

30. Egido, "Los Yepes," 37–38.
31. John of Ávila, that other Spanish Doctor of the Church of that period, had published a particularly popular catechism, set to verse, and able to be sung in order to enhance memorization.

off the streets and perpetuating yet another generation of the profoundly poor. Without this opportunity, John would have ended up like his brother. There were also, in lesser number, similar schools for poor girls in which the focus was household skills and good morals. Girls from wealthier families, on the other hand, could become boarders in schools within the monasteries of women—as the young Teresa did for about eighteen months in an Augustinian monastery of women.[32]

Such schools for the poor were rigorous, following a monastic discipline and overseen by a priest. The young John attended a school attached to a convent of Augustinian nuns. These nuns also had an outreach to *"mujeres perdidas"* (literally, "lost women," mostly prostitutes) in a city in which prostitution was a major problem because of poverty and the frequent trade fairs and presence of traveling merchants. As was typical, young John was expected to take his turn at serving Mass and cleaning the nuns' church. In addition, the boys were often expected to beg alms in the streets to support the school. Funerals of the wealthy would be a source of income for the boys and their schools, since the presence of an abundance of members of confraternities, clerics, religious, and altar servers was considered a sign of the deceased's social status. And such families—whether noble or simply aspiring to make the right appearance—were often the principal and essential donors of the schools.

The boys usually left the schools at about fourteen years old to pursue whatever trade they had learned. Some, like John, were able to go on for further studies. In John's case, with the

---

32. Serafín de Tapia, "Las primeras letras y el analfabetismo en Castilla, Siglo XVI," in *Historia*, ed. Teófanes Egido, 185–220, vol. 2 of *Actas del Congreso Internaticional Sanjuanista* (Valladolid, Spain: Junta de Castilla y León. Consejería de Cultura y Turismo, 1993), 192–93.

help of a generous priest, he was able to procure a job as a kind of resident orderly in a hospital for the poor (Nuestra Señora de la Concepción) while he studied (about 1559–1563) in a recently established Jesuit school. There he gained a sound humanistic education, including grammar, Latin, rhetoric, literature, and perhaps some philosophy as well as basics of etiquette. The Jesuits had arrived in Medina del Campo in 1550, but it is estimated that their school had more than 160 students at John's time there.[33]

The hospital in which John worked focused on the care (rather than real cure) of those with contagious disease, specifically venereal diseases such as syphilis (and thus the hospital's popular name "Las Bubas," referring to the boils that often afflicted its patients). It had about forty-five to fifty beds, not including accommodation made for patients of greater financial means who were also plagued with some contagious disease but could afford to bring their own bedding and pay for their care. It was one of thirteen or fourteen such hospitals in Medina del Campo—eleven of them funded by the confraternities. Some of them—despite the name "hospital"—were probably more akin to homeless shelters with food kitchens for the sick poor than to any modern sense of a health-care facility. This is not to say that they were not attended by a doctor or others sincerely dedicated to the care of the sick with training and experience beyond that of an orderly like the young John; rather, it is a reflection of the state of medicine at the time and the resources available to a privately funded institution in an age of great and widespread poverty. Again, John and other such aides would have been expected to beg for alms to support the institution.

---

33. Rodríguez, *San Juan de la Cruz*, 104–18.

This background helps us to understand a number of things about John of the Cross—or at least to place them in a solid context—whether his physical shortness of stature (due to possible early malnutrition), his later solicitude for the poor and sick, his compassion toward sinners, or his comfort with manual labor and humble tasks. In adulthood, he proudly introduced his brother Francisco, still living in poverty and who would have lacked the manner of the better educated.

Conclusion

Teresa of Jesus and John of the Cross are deservedly saints. Their sanctity is well attested. They are Doctors of the Church and among the greatest mystical writers in the Catholic tradition. And they were also human beings—in some ways quite extraordinary human beings but still very much flesh-and-blood people who were formed by their life experiences and the context in which they grew up. It cannot have been otherwise. We do them a disservice to whitewash elements of their family backgrounds or think that their later adult actions and emphases arose independently of their childhood experiences. Their first biographers in the century after they died inevitably looked at them through the lenses of their own time and culture, and with their own ideas about what constitutes true sanctity. In our time, we embrace Teresa and John as true guides and examples in our own path to sanctity by seeing them in their flesh-and-blood reality.

SELECT BIBLIOGRAPHY

English

Álvarez, Tomás. *St. Teresa of Avila: 100 Themes on Her Life and Work*. Translated by Kieran Kavanaugh. Washington, D.C.: ICS Publications, 2011. (See, in particular, pp. 45–86.)

Egido, Teófanes. "The Historical Setting of St. Teresa's Life." In *Spiritual Direction*, edited by John Sullivan, translated by Michael Dodd and Steven Payne, 122–82. Vol. 1 of *Carmelite Studies*. Washington, D.C.: ICS Publications, 1980.

Spanish

Álvarez, Tomás. "El pleito de hidalguía de los Cepedas: Padre y tíos de Santa Teresa." In *Estudios Teresianos I: Biografía e historia*, 65–102. Burgos, Spain: Editorial Monte Carmelo, 1995.

———. "La ejecutoria de hidalguía del padre de Santa Teresa." In *Estudios Teresianos I: Biografía e historia*, 103–39. Burgos, Spain: Editorial Monte Carmelo, 1995.

Egido, Teófanes. "Ambiente histórico." In *Introducción a la lectura de Santa Teresa*, edited by Alberto Barrientos, 63–155. 2nd ed. Madrid: Editorial de Espiritualidad, 2002.

———. "Claves históricos para la comprensión de San Juan de la Cruz." In *Introducción a la lectura de San Juan de la Cruz*, edited by Salvador Ros García, 59–124. Salamanca, Spain: Junta de Castilla y León, Consejería de Cultura y Turismo, 1993.

———. *El linaje judeoconverso de Santa Teresa: Pleito de hidalguía de los Cepeda*. Madrid,: Editorial de Espiritualidad, 1986.

———. "El tratamiento historiográfico de Santa Teresa: Inercias y revisiones." In *Perfil histórico de Santa Teresa*, edited by Teófanes Egido, 13–31. 3rd ed. Madrid: Editorial de Espiritualidad, 2012.

———. "La infancia de un santo del barocco." *San Juan de la Cruz* 47, no. 1 (2013–2014): 43–84.

———. "Los Yepes, una familia de pobres." In *Aspectos históricos de San Juan de la Cruz*, edited by Teófanes Egido, 25–41. Ávila, Spain:

Institución Gran Duque de Alba de la Diputación Provincial de Ávila, 1990.

Marcos Martín, Alberto. "San Juan de la Cruz y su ambiente de pobreza." In *Historia*, edited by Teófanes Egido, 143–84. Vol. 2 of *Actas del Congreso Internacional Sanjuanista*. Valladolid, Spain: Consejería de Cultura y Turismo de la Junta de Castilla y León, 1993.

Pacho, Eulogio. "Escenario histórico de Juan de la Cruz." In *Historia, textos, hermenéutica*, 53–99. Vol. 1 of *Estudios sanjuanistas*. Burgos, Spain: Editorial Monte Carmelo, 1997.

———. "Hagiografías y biografías de San Juan de la Cruz." In *Historia, textos, hermenéutica*, 27–52. Vol. 1 of *Estudios sanjuanistas*. Burgos, Spain: Editorial Monte Carmelo, 1997.

Velasco Bayón, Balbino. *San Juan de la Cruz: A las raíces del hombre y del carmelita*. Madrid: Editorial de Espiritualidad, 2009.

Wilhelmsen, Elizabeth Christina. *San Juan de la Cruz y su identidad histórica: Los telos del León Yepesino*. Madrid: Fundación Universitaria Española, 2010.

Chapter 4

Reform of the Church and Religious Orders

Neither the Protestant Reformation nor the Discalced Reform of the sixteenth century appeared out of nowhere. A spirit of reform was alive in the church in the late fourteenth and especially in the fifteenth century. The institutional church had been rocked by the scandals of the Avignon papacy (1309–1376) and the Great Schism (1378–1417) that followed it and by widely known papal and curial misbehaviors. The crowning achievement of medieval theology in the work of St. Thomas Aquinas (1225–1274) was followed by a period of decline in which Scholastic theology became increasingly unoriginal, dry, and speculative. The religious orders throughout Europe were decimated by the Black Death in the middle of the fourteenth century, and the religious who remained were generally forced to mitigate their rules and observance.

Adequate catechesis was inevitably a problem especially in rural areas. Without modern means of communication and with widespread illiteracy, religious education was difficult. Parish clergy were often poorly educated themselves. Like forms of popular religion in other European countries of the time, though perhaps with its own distinctive fervor, popular Spanish religion was highly devotional. Although often lacking the depth of real knowledge of the faith, people were fiercely devoted to saints and attracted to externals like grand processions. Teresa shared such devotion, but she had no patience with excessive devotions or superstitions (L 6.6, 13.16, 25.20–22; W 34.11). The culture was very concerned about the working and threats of the devil.[1]

By the fifteenth century, movements such as the Devotio Moderna were promoting a more personal faith and devotion beyond superstition and excessive focus on merely external rituals, a return to reading the Bible, and an invitation to a deeper prayer for laity and clergy alike—a kind of democratization of faith and the spiritual life.[2] Particularly influential in Spain was the translation and publication in 1490 of the classic *Imitation of Christ* by Thomas à Kempis that Teresa recommended in her *Constitutions* (Con 8). Meanwhile, there were focused movements toward reform of the clergy and of religious orders. Theologians were beginning to return to a study of the Bible, of the church fathers, and the works of Aquinas.

The "Catholic Kings" and Cardinal Cisneros

Ferdinand of Aragon and Isabella of Castile married in 1469, uniting the two major kingdoms of the Iberian Peninsula. One of the principal emphases of their reign—and that of their successors throughout the sixteenth century—was reform of the church and of its religious orders. In 1494, the pope recognized their efforts with the title "the Catholic Kings" (*Reyes Católicos*). Genuine religious zeal was partnered with political strategy as

---

1. Álvarez, *St. Teresa of Avila*, 29–32.
2. Pérez, "Mística y realidad histórica," 39.

the Spanish crown pursued a reform agenda that was at the same time under royal control and Spanish in focus. Their principal agent was Franciscan cardinal Francisco Jiménez de Cisneros, confessor to Queen Isabella and archbishop of the primatial see of Toledo. The process was advanced and encouraged by the arrival of their grandson and heir, Carlos V, from the Low Countries in 1516. Sympathetic to humanistic ideals, he and his Flemish courtiers promoted the inflow of books and reform ideas from northern Europe (at least until such ideas seemed to be linked with the rise of the Protestant reform).[3]

Reform of the Clergy

One of the principal means of reform pursued by the Spanish crown was the appointment of reform-minded bishops rather than the former practice of simply promoting clerics because of family and political connections. The more difficult challenge was the reform of the so-called lower clergy—that is, especially parish priests.[4] It was not uncommon for priests to have what was effectively a wife ("concubinage"). Recall the priest-confessor whom Teresa describes in the *Life* (chapter 5) who was involved in a publicly known relationship with a woman who had "bewitched" him with a charm. A 1512 synod in the Archdiocese of Seville

---

3. Juan Ignacio Gutierrez Nieto, "El proceso de encastamiento social de la Castilla del siglo XVI, La respuesta conversa," in *Congreso Internacional Teresiano (4–7 octubre, 1982)*, ed. Teófanes Egido et al., 1:103–20 (Salamanca, Spain: Universidad de Salamanca, 1983), 107–10; and Miguel Norbert Ubarri, *Jan Van Ruusbroec y Juan de la Cruz: La mística en diálogo* (Madrid: Editorial de Espiritualidad, 2007), 16–22.

4. For the state of the clergy at the time of Teresa, see, especially, Pérez, *Teresa de Ávila*, 150–74.

called on clerics to maintain the public appearance of virtuous living and chastity, particularly by not participating publicly in the marriages of their adult children, nor legally willing property to their concubines. Such widely known scandalous behavior was undoubtedly behind at least some of the anticlerical tones of popular literature of the time.[5]

Rural priests were likely to be largely uneducated. It is no wonder that basic catechesis was often neglected. Recall that the first two friars of the reform at Duruelo found that the people in the area were in need of such basic religious education (F 14.8). One of the typical procedures of the Inquisition was to question those accused to the tribunal about their knowledge of basic doctrine and prayers. Records indicate that such knowledge improved over the course of the century as new catechisms were published in the vernacular and renewed attention was given to religious education.[6] John of Ávila, now a Doctor of the Church and consulted by Teresa of Jesus for the publication of the *Life*, was a particular advocate for good religious education.

Priests often did not preach or did not do it well. This problem was apparently so rampant in Europe that the Council of Trent later called on priests to preach at least once a week. In many places, this was apparently an innovation. Teresa tells us that she herself was very fond of good sermons (L 8.12), and preaching was an important aspect of the ministry of John of the Cross throughout his adult life.

---

5. Payne, *Spanish Catholicism*, 36–38.

6. Payne, 44–45. See also Melquíades Andrés Martín, "San Juan de la Cruz y los movimientos espirituales de su tiempo," in *Aspectos históricos de San Juan de la Cruz*, ed. Teófanes Egido, 99–115 (Ávila, Spain: Institución Gran Duque de Alba de la Diputación Provincial de Ávila, 1990), 102.

Universities and the Renewal of Learning

The sixteenth century witnessed the multiplication of universities in Spain—from only six in 1459 to thirty-three only 150 years later. In them was fostered the study of the Fathers, the Bible, and theology. Cardinal Cisneros himself founded the University of Alcalá in 1499 (actually opened in 1508), which became a center of the new humanistic studies and especially the works of Erasmus of Rotterdam. There, scholars pursued the preparation of a massive polyglot Bible with the biblical text in critical ancient and modern languages to promote biblical study. Also at Alcalá, in 1502, Cisneros established a printing press from which was published the vernacular translations of theological and spiritual works that he himself promoted to widen theological knowledge and spiritual growth. These works included authors such as Augustine, John Climacus, Bernard of Clairvaux, Bonaventure, Angela of Foligno, and Hugh of Balma. And the import of books and publication of books in the vernacular would continue at a rapid pace—at least until the Inquisition and its "Index of Forbidden Books" slowed the process.

Reform of the Men's Religious Orders

Like the reform spirit present in the Spanish church before the reign of Isabella and Ferdinand, reforms movements within the religious orders were also already well advanced. But with the help of Cisneros who was himself imbued with the spirit of the Franciscan reform, they actively promoted it. They and their successors would favor those religious orders that came to be known as "observants," seeking to observe strictly their rules and founding traditions.

The middle of the fourteenth century had seen the serious decline in members in religious communities throughout Europe due to the Black Death. Some houses lost as many as 85 or 90 percent of their members. In many cases, the full rigors of their lives for those who remained could not be maintained, and their practices were relaxed or "mitigated" in order to survive in these unfavorable circumstances. Candidates with less preparation and perhaps with less zeal were accepted in order to rebuild numbers. But such members were less likely to yearn for the return to stricter observances.[7] Fewer members could pursue further theological study that might have served as a foundation for a sound spirituality. This was similar to the later case of the monastery of Teresa's profession where the many women who entered religious life because of being unmarriageable would not be likely to want to pursue a stricter form of life.

But already in the fourteenth century and especially in the fifteenth, a momentum for change began to grow among the communities of male religious. At first, as branches or movements within the various orders themselves, "observants" began to advocate and embrace a life in greater keeping with the strict observance of their original rules without mitigation. In contrast—and sometimes in active opposition—were the so-called conventuals who often wanted to embrace the religious life with seriousness but while maintaining the mitigations that had been granted. The reform-minded religious might also be called *recolectos* (reflecting their often more contemplative emphasis that might be an obscured characteristic of their founders) or *descalzos* (shoeless or barefoot—a practice

---

7. Melquíades Andrés Martín, *La teología española en el siglo XVI* (Madrid: Biblioteca de Autores Cristianos, 1976), 1:83–85.

meant to indicate an embrace of a spirit of poverty, austerity, and mortification).[8]

The austere reform of the Benedictines was among the first in Spain, beginning with the foundation of a monastery at Valladolid in 1381—a monastery that would become the center of a reform-minded congregation. The Franciscan reform in Spain may be dated at about 1380 when groups of Franciscans in Galicia and Valencia decided to return to their primitive rule. The movement spread quickly to Castile. A similar effort was initiated with secular clergy at the Council of Alcalá de Henares in 1379. The Jeronimites were an order officially formed in 1373 from a group of hermits with a founding spirit of reform, emphasizing austerity of life, manual labor, and the careful celebration of the liturgy. Between 1374 and 1414, twenty-three monasteries of the order were founded in Castile, five in Aragon and one in Portugal.[9] By the late fourteenth and early fifteenth century, almost all of the major religious orders—Benedictines, Cistercians, Franciscans, Augustinians, and Dominicans—had begun to experience the spirit of reform. In this, they were often encouraged and supported by reform-minded nobles and bishops.

The reform of religious orders was already well underway by the time that it was mandated by Council of Trent (1545–1563). By 1562, virtually all of the religious orders in Spain had seen reform or already had an established observant

---

8. José García Oro, "Observantes, recolectos, descalzos: La monarquía católica y el reformismo religioso del siglo XVI," in *Historia*, ed. Teófanes Egido, 53–97, vol. 2 of *Actas del Congreso Internaticional Sanjuanista* (Valladolid, Spain: Junta de Castilla y León. Consejería de Cultura y Turismo, 1993).

9. Melquíades Andrés Martín, *Los místicos de la Edad de Oro en España y América: Antología* (Madrid: Biblioteca de Autores Cristianos, 1996), 15.

internal movement—except, or at least unevenly, the Mercedarians, the Trinitarians, and the Carmelites, especially in southern Spain. King Philip II (who ruled from 1556 through 1598) was particularly attentive to the task of reforming the religious orders—though, like his predecessors, jealous of royal control and priorities. He supported the observant faction within orders over their conventual brothers. Teresa herself notes his special role in the establishment of the Discalced Reform (F 29.30–31).

By the beginning of the sixteenth century, religious communities had regained their numbers, and Spain had an abundance of religious communities. At the end of the sixteenth century, there were nearly three hundred houses of Franciscan men with a total of some 4,000 friars, a hundred houses of Dominicans with a total of about 2,400 friars, one hundred and fifty monasteries of Benedictines, fifty of Jeronimites, and thirty of Carthusians, plus the houses of many other religious men. The Jesuits were founded in 1539–1540, but they spread quickly in Spain. They soon had three Spanish provinces and by 1566 ran sixteen secondary schools (*colegios*) and a seminary. There were fewer houses of women religious, but there were many. And then there were the *beatas*—laywomen living a kind of religious life without vows and usually alone or in small groups.

The spirit of reform moved among virtually all of the religious communities with many widely shared characteristics: a return to the order's original rule, repudiation of subsequent mitigations, austerity in manner of living and in architecture, poverty in manner of dress and physical comforts, the embrace of fasting and bodily discipline, and the pursuit of a deeper spirituality, sometimes in the form of increased solitude and even eremitism. In many communities, this movement also involved a suspicion of academic learning and degrees—viewing these as dry and speculative in nature, as opposed to a simple interior faith and as encouraging academic ambitions and laxity of life that could be promoted by the need to be actively involved in university life and culture.[10] The notable exception to this last characteristic was the Dominicans whose reform was linked with a return to the study of Aquinas.

Certainly, the strongest force for reform among the religious orders were the Franciscans, whose reform was closely linked with the promotion of the prayer of recollection, that is, a wordless prayer with a contemplative spirit. (We will say more of this when we look at the spiritual antecedents of Teresa and John in chapter 7.) Their observants began to promote this form of prayer among the laity with a sense of a universal call to holiness or deep prayer. This development was extraordinary in a culture that had traditionally encouraged the laity simply to keep the commandments, participate faithfully in the sacraments and devotions, and say their prayers. Also from among these observant Franciscans came the authors of foundational vernacular works on the prayer of recollection that would have a major impact on Teresa of Jesus and most likely on the early formation of John of the Cross (though we know almost nothing explicitly of his reading).

Parallel to the distinction between observants and conventuals was the distinction between the so-called *letrados* (those with academic learning) and the *espirituales* (those with spiritual experience). Many of the observant religious were promoting deeper interior prayer by all Christians, believing that the deep experience of personal prayer could yield a knowledge of God that could not be obtained by academic learning,

---

10. Ruiz Salvador, *God Speaks*, 120.

especially what they viewed as dry and speculative Scholasticism. The *letrados*, on the other hand (whether from among the conventuals or the observants, though usually possessing academic degrees), believed that subjective experience could easily deceive—especially when not accompanied by the formal theological education to keep it within the boundaries of orthodoxy.[11] In a time of poor catechesis, such concern was not unwarranted, but at the same time, the attitude of the *letrados* often reflected a widespread disdain among the educated classes for the "illiterate masses" (*idiotas*), that is, the uneducated or even simply those without a formal university education.[12]

The unfolding of the Franciscan reform with its emphasis on the prayer of recollection, available to the laity, often placed them in close association with the spirituals. The Dominican reform, on the other hand, had been linked with a renewal of theological studies focused on a return to Aquinas. Subsequently, they led the way in addressing many of the pressing moral problems of the day such as issues raised by emerging capitalism, slavery, and the rights of indigenous peoples in the Spanish colonies. Another result was associating the Dominicans with the *letrados*. (A notable exception was Luis de Granada, who was both highly learned and, at the same time, a promoter of deeper prayer among the laity.) Indeed, they became leaders and supporters of the Inquisition in its effort to uncover false mystics.[13]

---

11. Joseph Pérez, "Cultura y sociedad en tiempos de Santa Teresa," in *Congreso Internacional Teresiano (4–7 octubre, 1982)*, ed. Teófanes Egido et al., 1:31–40 (Salamanca, Spain: Universidad de Salamanca, 1983), 36–40.

12. Pérez, "Cultura y sociedad," 32. See also Pérez, "Mística y realidad histórica," 59–60.

13. Pérez, "Cultura y sociedad," 35.

In John of the Cross and Teresa of Jesus, we find the two perspectives balanced. John was both university educated and a mystic and a teacher of mystical prayer. Teresa lacked formal theological training, but she valued and insisted on consultation with people who had such learning. For her, such dialogue was a check against being led astray as well as a source for vocabulary and categories for understanding and conveying her experience. In fact, being able to present the list of the *letrados* whom she had consulted was a line of protection against the Inquisition (ST 58), but her relationships with such men seem more basically to have been an instinctual pursuit of balance rather than a strategy for protection.[14]

Beatas and the Reform of the Women's Religious Orders

Before the sixteenth century, women's communities experienced less formal, systematic reform than the men's communities. Sometimes this depended on their relationship with the associated male branch of the same order and its reform. Even more than their male counterparts, women's communities were often more tied to the aristocratic families that served as their principal donors and often provided their superiors in a kind of family monopoly in office. Such entanglements brought resistance to change of the established order. Certainly, most of the more prominent monasteries of women had become centers for noble women—some of whom had a sincere vocation, while others entered due to being unmarriageable for a variety of reasons. Such entanglements encouraged frequent visits of family

---

14. Pérez, "Cultura y sociedad," 38.

members to the cloister and even comings and goings to visit family. Wealthy donor families also expected their beneficiaries to offer additional prayer for them and for deceased members that could significantly multiply the amount of time dedicated by the community to such exercises. The Monastery of the Incarnation in which Teresa first entered is typical of all of the above characteristics.

Meanwhile, smaller and rural monasteries of women without such aristocratic entanglements and support often simply could not survive. And through the course of the fifteenth and sixteenth century, such monasteries largely disappeared. To some degree, they were replaced by *beatas* and *beaterios*. A *beata* was a lay woman, without formal religious profession, who lived a manner of life much like a religious but in her own home. *Beatas* might be widows, women who could not afford a dowry to enter a religious community, or women who were simply unmarriageable for some reason. (As increasing numbers of men went off to the Americas or to fight Spain's many foreign wars, this became more and more a reality.) Such women could be virtually hermits, or they might be actively engaged in care of the sick and poor or in offering spiritual counsel to other laity. Sometimes, a group of *beatas* would come together to live an informal common life in a *beaterio*.[15]

Such individuals and groups might be associated with a monastery of men or women from an established religious order that would provide guidance. But such associations were not always the case. Without such direction, uneducated and

---

15. Kieran Kavanaugh, "Faith and the Experience of God in the University Town of Baeza," in *John of the Cross*, ed. Steven Payne, 48–64, vol. 6 of *Carmelite Studies* (Washington, D.C.: ICS Publications, 1992), 54–55.

illiterate *beatas* could become prey to unorthodox beliefs as well as to unscrupulous clergy who took advantage of them. It is for this reason that the *beatas* were sometimes more likely to gain the unwanted attention of the Inquisition. Both Teresa and John naturally encountered *beatas* in the course of their journeys—for John, especially in southern Spain where there were many—and many who came to be accused before the Inquisition because of a particular fascination with extraordinary spiritual experiences.

More focused efforts to bring systematic reform to women's communities began in the sixteenth century. These often met with stiff resistance from the aristocratic families that maintained them (and populated them). But reform-minded bishops and, later, male observants of the same order were persistent.[16]

Spain and the Protestant Reformation

The Protestant reform never made serious inroads in Spain, though it was a focused and constant concern of the Spanish crown. Recall that Teresa tells us (W 1.2) that one of the reasons for the establishment of her reform was to counter the spread of the "Lutherans." (This was Teresa's general term for Protestants, about which Teresa apparently knew very

---

16. José García Oro, "La vida monástica feminina en la España de Santa Teresa," in *Congreso Internacional Teresiano (4–7 octubre, 1982)*, ed. Teófanes Egido et al., 1:331–49 (Salamanca, Spain: Universidad de Salamanca, 1983), 337–38. See also José García Oro, "Reformas y Observancias: Crisis y renovación de la vida religiosa española durante el Renacimiento," in *Perfil histórico de Santa Teresa*, ed. Teófanes Egido, 49–52, 3rd ed. (Madrid: Editorial de Espiritualidad, 2012).

little—and of whom there were actually very few in Spain.) When small Protestant groups were discovered in the major cities of Valladolid and Seville in 1558—with members from noble families—King Philip II and the Inquisition reacted strongly. Prominent trials and a handful of public executions, the publication of the Index of Prohibited Books, the effort to prevent the import of Reformation literature, and a ban on Spanish students attending all but a handful of foreign universities followed. But despite the concern, real Reformation ideas never seemed to have gained a prominent foothold on the peninsula. It is unlikely that any of the efforts mentioned above were the main reason for this success because they were too difficult to enforce in an age when national borders were much more porous for private citizens. A more likely reason is that, as we have seen, reform movements were already well underway in Spain by the time that the Reformation would have reached its borders.[17]

Conclusion

In this chapter, we have been laying the foundations for more focused discussions of such topics as the reform of the Carmelites, the Monastery of the Incarnation, the spiritual antecedents of Teresa and John, potentially heretical movements from which they are to be distinguished, and the Inquisition and its concerns. Sixteenth-century Spain was a complex and varied landscape, and the reform agenda and mystical insight of these two great Carmelite mystics must be understood in its context.

---

17. Pérez, "Mística y realidad histórica," 54–68; and "Cultura y sociedad," 31–32.

SELECT BIBLIOGRAPHY

English

Álvarez, Tomás. *St. Teresa of Avila: 100 Themes on Her Life and Work.* Translated by Kieran Kavanaugh. Washington, D.C.: ICS Publications, 2011.

Payne, Stanley G. *Spanish Catholicism: An Historical Overview.* Madison, Wisc.: University of Wisconsin Press, 1984.

Spanish

García Oro, José. "La vida monástica feminina en la España de Santa Teresa." In *Congreso Internacional Teresiano (4–7 octubre, 1982)*, edited by Teófanes Egido et al., 331–49. Vol. 1. Salamanca, Spain: Universidad de Salamanca, 1983.

———. "Observantes, recolectos, descalzos: La monarquía católica y el reformismo religioso del siglo XVI." In *Historia*, edited Teófanes Egido, 53–97. Vol. 2 of *Actas del Congreso Internaticional Sanjuanista*. Valladolid, Spain: Junta de Castilla y León. Consejería de Cultura y Turismo, 1993.

———. "Reformas y Observancias: Crisis y renovación de la vida religiosa española durante el Renacimiento." In *Perfil histórico de Santa Teresa*, edited by Teófanes Egido, 33–55. 3rd ed. Madrid: Editorial de Espiritualidad, 2012.

Pérez, Joseph. *Teresa de Ávila y la España de su tiempo.* 3rd ed. Madrid: Editorial EDAF, 2015.

Chapter 5

The Carmelites

The reform of religious orders throughout the history of the church has always involved an effort to return to the original inspiration and vision of the founders in light of the needs and realities of the present. In that respect, the Carmelite Reform, initiated by Teresa of Jesus together with John of the Cross, is no different. Teresa's reform looked back to the contemplative and eremitical roots of the first hermits at Mount Carmel, influenced certainly by the reform of other religious orders and spiritual trends of her own time. But the Carmelite life had by necessity undergone changes when the hermits were forced to leave the Holy Land and take up their new life in Europe. Many of these were adaptations that Teresa simply presumed in looking back on the founding vision of the order. In order to understand the Teresian Reform—as well as the historical context of the conflicts between Calced and Discalced that have such a prominent place in the biographies of both Teresa and John—we must understand the history of the Carmelites in general and, more specifically, the state of the Carmelites in Spain in the middle of the sixteenth century.

The Origins

The period from the late tenth century to the twelfth saw a flowering of the eremitical life in Europe, notably with the foundation of the Camaldolese by St. Romuald (ca. 950–1027) and the Carthusians—which is the religious order that so attracted the young John of the Cross—by St. Bruno (ca. 1030–1101).[1] Many Christians were going out to the "desert" in search of solitude, contemplative prayer, and a life of poverty and penance at a time when many medieval monasteries seemed to them to be too comfortable, too focused on liturgical prayer and elaborate rituals, and too caught up in lands and relations with aristocratic donors. Western France was a particular center of this hermit movement. And it was from this same region that many young men traveled to the Holy Land as Crusaders seeking to retake it for Christianity.[2]

The Crusades were a series of wars, essentially between 1096 and 1291, to reconquer and hold territories in the Holy

---

1. The history of the Carmelites, unlike many of the topics addressed in this book, can be studied in depth in a number of English-language works that will be listed in the select bibliography at the end of the present chapter. Friedman in particular provides a closer study of the thirteenth-century origins in the Holy Land. Elias Friedman, *The Latin Hermits of Mount Carmel: A Study of Carmelite Origins* (Rome: Institutum Historicum Teresianum, 1979). See also: Patrick Mullins, *St. Albert of Jerusalem and the Roots of Carmelite Spirituality*, vol. 34 of Institutum Carmelitanum, *Textus et Studia Historical Carmelitana*. Rome: Edizioni Carmelitane, 2012.

2. Joachim Smet, *The Carmelites: A History of the Brothers of Our Lady of Mount Carmel* (Darien, Ill.: Carmelite Spiritual Center, 1976), 1:1. See also: Joachim Smet, *The Mirror of Carmel: A Brief History of the Carmelite Order.* (Darien, IL: Carmelite Media, 2011), 4–5. [The latter is a one-volume digest of the former from which footnotes have been omitted.] Also: Mullins, *Albert of Jerusalem*, 67–108.

Land controlled by Muslim forces. Crusaders captured Jerusalem in 1099. Although their triumph in that particular city was short lived, they erected Christian kingdoms that lasted until the fall of the city of Acre in 1291. Following the successes of the Christian armies, the first European hermits seem to have arrived in the Holy Land at the beginning of the twelfth century. And later in the same century, following the Third Crusade (1189–1192), they began to populate the area of Mount Carmel—preceded, it seems, before Muslim occupation, by earlier Byzantine hermits.[3] European pilgrims to the liberated Holy Places and former Crusaders soon became donors or new recruits.

The First Book of Kings (18:20–40) records that it was at Mount Carmel that the prophet Elijah had bested the prophets of Baal, and the site came to be associated with him. The same prophet was also reported to have had a mysterious mountain encounter with God at Mount Horeb (Sinai) where God spoke to him in a "sound of sheer silence" (1 Kgs 19:12 NRSV). The idea began to emerge in patristic literature that Elijah was a prophet, a hermit, and a mystic—and under his leadership was formed a group of prophet-hermits. The idea had already begun to circulate in Europe that Elijah, therefore, could be considered the "father of hermits."[4] It was no coincidence, then, that the Carmelites began to see the prophet as a central figure in their own identity and eventually as their "Father Elijah."

---

3. Friedman (*Latin Hermits*, 60–103) covers the pre-Latin monastic foundations at some length.

4. Smet, *Carmelites*, 1:1; *Mirror*, 6.

The Rule of St. Albert

The first European hermits at Mount Carmel left little in the way of written records about their manner of life. We know that they lived and ate separately but gathered regularly for Mass and for spiritual conversation. They elected a leader to help oversee the details of their semi-communal life and their mutual assistance. At some point, it appears that they asked the Patriarch of Jerusalem (actually resident in Acre), Albert Avogadro (1149–1214), to write a "formula of life"—what has come to be known as the Rule of St. Albert or the Albertine Rule (to distinguish it from its mitigated forms in the decades ahead).[5] Albert wrote this extremely short document sometime during his tenure as patriarch (1206–1214). It affirms the eremitical, ascetical, and contemplative nature of the life, focused on meditation on the Word of God and daily Eucharist. Devotion to Elijah and to the Blessed Virgin Mary is not explicit in the document, but early evidence suggests that both were central from the very beginning.[6]

Although this primitive rule was not really a legislative document for truly governing a religious community, it was sufficient to transform this loosely organized group of hermits into a recognized religious body. And its authorship by the Patriarch of Jerusalem, simultaneously appointed by the pope as a papal legate, assured its status before the Fourth Lateran Council in 1215

---

5. For a full English text of the Rule of St. Albert, see John Welch, *The Carmelite Way: An Ancient Path for Today's Pilgrim* (Mahwah, N.J.: Paulist Press, 1996), 175–81. In English and Latin: Mullins, *Albert of Jerusalem*, 345–53; and Michael Mulhall, ed., *Albert's Way: The First North American Congress on the Carmelite Rule* (Barrington, Ill.: Province of the Most Pure Heart of Mary, 1989), 1–21. See also www.carmelites.ie/Rule.pdf.

6. Friedman, *Latin Hermits*, 179–80; Mullins, *Albert of Jerusalem*, 16–17.

forbade the foundation of new religious orders.[7] Pope Honorius III affirmed the hermits in their "rule" in 1226 in face of the council's subsequent mandate. Pope Gregory IX reaffirmed this approval in 1229, addressed to them as "Prior and Hermits of Mount Carmel."

Transfer to Europe and the First Mitigation

But the Christian kingdoms in the Holy Land were not to survive much beyond the formal initiation of the Carmelites. As Muslim forces increasingly impinged upon them, the hermits began to migrate to Europe, beginning about 1238.[8] Aided by Crusader nobles, the hermits moved first to the areas from which their patrons originally came: Cyprus, Sicily, France, and England. (Spanish nobles had not participated in the Crusades, since they were fighting their own "crusade" against Muslim occupation in the southern part of the Iberian Peninsula. This explains the relatively late arrival of the Carmelites in Spain.) This migration to Europe was complete by 1291.

The new context demanded change. The Carmelites quickly realized that they could not effectively found communities in remote places in Europe as they had in the Holy Land. In their new context, such isolation would have deprived them of both

---

7. At the Council of Lyons in 1274, twenty-two orders were suppressed because they had been founded after 1215.

8. Mullins, *Albert of Jerusalem*, 21–23. Rohrbach claims that it was the inner dynamics of the order's growth that was the fundamental reason for the migration. Peter-Thomas Rohrbach, *Journey to Carith: The Story of the Carmelite Order* (1966; repr., Washington, D.C.: Institute of Carmelite Studies, 2015), 55. Kieran Kavanugh, in his preface to this latter work, concludes that, despite being dated in some details and interpretations of events, it remains "unsurpassed as a concise and readable overview."

recruits and donors. Further, following a period of rapid multiplication of religious communities, Rome was opposed to founding new monastic and eremitical orders. And so the Carmelites found themselves identified as mendicants—"friars" like the Franciscans, Dominicans, and Augustinians. They began to found their monasteries in urban areas (as Teresa of Jesus later did, to ensure the economic viability of her communities), to live a more communal form of life, and to offer apostolic service (beginning probably with the people in their immediate environs). Rather soon after arriving in Europe, in 1247, the general chapter of the order petitioned the pope for an adaptation of their Rule in line with their changed circumstances. And in that same year, Pope Innocent IV revised the Carmelite Rule—the "first mitigation" or the "mitigation of 1247" ("mitigation," in the sense of a lessening or reduction of severity, strictness, or burden).

The revised Rule, while practically acknowledging new realities, tried to maintain the contemplative and eremitical spirit of the Albertine Rule even while it adapted Carmelite practice to established mendicant patterns, including the elimination of the requirement to establish new communities only in solitary places, the new requirement of the common recitation of the Divine Office as well as common meals in a common refectory, and importantly the expectation of an apostolic outreach. This created a tension that has run through subsequent Carmelite history. For the friars, it is a tension between contemplation/solitude and outreach/ministry. We see this tension, dynamically lived, in Teresa's brief account of the first Carmelite friars at Duruelo. She describes how John of the Cross and Antonio de Jesús followed a life of intense prayer and asceticism even as they engaged in an active evangelical and catechetical ministry to the people around them (F 14). For the Carmelite women, we see Teresa's foundational vision involving both the life of intense prayer and an evangelical concern for the church and its unity, missions, and ministers (W 1–3). Further, there is a similar tension between solitude and community.[9]

It is the mitigated rule of 1247 that Teresa sometimes identified as the "primitive rule" or the "rule without mitigation." And her reform was focused on restoring its spirit. Some have claimed that, in fact, she was ignorant of the existence of the Albertine Rule, but this is not true. It was typical of Teresa's time to speak of the Rule of 1247 as the "primitive rule" in relation to the later, second mitigation of 1432. And it appears that her only access to the texts of the versions of the Rule were in a poor Castilian translation that referred to the 1247 form as "without mitigation."[10] In fact, living in sixteenth-century Spain, return to the Rule of St. Albert, written for hermits living at Mount Carmel, would have been quite impossible. For all of their high ideals and determination, both John and especially Teresa were eminently practical.

The arrival of the Carmelites in Europe also brought problems of identity in relation to other, established religious orders.[11] Each of these other communities had an identifiable founder, for example, St. Francis, St. Dominic, and St. Benedict. But the Carmelites had none. And so the prophet Elijah and the

---

9. Keith J. Egan, "The Spirituality of the Carmelites," in *High Middle Ages and Reformation*, ed. Jill Raitt with Bernard McGinn and John Meyendorff, 50–62, vol. 2 of *Christian Spirituality* (New York.: Crossroad, 1989), 53.

10. Welch, *Carmelite Way*, 18; Patrick Mullins, "St. Teresa of Ávila and Earlier Carmelite Traditions," in *St. Teresa of Ávila: Her Writings and Life*, eds. Terence O'Reilly, Colin P. Thompson and Lesley Twomey, 14–31, (Cambridge: Legenda [Modern Humanities Research Association], 2018), 25; Tomás Álvarez, "Santa Teresa ante la regla de Carmelo," in *Estudios Teresianos I: Biografía e historia*, 169–92 (Burgos, Spain: Editorial Monte Carmelo, 1995), 177–78.

11. Smet, *Carmelites*, 1:18–19.

centrality of devotion to the Virgin Mary—in fact, present from their beginnings—began to play a more explicit role in their foundational legends. It appears, for example, that the Carmelites' constitutions of 1281 were the first official document to claim an unbroken succession of monks from the time of Elijah and Elisha—that is, that the Carmelites were "founded by" Elijah the prophet.[12]

The Institution of the First Monks

Around 1390, the Carmelite provincial of Catalonia in Spain, Philip Ribot (d. 1391), published the *Institution of the First Monks* (*Liber de institutione primorum monachorum*), which drew together available materials into a critically important work that explained both the foundational legends and fundamental elements of Carmelite history and spirituality.[13] He identified himself not as the work's author but as the editor of a text written by a supposed forty-fourth Patriarch of Jerusalem in 412. This explanation of the origins of the document was considered genuine through the time of Teresa of Jesus and John of the Cross, and because it claimed existence prior to the Albertine Rule, it was believed to have been formative even for that foundational document. It began to circulate immediately in the 1390s and became central to the formation of Carmelite men and women for generations.[14]

---

12. Friedman, *Latin Hermits*, 200–201; Mullins, *Albert of Jerusalem*, 29–31.

13. For overviews of the text, see especially Welch, *Carmelite Way*, 49–62; Egan, "Spirituality of the Carmelites," 54–56; Smet, Mirror, 19–21; and Rohrbach, *Journey to Carith*, 85–88.

14. Daniel de Pablo Maroto, *Ser y misión del Carmelo Teresiano: Historia de un carisma* (Madrid: Editorial de Espiritualidad, 2011), 26–27.

The *Institution* lays out a foundational vision of the Carmelites that highlights their foundation by Elijah and the centrality of Marian devotion. Its vision of the Carmelite life undergirds the "mixed life" of the eremitical and the prophetic—of contemplation and apostolic outreach—being lived by the Carmelites after 1247, with the presentation of Elijah as its forerunner. It presents a spirituality with a strong spirit of solitude and withdrawal, asceticism, purification of heart, pursuit of the gift of union with God in love, and a focus on the experiential encounter with God that lays the groundwork for the more explicitly mystical focus of Teresa and John.[15]

It is most probable that Teresa of Jesus and John of the Cross read the *Institution*. Although neither of them quotes from it, in light of its popularity and importance to the order, it is hard to imagine that they did not. An extant copy of the document, in Castilian translation, indicates that it is "from Ávila," which argues for the idea that Teresa read it herself or heard it read in the common refectory of the Incarnation—though others doubt that this evidence is conclusive.[16]

Decline and the Mitigated Rule of 1432

The fourteenth century saw a decline in the numbers, religious fervor, and observance of the Carmelites and other religious orders. Several events contributed to this decline. Around the year 1347, the so-called Black Death or plague arrived in Europe. It is estimated that, within the five years or so of its major

---

15. Egan, "Spirituality of the Carmelites," 56.

16. Mullins, "St. Teresa of Ávila," 19–20; Maroto, *Ser y misión del Carmelo Teresiano*, 27.

outbreak, somewhere between a third or as much as 60 percent of Europe's population was decimated. The effects of this catastrophe can hardly be exaggerated. Whole religious communities were wiped out or so depopulated that they couldn't continue. The effects were devastating at a number of levels: fewer numbers, fewer recruits, fewer donors, depleted resources, and farming and other economic enterprises unable to continue for lack of workers. It became difficult to maintain regular observances of the religious life as well as the intellectual and spiritual formation of the religious. Religious orders—together with all of the countries and institutions of Europe—took a very long time recover.

The Hundred Years' War from 1337 until 1453 between England and France involved sporadic but fierce fighting as well as pillaging and destruction of towns and their economic structures. As many as fifty Carmelite monasteries were destroyed, and again, more generally, there were both fewer recruits and fewer donors. The church in the same period experienced the so-called Avignon papacy (1309–1377) with popes residing in France, followed by the Great Schism (1378–1417) in which rival cardinals were claiming to be pope. The latter divided the European church and its religious orders. The former represented one aspect of a general period of decline in the wider church that could not but have an effect on religious orders. In light of these events, it is little wonder that the spirit and observance of religious communities were in serious decline.

Legislation from the Carmelite general chapters in the mid- to late fourteenth century reveals the decline in spirit and observance including laxity in observance of silence and poverty, useless visiting of towns, and failure to attend common prayer and meals. Finally, in 1432, Pope Eugenius IV approved the second mitigation of the Carmelite Rule, which generally lowered the standards of observances, reducing both solitude and austerity. In a way, it represents the final transformation of their way of life from eremitical to mendicant. More broadly, it was an acceptance of the decline that had been experienced in the previous century. Some friars did object to the mitigation, but it was confirmed by further decrees from Rome in 1459 and 1476.[17] It was this second mitigation that Teresa of Jesus rejected.

Carmelite historian Joachim Smet has strong words for the 1432 mitigation:

> The mitigation of 1432 came at a time when the spiritual vitality of the Order was low. . . . The mitigation brought the rule up to date with the real implications of the mitigation of 1247, but historically it has probably done more harm than good. It has been the source of every subsequent division in the Order. Then and since, mistakenly or not, it has been regarded by many interested in dedicating themselves wholeheartedly to the Carmelite ideal as a betrayal of the contemplative spirit of the Order.[18]

Efforts at Reform

A number of reform efforts arose in the fifteenth and early sixteenth centuries, though often concentrated in groups of monasteries rather than across the entire order. A reform movement

---

17. Rohrbach, *Journey to Carith*, 1–12. See also Smet, *Carmelites*, 1:79–84.
18. Smet, *Carmelites*, 1:86.

began in Mantua in Italy in the early fifteenth century. In 1442, the group of monasteries associated with this movement became a semiautonomous congregation with its own vicar general. In its beginnings, it was permitted not to live the mitigation of 1432, but not long after, in 1465, it accepted the mitigation and remained observant though without the rigors of its original spirit. Similar was the reform of Albi in France. It too became a semiautonomous congregation with its own vicar general, but again it too lost its original fervor.

John Soreth (1395–1471) was elected prior general of the order in 1451. He supported the efforts of the reform groups within the Carmelites but sought a wider reform of the entire order. He called in particular for the renewal of the common life in Carmelite communities, renunciation of private property, commitment to the life of contemplation, and careful observance of the order's Rule, constitutions, and liturgical norms. His efforts were particularly effective in Germany and in the Low Countries. Notably, they did not reach Spain.

But Soreth's most lasting contribution to the Carmelites may have been the establishment of the Carmelite nuns during his tenure.[19] There had, in fact, been a long history of laypeople, men and women, associated with the order. But the friars had initially resisted incorporating women's communities into the order, because it would bring with it the need to provide chaplains and confessors, as well as the expectation of assistance with the nuns' foundations and maintenance and ongoing practical oversight. In fact, in 1261, the friars had been given official exemption from acquiring a feminine branch. But in 1452, the friars requested and received papal approval (*Cum nulla*,

---

19. Rohrbach, *Journey to Carith*, 117.

October 7, 1452) to receive women's communities. (Note that this is only about sixty years before the birth of Teresa of Jesus and the incorporation of the Monastery of the Incarnation in Ávila into the Carmelite Order.)

Reform efforts continued in the sixteenth century under Nicholas Audet (1481–1562) who served as prior general between 1524 and 1562—his efforts complicated by the onset of the Reformation. He initiated a series of visitations of the houses of the order, though his success was spotty. The province of Castile in Spain embraced his reform, though at the cost of about half of the friars of that province who left rather than embrace the changes. As part of Audet's general effort to improve the academic level and intellectual formation of the young friars, in 1548 the general chapter named the Monastery of St. Andrew at the University of Salamanca as the central Carmelite study center in the Iberian Peninsula (not long before the young John of the Cross was sent to study there).

State of the Order in Spain at the Time of Teresa and John

As we noted early, the Carmelites came relatively late to Spain. Their first foundation was made in the kingdom of Aragon on the Mediterranean coast in the mid-1250s, and the order spread quickly throughout the peninsula. The first foundation was made in the kingdom of Castile in 1315, and by 1416, there were already enough houses to create a separate province of Castile/Andalusia. In 1498, these were split into two separate provinces.

Until the marriage of Queen Isabella and King Ferdinand in 1469 united the two principal kingdoms of the peninsula, Spain was very much inwardly focused—smaller kingdoms in conflict with one another and with the Muslim kingdoms to the south. In this context, Spain remained something of a backwater in the Carmelite world. The reform movements in the order during the fifteenth century, including that of John Soreth, seem not have had much success there. Few Spaniards studied at the order's houses at major European universities. The provincial of Castile attended the order's general chapter only four times between 1476 and 1564,[20] and no prior general visited there during the entire fifteenth century. An early sixteenth-century report on the Carmelite houses of Toledo, Ávila, and San Pablo de la Moraleja judged them to be in deplorable condition, with a number of friars giving public scandal.[21] It appears that the wider efforts at reform initiated by Cardinal Cisneros under royal mandate also had little impact.[22]

But the reform efforts of Audet in the first half of the sixteenth century did affect at least the Carmelite province of Castile to which Teresa and John belonged. As we have said, about half of the friars of the province had left rather than embracing this reform, leaving only about one hundred friars (F 2.5). The claim of reform could not be said equally of the other three Spanish provinces, notably that of Andalusia in the south of Spain.[23] When the prior general Giovanni Battista Rossi (Rubeo) did visit Spain during the time of Teresa (1566–1567), he found the

---

20. Smet, *Carmelites*, 1:139–42.

21. Welch, *Carmelite Way*, 15.

22. Smet, *Carmelites*, 1:139–42.

23. Otger Steggink, *La reforma del Carmelo español: La visita canónica del General Rubeo y su encuentro con Santa Teresa (1566–1567)* (Rome: Institutum Carmelitanum, 1965), 48–49. This text also appears in a revised edition published in 1993.

Castilian province largely in good order while the Andalusian province gave him notable problems, as it would Jerome Gratian in his role as visitator there, as we will see below.

When the Discalced Reform began, there were four Spanish provinces (Castile, Aragon, Catalonia, and Andalusia), with about forty-eight houses of men and about 550 religious. This included the nine houses and about one hundred friars of Castile. In addition, there were twelve monasteries of women (including *beaterios* of women, associated with Carmelites), including three in Castile (the oldest of which was the Incarnation in Ávila).

It was typical of Baroque hagiographies to present stark contrasts between the new and the old, between the reform and the original branches of religious orders. Such had been the case in many earlier biographies of Teresa and John, suggesting that they rejected the decadent houses of the Carmelites, but this is not the case—again, at least for the province of Castile to which they belonged.[24] In fact, it has been suggested that the reform and spirituality of Teresa and John of the Cross were the flowering of the reform spirit that had already been moving in the Carmelites of Castile and of the order in general.[25]

Crossed Jurisdictions

One of the most well-known incidents in the life of John of the Cross must certainly be his imprisonment in the city of Toledo by the Calced Carmelites in the relatively early stages of

---

24. Pablo María Garrido, "El Carmelo español en tiempo de Santa Teresa," in *Congreso Internacional Teresiano (4–7 octubre, 1982)*, ed. Teófanes Egido et al., 1:407–29 (Salamanca, Spain: Universidad de Salamanca, 1983), 407.

25. Garrido, 411–12.

the Teresian Reform.[26] It is only one window into the unfortunate conflict between the Discalced and the Calced in the early years of the reform. The works of Teresa and her early biographies highlight this conflict even more clearly and at greater length. But the fact is that, while Teresa and John had detractors and opponents among the Calced, they also had admirers and supporters.[27] And while it is understandable that many of the Calced would have felt a sense of implicit criticism and even betrayal at the foundation of separate houses of the reform, a substantial portion of the difficulties between Calced and Discalced can be traced to the complicated jurisdictional tangle in which the reform unfolded.

As we have seen, efforts at the reform of the Carmelite Order from within were well underway. These coincided with papal efforts at reform, especially during and after the Council of Trent. Meanwhile the Spanish crown, under King Philip II, was continuing its efforts to reform the church in Spain and its religious communities—while trying to maintain control of this

---

26. Kieran Kavanaugh, O.C.D., provides a brief summary of these jurisdictional disputes in the introduction of *The Collected Works of Saint John of the Cross*, trans. Kieran Kavanaugh and Otilio Rodriguez, rev. ed. (Washington, D.C.: ICS Publications, 1991), 17–20. Smet, *Carmelites* (2:1–131) provides a lengthy analysis of the establishment of the Discalced Reform and the sometimes-troubled relationships between Calced and Discalced during that period. Smet's work forms the basic outline of this present chapter, with additions from other sources, as noted in footnotes. In Spanish, see the discussion offered by Otger Steggink, O.Carm., in two works: *La reforma del Carmelo español* and "Dos corrientes de reforma en el Carmelo español del siglo XVI: La observancia y la descalcez, frente a la 'Reforma del rey,'" in *Aspectos históricos de San Juan de la Cruz*, ed. Teófanes Egido, 117–42 (Ávila, Spain: Institución Gran Duque de Alba de la Diputación Provincial de Ávila, 1990).

27. Pablo María Garrido, *St. Teresa, St. John of the Cross, and the Spanish Carmelites*, trans. Joseph Chalmers (Darien, Ill.: Carmelite Media, 2015), 5–6.

process within its borders and protect what it viewed as royal prerogatives. The result was conflict among and between people sincerely pursuing reform, though with differing visions and timetables. Under whose jurisdiction did the reform fall? And what was to happen when authority, permissions, and mandates flowing from the Carmelite prior general and its general chapter conflicted with those coming from papal nuncios and the officials appointed by them—while at the same time the king was seeking to limit the perceived interference by church authority from Rome, whether the pope or the Carmelite general?

Giovanni Battista Rossi (known as Rubeo in Spain) became vicar general (acting general) of the order in 1562 on the death of the prior general, Nicholas Audet. Rubeo was elected prior general in his own right in 1564 and took up the efforts of his predecessor to continue the reform of the order. In this, he was committed to pursue the spirit of the Council of Trent—focused not so much on return to primitive observance but more on faithful adherence to established obligations, including the reforms that had been instituted by his predecessors. He had an early commitment to visit the Carmelite communities of men and women in Spain.

In fact, Teresa had a different view of reform. She wanted not simply to embrace fully the reforms that followed the mitigations of 1432. Rather, she hoped to restore what she understood to be the pristine purity of the "primitive rule"—which she understood to be the mitigated rule of 1247 (L 36.26).[28] This included a greater emphasis on solitude, contemplation, and an eremitical spirit. In this, Teresa's reforming vision found

---

28. Teresa had the date wrong: she said 1248 though it was in fact 1247. Smet, *Mirror*, 85–86.

a closer ally in King Philip whose own preference for all of the orders in Spain was a return to the "ancient" observances.

Rubeo was himself, at first, supportive of Teresa's efforts, and he accepted that the nuns would be called *discalced*. But he never wanted the friars of the reform to bear the same name, fearing that it seemed disparaging of the Calced (in the same way that he did not want the friars of the established observance to be called "of the cloth" or "mitigated"). Rather, he wanted the friars of the reform to be called "contemplative Carmelites."[29] In fact, Rubeo was shrewd enough to see the potential for conflict especially in his approval to found friars of the reform. But he envisioned these friars and nuns as living under the same provincial, not seeing or presenting themselves as following a more authentic or more perfect form of Carmelite life. Perhaps he was naïve in this hope—though there were precedents, as we have seen, of semiautonomous Carmelite groups under their own vicar generals.

Meanwhile relations between Spain and the papal court were strained. Papal international politics and actions often ran contrary to Spanish interests. Decades of papal and curial scandals in Rome had undermined the crown's respect for papal authority and motives, even after the reforms of Trent. In the previous century, Spanish monarchs had consistently asserted royal prerogatives over the Spanish church and its reform—which was viewed in Rome as a usurpation of its power.[30] In fact, King Philip wanted all the religious communities in Spain to accept the stricter reform of the "observants" under the authority of the crown. The Council of Trent, on the other hand, promoted a

---

29. Rohrbach, *Journey to Carith*, 171–72.
30. Steggink, *La reforma del Carmelo español*, 51–54.

more moderate reform of the orders (as did Rubeo) under the supervision of their own general superiors.[31] But at the same time, the papacy could not afford to alienate the Spanish king completely—and so the demands of the Spanish crown were often met with negotiations, concessions, and resulting overlapping jurisdictions.

In February 1566, Rubeo, already prior general, was granted formal papal authority to visitate and reform the whole order. (This authority had not been revoked later when in 1569 two Dominicans were appointed by the papal nuncio as visitators of the Carmelites in Spain.) And so, in 1566, Rubeo's visitation of Spanish provinces began—with personal interviews with religious, examination of financial records, and efforts to correct, on the spot, lack of observance in ownership, frivolities in habit, or lifestyle. He found that the province of Castile had largely embraced the reform of his predecessor Audet, as had those of Aragon and Catalonia. The province of Andalusia, in the south of Spain, on the other hand, had largely not embraced earlier reforms and was also torn by factions. Rubeo called for and himself oversaw a provincial chapter there to issue reform regulations, though this failed to end the factions or bring about lasting reform in that province.

The visitation in Castile began early in 1567, beginning with the house of studies at Salamanca, where John of St. Matthias (as John of the Cross was known in the order before he joined the reform) was one of its eleven students. In mid-February, Rubeo arrived at the Incarnation in Ávila. Records of his interviews with half of the 180 nuns are extant. Rubeo found much of what Teresa herself reported in the *Life*: a monastery overflowing in

---

31. Steggink, 310.

dire economic circumstances with nuns buying and selling better cells, leaving personal property to relatives by will, involved in frivolities in dress, class distinctions in lifestyle, personal maids and at least one nun with a black slave girl, frequent visits to family (often to relieve financial strains on monastery), frequent visits in the parlor (or even out of windows to the street), and a general lack of a carefully observed cloister. Of the ninety nuns interviewed, forty asked the general to be dispensed from choir.[32] Still, he found a community with many dedicated religious who deplored the shortcomings in observance, many of them beyond their control because of population, finances, and societal/cultural expectations. It was, in general, a religious house at peace and harmony, with good morals and fervent devotion. In fact, concluding the visitation of the province of Castile, Rubeo judged it to be, as a whole, in a good state—reduced in number following the reforms imposed by his predecessor but not lacking in fervor and certainly not decadent.

But even while Rubeo's visitations in Spain were in progress, in 1567, King Philip received papal permission to reform the Merecedarians, Trinitarians, and Carmelites under the oversight of the local bishops with the assistance of Dominicans—even though this was contrary to Trent's directives to entrust reform to each order's own religious superiors and ignored the spirit of reform among the Carmelites, represented by Rubeo's simultaneous visitations as both prior general and with the papal authority he had received in 1566. In fact, the Carmelites in Andalusia, following Rubeo's largely unsuccessful visitation there, had appealed to the king, and it may be that Rubeo's

---

32. Smet, *Carmelites*, 2:18–19.

perceived failure there, early in his visitations, may have spurred the king to take the reform into his own hands.

The royal effort at reform, however, quickly proved to be a mess. Some local bishops who had at times been at odds with the religious within their dioceses took the opportunity to seek revenge. Secular priests and religious of other orders, charged with oversight of the reform of individual communities, often lacked any real knowledge of the charism and history of that order. The "secular arm"—royal power—was sometimes too quickly used to enforce "reform." Rubeo appealed to the pope, and in 1571 the pope, himself a Dominican, formally revoked his earlier permission for the "royal reform" process and instead handed over the process to the observant Dominicans (again, bypassing the legitimate superiors within the respective orders themselves).

Already in August 1569, the pope had appointed three Dominican visitators with broad authority: one each for the provinces of Castile, Andalusia, and Aragon-Catalonia together. Meanwhile, Rubeo still remained both superior general and papal visitator of the Carmelites. It is difficult to imagine how confusion would not result. The Dominican Pedro Fernández, papal visitator in Castile, acted with discretion, collaborating with the Carmelite friars and respecting their normal structures. The result was a relatively smooth and successful visitation and promotion of further reform within the province.

The same cannot be said of the work of Francisco Vargas, papal visitator for Andalusia. He faced the greater challenge in a province less open to reform and far less cooperative with his mission. This had been Rubeo's experience as well. But Vargas exacerbated the difficulties by proceeding with less discretion—notably, for example, by promoting the foundation of Discalced houses by friars from the province of Castile (over which he had no authority) in Andalusia—against the expressed wishes of Rubeo and over the objections of the Calced friars there. He further muddied the jurisdictional waters both by seeking the support of the king in his reform efforts and by meeting with the friars opposed to their own general, Rubeo. Perhaps daunted by the challenges, Vargas sought and received authority from the papal nuncio in Spain, Nicolas Ormaneto, to appoint the young Discalced friar Jerome Gratian as a fellow visitor and as vicar provincial of both the Calced and Discalced in Andalusia. Meanwhile, to add to the layers of confused jurisdictions, the friars of Andalusia retained their own previously designated provincial. At the time, Gratian was just twenty-seven years old, only three months out of the novitiate, Discalced, and from the province of Castile. None of it was likely to ingratiate him to the Calced friars of the province. Gratian further aggravated the tensions—probably feeling that his authority was from the papal visitator and the nuncio—by failing to communicate with his own general, Rubeo.

In August 1574, Pope Gregory XIII brought an end to the Dominican visitation, returning the work of reform to the Carmelite prior general and his delegates. At the same time, however, he also reaffirmed the authority of the papal nuncio Ormaneto to reform religious orders. Meanwhile, the king, jealous of his own prerogatives and with his own reform agenda, objected to the end of the papal visitation in Spain without his approval, declaring its elimination as invalid without his *placet* (approval). With the authority of the Dominican visitators removed, the Carmelite general chapter meeting at Piacenza in Italy ordered the closing of all Discalced houses founded in Andalusia and the removal of their superiors established contrary to his wishes.

Gratian, however, continued to act with the authority delegated to him by the papal nuncio—not always with the greatest discretion in his dealings with the Calced.[33]

In December 1575, Rubeo appointed Jerome Tostado of the province of Catalonia as the general visitator for the Spanish provinces—a visitation that the king opposed. In August 1577, following the death of the nuncio Ormaneto, the new nuncio, Philip Sega, arrived with instructions to end the extraordinary papal visitations and leave the work of reform to those appointed by the Carmelite general. Gratian's authority was revoked. Meanwhile, King Philip refused to grant royal authority to Tostado to visitate the communities in Castile and Andalusia.

Finally, the confusion came to an end when in July 1579, Sega recommended to the pope the erection of a separate province for the Discalced friars and nuns—a resolution that the king had separately promoted. On June 22, 1580, Pope Gregory XIII created the separate Discalced Province. On July 10, 1587, Pope Sixtus V created a separate and still more autonomous Discalced Congregation, still within the same order but with its own vicar general with powers akin to those of a prior general over the larger order. On December 20, 1593, Pope Clement VIII erected the Order of Discalced Carmelites with its own general. And so ended the complicated overlay of jurisdictions in which we can better understand the unfolding of the reform and the biographies of Teresa of Jesus and John of the Cross.

---

33. Smet (*Carmelites*) believes that, if Gratian had acted with more discretion, the unity of the order could have been preserved.

SELECT BIBLIOGRAPHY

English

Egan, Keith J. "The Spirituality of the Carmelites." In *High Middle Ages and Reformation*, edited by Jill Raitt with Bernard McGinn and John Meyendorff, 50–62. Vol. 2 of *Christian Spirituality*. New York: Crossroad, 1989.

Friedman, Elias. *The Latin Hermits of Mount Carmel: A Study of Carmelite Origins*. Rome: Institutum Historicum Teresianum, 1979.

Garrido, Pablo María. *St. Teresa, St. John of the Cross, and the Spanish Carmelites*. Translated by Joseph Chalmers. Darien, Ill.: Carmelite Media, 2015.

McGreal, Wilfrid. *The Fountain of Elijah: The Carmelite Tradition*. Traditions of Christian Spirituality. Series edited by Philip Sheldrake. London: Darton, Longman and Todd, 1999.

Mulhall, Michael, ed. *Albert's Way: The First North American Congress on the Carmelite Rule*. Barrington, Ill.: Province of the Most Pure Heart of Mary, 1989.

Mullins, Patrick. *St. Albert of Jerusalem and the Roots of Carmelite Spirituality*. Volume 34 of Institutum Carmelitanum, *Textus et Studia Historical Carmelitana*. Rome: Edizioni Carmelitane, 2012.

O'Reilly, Terence, and Colin P. Thompson and Lesley Twomey, eds. *St. Teresa of Ávila: Her Writings and Life*. Studies in Hispanic and Lusophone Cultures, 19. Cambridge, England: Legenda (Modern Humanities Research Association), 2018.

Rohrbach, Peter-Thomas. *Journey to Carith: The Story of the Carmelite Order*. 1966. Reprint, Washington, D.C.: ICS Publication, 2015. Kieran Kavanaugh, O.C.D., in his foreword to this reprint edition praises the continuing value of this text. At the same time, he notes that some of its account of the early history of the order is in need of updating in light of subsequent scholarship. He also cautions that Rohrbach's assessment of the state of the Calced in Castile at the time of Teresa and John needs to be nuanced.

Smet, Joachim. *The Carmelites: A History of the Brothers of Our Lady of Mount Carmel*. 4 vols. (in 5 bindings; vol. 3 has separate part 1 and part 2). Darien, Ill.: Carmelite Spiritual Center, 1976–1988.

———. *The Mirror of Carmel: A Brief History of the Carmelite Order.* Darien, Ill.: Carmelite Media, 2011. [This is a one-volume, condensed version of text above, without its footnotes.]

Welch, John. *The Carmelite Way: An Ancient Path for Today's Pilgrim.* Mahwah, N.J.: Paulist Press, 1996.

———. "To Renew a Tradition: The Reforms of Carmel." In *Carmel and Contemplation: Transforming Human Consciousness*, edited by Kevin Culligan and Regis Jordan, 3–23. Vol. 8 of *Carmelite Studies*. Washington, D.C.: ICS Publications, 2000.

Spanish

Álvarez, Tomás. "Santa Teresa ante la regla de Carmelo." In *Estudios Teresianos I: Biografía e historia*, 169–92. Burgos, Spain: Editorial Monte Carmelo, 1995.

Garrido, Pablo María. "El Carmelo español en tiempo de Santa Teresa." In *Congreso Internacional Teresiano (4–7 octubre, 1982)*, edited by Teófanes Egido et al., 407–29. Vol. 1. Salamanca, Spain: Universidad de Salamanca, 1983.

Maroto, Daniel de Pablo. *Ser y misión del Carmelo Teresiano: Historia de un carisma.* Madrid: Editorial de Espiritualidad, 2011.

Steggink, Otger. "Dos corrientes de reforma en el Carmelo español del siglo XVI: La observancia y la descalcez, frente a la 'Reforma del rey.'" In *Aspectos históricos de San Juan de la Cruz*, edited by Teófanes Egido, 117–42. Ávila, Spain: Institución Gran Duque de Alba de la Disputación Provincial de Ávila, 1990.

CHAPTER 6

The Monastery of the Incarnation

eresa of Jesus had been a nun of the Carmelite Monastery of the Incarnation in Ávila for twenty-seven years (1535–1562) when she began the Discalced Reform with the foundation of the Monastery of St. Joseph in the same city.[1] In the *Life*, she speaks with great affection of the community and praises the religious spirit and sanctity of many of its nuns. In fact, she had known some truly exemplary nuns (L 7.3). Even

---

1. The most thorough history of the Monastery of the Incarnation was written by one of its recent, now deceased, chaplains: Nicolás González y González, *Historia del monasterio de la Encarnación de Ávila* (Madrid: Editorial de Espiritualidad, 1995). This is the one-volume updating of an earlier two-volume work: *El Monasterio de la Encarnación de Ávila* published in 1976. In another work, the same author provides copies of extant documents concerning the foundation and history of the Incarnation until the time of Teresa: *La ciudad de las Carmelitas en tiempos de Doña Teresa de Ahumada: Documentación histórica u gráfica del monasterio de la Encarnación de Ávila en el periodo de treinta años, en el que vivió santa Teresa de Jesús (1535–1562 y 1571–1574)* (Avila, Spain: Diputación de Ávila. Institución Gran Duque de Alba, 2011), 247–358. See also Steggink, *La reforma del Carmelo español*, though the author takes a wider lens to look at the Incarnation at the time of Teresa within the context of the history of the order and the jurisdictional struggles at the time of the reform.

when Teresa reluctantly returned as prioress and worked to bring some reform to the monastery—without trying to bring her own Discalced vision—she spoke with affection and respect of the nuns.[2] But she was not without criticism. And it has been somewhat traditional—at least in more popular presentations—to take her more critical comments "and run with them" to suggest that the Incarnation was somehow decadent or in scandalous need of reform. But this does not seem at all to be the case.

It is true that the monastery had its areas of laxness in observance. As we will see, in the visitation of the monastery by the Carmelite general Rubeo (Giovanni Battista Rossi) in 1566–1567, many of its nuns said the same. But as we have seen, Teresa and Rubeo—and with him, many of the nuns of the Incarnation—seem to have had different views of what Carmelite reform would mean. Rubeo's aim was to bring the Incarnation more fully into conformity with the mitigated rule of 1432 and subsequent reform decrees. Teresa, on the other hand, wanted her reform to return more fully to the eremitical and contemplative focus of the mitigated rule of 1247 with an eye to the founding vision of the Carmelites, as she understood it. This was consistent as well with the wider "observant" reform of religious orders at the time and with the more contemplative spirituality that was partnered with it. This wider reform and spirituality were embedded in Teresa's reading of Francisco de Osuna and others as well as in her many contacts with observant Franciscans, Dominicans, and Jesuits. As we have seen, all of the reform movements in the religious communities of the time were directed

---

2. Ltr 38 (November 7, 1571) to Doña Luisa de la Cerda.

to the reclaiming of their primitive rules without subsequent mitigations.[3]

Teresa of Jesus did not launch her reform because the monastery of her profession and early religious life was decadent. She did share many of the concerns that other nuns of the community themselves expressed to their prior general at the time of his visitation. But Teresa wanted something more than what the Incarnation, even in a more fully reformed state, could provide her. Unless we see this, we do a disservice to the monastery of the Incarnation that Teresa herself never intended—and we would fail to see the true nature of Teresa's own reform. We would further misunderstand the initial displeasure of many of the nuns of the Incarnation when Teresa was later appointed prioress there. They were not decadent nuns, fearful of reform, but they did not share the specifically Discalced vision of reform that had been initiated elsewhere by their new prioress.

A Little Village in Itself

The feminine branch of the Carmelites was only formally established in 1452—only sixty years before Teresa's birth.[4] The monastery of the Incarnation was founded first in 1479 as a *beaterio*—that is, as a community of pious women living together

---

3. Teófanes Egido, "Significado eclesial y social de la fundación del Monasterio de San José," in *Vivir en Ávila cuando Santa Teresa escribe el libro de su "Vida,"* ed. Rómulo Cuartas Lodoño and Francisco Javier Sancho Fermín, 169–207, Colección Claves (Burgos, Spain: Editorial Monte Carmelo, 2011), 174–77.

4. A great deal of firsthand knowledge of the state of the Incarnation at the time of Teresa is provided by the extant notes from the interviews of ninety nuns of the Incarnation during the canonical visitation of Rubeo during that time. Steggink, *La reforma del Carmelo español*, 201–16.

without formal religious profession. As was not unusual in the time, it was founded by a wealthy widow, Doña Elvira González, together with women drawn from family and friends. Both the Dominican and the Augustinian convents in Ávila had a similar history. In 1485, it moved to another location and became more formally a monastery of women. Ten years later, in 1495, the community received the deed to what had been a Jewish cemetery before the expulsion, outside the city walls. The little community moved to that location and was formally accepted as a Carmelite monastery of women in 1515, the year of Teresa's birth. This was the location that Teresa came to know (and that is still its location to this day).

The monastery subsequently grew quickly, and it became a favored place for the daughters of the prominent families of Ávila. Its prioresses were generally drawn from the nobility of the area. It had a good reputation in the city, and the ever-increasing size of the community lent it a certain sense of prominence. When Teresa entered the monastery in 1535, there were about forty nuns. Only five years later, in 1540, there were 120. In 1545, the number had increased to 165. By 1566, there were almost two hundred nuns—in addition to the personal servants and boarders living in the monastery. Already in 1547, the prioress had noted overcrowding. After all, the community had grown by almost five times in only thirty years.

There were many reasons that a young woman would choose to enter the monastery, and girls as young as twelve could be admitted. Some, of course, were drawn by a sincere sense of personal vocation. But others were unable to marry for a variety of reasons—whether simply unable to find a suitable husband in a time when men were being drawn into foreign wars and to the New World, because a wealthy family could not afford adequate dowries for the marriage of multiple daughters in keeping with their sense of social rank, or because the woman's reputation was tarnished through some supposed indiscretion. In any case, except for widows, nuns, and *beatas*, single women were the exception in Spanish society of the time. Perhaps, as Teresa herself suggests, some women had an unconscious sense that the life of a nun would bring greater freedom than that of a married woman in the culture.[5]

In addition to the nuns and others living in the monastery itself, many other individuals were housed on the monastery precincts and grounds. There were homes for the lay administrators of the nuns' properties; for those who collected the rents/income from the nuns' lands, servants, gardeners, and caretakers of the monastery's livestock; for those who processed the nuns' grain and produce; and for chaplains, confessors, a doctor, a surgeon, and a notary. The presence of assorted mules, pigs, goats, sheep, and chickens virtually made of the monastery and its grounds a small village of its own.

The Spiritual and Liturgical Life of the Monastery

It appears that the Divine Office and Eucharist were celebrated by the nuns of the Incarnation faithfully and reverently. There was a devout Marian and eucharistic piety in the community. The nuns received Communion once or twice a month—which was considered frequent at the time. In fact, there were fifteen to twenty days per year set for the nuns to receive Communion, and they were all generally expected to receive on those days. Teresa

---

5. See, for example, the insight that Teresa describes in L 34.4.

herself followed this practice for many years at the Incarnation, but later in her time there she began to receive daily. In order to avoid notoriety for this at-the-time unusual practice, she often received at an earlier Mass rather than at the conventual Mass where she would have been more likely to be noticed.

The nuns ate only one meal a day, three days a week, from September 14 until Easter. They observed abstinence from meat on four days per week and fasted during Advent and Lent. They had public reading in their refectory. They took the discipline (self-flagellation) three times a week, a common ascetical practice among serious religious of the period.[6] There was mandated silence in the church, the choir, the cloister, the refectory, and the cells (though, as we shall see, this was not always well observed).

The nun's constitutions mandated that each nun confess each week or at least every other week. For this purpose they had two regular Carmelite confessors (John of the Cross and another Discalced friar would replace their two Calced counterparts when Teresa later became prioress—much to the consternation of the Calced and, initially, to many of the nuns who feared they would be too harsh). But the nuns could also avail themselves of several other approved confessors from among the city's secular and religious clergy. It appears that many of the nuns actually preferred these outside confessors, feeling that they were better formed, showed a better religious spirit, and perhaps were less prone to show favoritism among the nuns. In Rubeo's visitation, for example, he reports that one of nuns opined that the friars would do well to read more spiritual books.[7]

---

6. Otger Steggink, "Arraigo carmelitano de Santa Teresa de Jesús," in *The Land of Carmel: Essays in Honor of Joachim Smet, O.Carm.*, ed. Paul Chandler and Keith J. Egan, 247–84 (Rome: Institutum Carmelitanum, 1991), 261.

7. Steggink, 267.

A central and important part of the community's common prayer was prayers for deceased donors and their families. The community sometimes contracted with wealthy families for specific prayers and devotions over many years, and these agreements would be witnessed by a notary. This practice, typical of the time, more tightly tied the monastery to the wealthy families of the city and to its culture. It provided an important source of income, especially for special projects like repairs and building. But at the same time, it provided an overlay of prayers and devotions that could require a great deal of time beyond the communal and personal prayer of the nuns.

A particularly glaring example of the institutionalization of this practice involved a wealthy landowner, Bernardo Robles, who, in 1530, made a very sizeable donation to the monastery in order to build a much needed church and choir with the promise of more funds upon his death. In return, the nuns agreed that, upon his death, his body could be interred in their church. And in perpetuity, day and night, a nun would kneel before the Blessed Sacrament with a lighted candle in her hand, praying for his soul. Robles died in 1531, and the nuns faithfully fulfilled the agreement for a year and a half. This meant, of course, that a different nun would have to be awakened each hour through the night. Eventually, feeling overburdened, the nuns petitioned Rome for and received a mitigation—against the strong objections of the deceased man's family. The conflict between the nuns and the family dragged on until 1545 when the final compromise was reached that the nuns agreed to pray the seven penitential psalms in choir and to offer Mass once a week for the deceased as well as keeping a special lamp burning before the Blessed Sacrament. In 1574, while prioress of the Incarnation, Teresa was able to obtain a further mitigation that required offering the regular psalms of the Divine Office for Robles and to reverently keep the special lamp burning before the Blessed Sacrament. In her reform, Teresa wanted none of this kind of entanglement with the wealthy, nor the added layers of required prayers.

Social Hierarchy

The social hierarchy so prevalent in society was mirrored within the monastery. Nuns who came from prominent and wealthy families, like Teresa, were addressed by the title Doña (Lady) and retained their claim on their illustrious family names. And so, Teresa was "Doña Teresa Sánchez de Cepeda y Ahumada." Their former status in the world was recognized by more prominent places in choir. They were able to live in ample private cells, sometimes with more than one room. Teresa herself had a cell with two separate levels. This allowed her, like other nuns, to provide accommodations even for an extended time to female family members (as she did for several years for her sister Juana). These cells could, in fact, be bought and sold between nuns. The nuns with the necessary means could prepare—or have prepared by personal servants—their own meals in their cells with food provided by family. One nun was reported to maintain a slave.

Meanwhile the nuns from poorer backgrounds lived in common dormitories and shared the common recreation space of the monastery. They ate whatever it was that the monastery provided in the common refectory. And their upkeep and sustenance were subject to the economic ups and downs of the community.

There was no precise uniformity in habit. This was a source of some complaint during Rubeo's visit. The nuns of humbler origins wore simple habits provided by the monastery. In times of financial difficulty for the community, they might find it difficult to have adequate shoes. Meanwhile, the nuns from families of means could wear habits of finer cloth, sometimes with fancy collars, lace, decorated belts, rings, and even colored petticoats.

What concerned Teresa especially was the concern for personal honor, so rampant in society, which remained prominent in the monastery. Nuns could take great offense if their family status and rank were not recognized appropriately by being offered the correct greeting or their proper place. Teresa would react strongly by eliminating all titles in the monasteries of the reform and mandating a spirit of egalitarianism.

Dire Economic Circumstances and Its Impact on Observance

During Rubeo's visitation of the monastery in 1566–1567, the nuns reported severe financial difficulties. He found some deficiencies in the community's financial administration, but clearly the main problem was that the large number of members seriously taxed the monastery's financial resources.

The income from the monastery's extensive lands was significant. Such lands came to the monastery through dowries or inheritance by individual nuns. But much of what they received was not in the form of money but rather in grains and vegetables, which had to be transported and processed. On the days that the nuns ate meat, they required about 110 pounds of it, plus a large sack of potatoes and about one hundred loaves of bread. The income from their lands could only cover about a third of the regular budget of the monastery—and this only if the income were not decimated by bad harvests (which were frequent in the mid-sixteenth century). The nuns from wealthier families also brought ample dowries, and there were many of them. But beyond just the salaries of the many employees and servants and the maintenance of the nuns, there were costly expansions and constant repairs to be made. The monastery was forced to sell some of its lands, and still the community accrued a large debt. In 1565, the monastery petitioned the city government for financial assistance.

An extant vow chart from the time of Teresa shows that the nuns took a vow of obedience to the Carmelite general, the prioress, and their successors according to the Rule. There was no formal vow of poverty or of enclosure, though these would have been general expectations, to some degree, flowing from the rule and constitutions. Although the nuns did not vow poverty, they were expected to give up the right to disposition over any money or property received—using them only with the permission of their superior. But because of the monastery's economic situation, even these restrictions were only loosely enforced. It became virtually necessary for individual nuns to seek help from outside for their own upkeep.

The nuns from wealthy families did not themselves feel so acutely the privations caused by economic problems. They could depend on income from family or even from their own properties. But those without outside assistance experienced poverty even in the cloister. Nuns complained to Rubeo that the monastery lacked the funds to provide them with adequate medical treatment or relief. Individually, some nuns sought additional income themselves through educating girls in their cells, taking in sewing, or even personally seeking alms.

The structures and spirit of poverty were not the only casualties of the economic circumstances. The spirit of enclosure—so essential for a life of tranquility, silence, and contemplation—likewise suffered. It became necessary for the nuns to be able to come and go more frequently and for longer periods in order to relieve the monastery of the burden of their upkeep or to seek the goodwill of wealthy family and other donors toward the monastery and its needs. When the Council of Trent mandated strict cloister for nuns, it was practically impossible to realize because of the very real need for the nuns to be able to seek outside assistance. King Philip II was opposed to implementing this conciliar ruling precisely for this reason.

One response to the Incarnation's financial distress was to have nuns leave the cloister in order to eat with families and friends or even to live with them for a time. Between 1560 and 1565, as many as fifty nuns—about a third of the community—were living outside the cloister. Or nuns were sent out as companions to wealthy women who had lost husbands or children—as Teresa was ordered to do for Luisa de la Cerda in 1561. This relieved the monastery of providing for them but also served as a way to promote good relations with wealthy donors. Such visiting outside the monastery would rather naturally slip into comings and goings for more frivolous reasons.

The monastery maintained visiting parlors in which the nuns could conduct the monastery's business with the outside world, speak with their confessors, and visit occasionally with family and friends. But in hard economic times, it was especially important for the nuns to maintain good relations with wealthy family and friends. But these visiting parlors became places for frequent, more frivolous visits—a social pastime for the upper classes of Ávila to pay a call on the nuns. Teresa herself confesses to being a frequent participant in such conversations in the parlors. It appears that men who were not family members—people of less than good repute or intention—would also come calling on the nuns. (Here we must recall that not all of the nuns entered the monastery because of a personal sense of vocation but were rather forced by other circumstances into the community.) The visiting and idle conversations extended beyond the visiting parlors to conversations from the lower windows of the monastery to people on the street below, at the door of the sacristy, or through the water conduits that allowed water to flow from outside the monastery walls into the nuns' gardens.

All of this—much of it begun or necessitated by economic stress—was bound to undermine the broader sense of observance and the spirit of recollection in the monastery.

But Neither Decadent nor Scandalous

Although the nuns themselves complained to Rubeo about some of the abuses or failures in observance mentioned above, they judged the community in general to have a good spirit and a solid, if sometimes shaky, observance. Rubeo's final overall evaluation too was positive.

The fact is that the nuns of the Incarnation had neither strict cloister nor a vow of strict poverty. Their unfortunate financial circumstances allowed this fact to open the door to a serious loosening of observance and even abuses in a number of areas. The majority of nuns, along with Rubeo, saw this reality. Teresa too saw it. And in her reformed monasteries, there would be both strict cloister and poverty. But the reform of Teresa was aimed at something more fundamental than bringing the monastery of her profession into better conformity with the mitigated rule of 1432. Her sisters in the community saw for themselves the same problems that Teresa saw, but she wanted something more fundamental than most of them did: a deeper reform, a return to an earlier form of the rule, and the broader and deeper reclaiming of the contemplative and eremitical spirit of the first Carmelites.

SELECT BIBLIOGRAPHY

English

Álvarez, Tomás. *St. Teresa of Avila: 100 Themes on Her Life and Work.* Translated by Kieran Kavanaugh. Washington, D.C.: ICS Publications, 2011. (See pp. 97–100.)

Spanish

González y González, Nicolás. "El ambiente religioso del Monasterio de la Encarnación en los tiempos de Santa Teresa." In *Vivir en Ávila cuando Santa Teresa escribe el libro de su "Vida,"* edited by Rómulo Cuartas Lodoño and Francisco Javier Sancho Fermín, 135–68. Colección Claves. Burgos, Spain: Editorial Monte Carmelo, 2011.

———. *La ciudad de las Carmelitas en tiempos de Doña Teresa de Ahumada: Documentación histórica u gráfica del monasterio de la Encarnación de Ávila en el periodo de treinta años, en el que vivió santa Teresa de Jesús (1535–1562 y 1571–1574).* Avila, Spain: Disputación de Ávila. Institución Gran Duque de Alba, 2011.

———. *Historia del monasterio de la Encarnación de Ávila.* Madrid, Spain: Editorial de Espiritualidad, 1995. This is the one-volume update of an earlier two-volume work: *El Monasterio de la Encarnación de Ávila.* 2 vols. Ávila, Spain: Obra Social y Cultural de la Caja Central de Ahorros y Prestamos de Ávila, 1976.

Steggink, Otger. "Arraigo carmelitano de Santa Teresa de Jesus." In *The Land of Carmel: Essays in Honor of Joachim Smet, O.Carm,* edited by Paul Chandler and Keith J. Egan, 247–84. Rome: Institutum Carmelitanum, 1991.

———. *La reforma del Carmelo español: La visita canónica del General Rubeo y su encuentro con Santa Teresa (1566–1567).* 2nd exp. ed. Ávila, Spain: Institución Gran Duque de Alba de la Disputación Provincial de Ávila, 1993.

Chapter 7

Spiritual Antecedents

Teresa of Jesus and John of the Cross undoubtedly represent the apex of the mysticism of Spain's golden age in the sixteenth century. They are, no less, among the principal figures in the history of Christian mysticism. But they were the "apex" of sixteenth-century Spanish mysticism in the sense that others preceded them. Teresa and John were inheritors and beneficiaries of a tradition, not only in Spain in the decades before them, but also in the broader Christian tradition in which they were formed. It is true that Teresa and John have a distinctive genius, but what they experienced, taught, and wrote did not suddenly come down out of heaven as a unique gift to them. Each of them, of course, had a unique, intimate, personal experience of God, but that experience was itself shaped—as was their understanding of it and their vocabulary for explaining it—by the long tradition of which they were especially gifted inheritors. It is to this tradition that we now turn as further context for a better understanding and appreciation of their distinctive contribution to the tradition that preceded and succeeded them.

In previous chapters, we looked at the reform movements at work in the church before and during the time of Teresa and John—in the church generally, among religious orders, and within the Carmelites themselves. But now we look more particularly at the spiritual movements that grew in the fertile soil of this wider reform and that shaped these two great mystical teachers. We will look particularly at the sixteenth-century Spanish mystical movement that influenced and shaped Teresa and John, especially the Franciscan movement that promoted the "prayer of recollection." This was represented especially by Francisco de Osuna, whose work was so critical for Teresa's own spiritual journey. But first we must examine the larger spiritual tradition that was the foundation for the unfolding of Spanish mysticism of the Golden Age.

The Pervasive Influence of Pseudo-Dionysius

Peter Tyler understands the mysticism of Teresa and John within the context of what he calls the unknowing-affective (or deconstructive-affective) mystical tradition.[1] It is a lineage that is grounded in the work of Pseudo-Dionysius, who throughout the Middle Ages until after the time of Teresa and John was believed to be Dionysius the Areopagite who was converted by the preaching of St. Paul (Acts 17:34). This belief gave his writings a near-scriptural authority. In fact, it is now believed that this so-called Dionysius really dates from the fifth century, probably writing in Syria. He is considered the father of the Christian apophatic tradition (that is, the tradition that seeks union with God by a "negative" path, a path of unknowing, or of darkness and night). One of his most well-known works, *Mystical*

---

1. Peter Tyler, *The Return to the Mystical: Ludwig Wittgenstein, Teresa of Avila, and the Christian Mystical Tradition* (New York: Continuum, 2011), 63–128. Tyler traces this unknowing-affective tradition from Pseudo-Dionysius into the flowering of mysticism in sixteenth-century Spain.

Theology, was one of the very few books that John of the Cross explicitly cites.

The works of Pseudo-Dionysius were translated, studied, and commented on throughout the Middle Ages, and this tradition flowered in late medieval affective mysticism exemplified by Bernard of Clairvaux and other commentators on the biblical Song of Songs. In this Dionysian tradition, love does what normal intellectual knowing cannot. We cannot know the transcendent God with our intellects, our normal understanding, but we can "grasp" God with love. Deepening spiritual and ultimately mystical knowing of God is a loving knowledge, a knowledge born of love. In our usual way of speaking, we can say that we can know a million facts about another person, but someone who loves that other person can know him or her more intimately and deeply than we do, even without all of the facts. By love, the person "grasps" another in a real knowing, but not in the normal sense of facts, figures, empirical data, and concepts. To the normal intellect, then, this type of loving knowledge can be called "obscure" or "mystical" (in the original sense of the word as "secret" or "hidden").

John of the Cross stands most clearly in this tradition. As Peter Tyler speaks of it, this is a path of unknowing or of deconstruction. We cannot know God deeply with our intellects, and so, we must systematically lay aside any image or concept that supposes any ultimate knowledge of God. This does not make our normal way of knowing about God wrong, just infinitely less than the reality. As the anonymous author of the medieval classic *The Cloud of Unknowing*—another clear example of this same tradition—says it, we must pierce the cloud of unknowing that stands between us and God. We must leave all images and concepts behind a "cloud of forgetting" and enter the darkness of unknowing. While less explicitly stated, Teresa too ultimately insists that the work of the intellect must cease when the soul enters into the deeper union of love.[2]

But at the same time, this mystical path is a way of love. And so, as Tyler says, it is a deconstructive but affective path—not ultimately a journey of deepening emotions (as we might normal understand "affect" or even "love") but rather the ever-deepening and more complete reaching out by the human will to embrace God and be embraced in turn and surrendered to the divine will. This yields, increasingly and ultimately only by divine gift, a true and deep loving knowledge that does not involve knowledge of doctrines about God or clearer images of God. Rather it is a grasping and being grasped beyond human knowing by a God who always remains beyond the ability of our human intellects to contain. It is this deep yearning and striving of the human will toward God that is symbolized by the many mystical commentaries on the biblical Song of Songs that have been the fruit of this apophatic tradition.

The inheritance of Pseudo-Dionysius passed through the Middle Ages along a number of related streams: the so-called Victorines such as Hugh of St. Victor (d. 1141) and Richard of St. Victor (d. 1173); the Cistercian Bernard of Clairvaux (d. 1153); the great Franciscan Doctor of the Church St. Bonaventure (d. 1274); Jean Gerson (d. 1429) of the University of Paris; and the German and Flemish mystics such as Meister Eckhart (d. ca. 1328), John Tauler (d. 1361), Henry Suso (d. 1366), and John van Ruysbroeck (d. 1381). Many of their works, as we will see, were being translated and published in Spain in the early sixteenth century.

---

2. Tyler, 143.

But the Pseudo-Dionysian stream that most influenced Spanish mystics of the sixteenth century is found in the work of the Carthusian Hugh of Balma (d. ca. 1305), which may also have influenced the author of *The Cloud of Unknowing*. Hugh's *Viae Lugent Sion*, also known sometimes as the *Mystical Theology*, was translated and published in Spain in 1514 under the title *Sol de Contemplativos*. This work was cited by both Francisco de Osuna and Bernardino de Laredo whose works played an important role in Teresa's mystical understanding. Osuna draws from and explicitly refers to the works of Hugh, Gerson (specifically, his *De Mistica Theologia*), and Pseudo-Dionysius himself—though his emphasis is more on the mystical path as an "art of love" than on unknowing.[3] Still, consistent with this tradition, Osuna maintains that we cannot gain intellectual knowledge of God but only a hidden, loving knowledge of God—the *sabor* (taste for God) rather than the *saber* (knowledge of God). Laredo on the other hand relies not on Gerson but more directly on Hugh, who Laredo says stands in the tradition of St. Paul, Pseudo-Dionysius, the Victorines, Gregory the Great, and Gerson.[4]

The flowering of sixteenth-century Spanish mysticism, then, was promoted by the earlier effort of Cardinal Francisco Jiménez de Cisernos to promote the translation and publication of just such works of spirituality and mysticism. This literature came to influence not only Osuna and Laredo but also other mystical writers of the period. Teresa read such works and certainly

---

3. It is not clear if Osuna and other Spanish writers of the period read Pseudo-Dionysius directly—which is possible—or through the works of Hugh of Balma, Bonaventure, and others. Melquíades Andrés Martín, *Los recogidos: Nueva visión de la mística española (1500–1700)* (Madrid: Fundación Universitaria Española, 1975), 779.

4. Tyler, *Return to the Mystical*, 113–24.

spoke of them with her many learned confessors and counselors. Although John says little directly about what he had read, it is likely that he was familiar with many of the published works of contemporary Spanish writers as well as many of those other books on prayer and mysticism that were flooding Spain at the time (until at least the Index of 1559).

The Unfolding of Spanish Mysticism

Two important studies of sixteenth-century Spanish mysticism were published in recent years in Spain by Melquíades Andrés Martín[5] and by Eulogio Pacho.[6] There is nothing in English that approaches the depth and breadth of these works for understanding the vibrant spiritual context in which Teresa and John were formed and taught.[7] We will understand and appreciate them even more deeply once we have identified the antecedents, general characteristics, and major figures of the golden age of Spanish mysticism.

---

5. Melquíades Andrés Martín, *Historia de la mística de la Edad de Oro en España y América*. (Madrid: Biblioteca de Autores Cristianos, 1994). This volume was followed by an anthology of excerpts from 133 spiritual and mystical writers of that period with some accompanying introduction and commentary: *Los místicos de la Edad de Oro en España y América: Antología* (Madrid: Biblioteca de Autores Cristianos, 1996). This follows on his earlier, 1975 work, *Los recogidos*, cited above. In addition to a number of important articles on sixteenth-century Spanish mysticism (see the general bibliography), he is also the author of a classic study of the academic theology of that period: *La teología española en el siglo XVI*, 2 vols. (Madrid: Biblioteca de Autores Cristianos, 1976–1977).

6. Eulogio Pacho, *Apogeo de la mística cristiana: Historia de la espiritualidad clásica española 1450–1650* (Burgos, Spain: Editorial Monte Carmelo, 2008). This is an impressive work of about 1,400 pages!

7. This is not to deny the continuing value of the now almost one-hundred-year-old work of E. Allison Peers: *Studies of the Spanish Mystics*, 2 vols. (London: Sheldon Press, 1927, 1930).

Andrés Martín understands the distinctive mysticism of Spain in the sixteenth century as developing or unfolding through five stages:[8]

1. Initial Formation and Consolidation (1480–1523)

In this period, we see the emergence of key ideas and terms from within the spirituality of the Observants or reformed groups of religious, most especially the Franciscans in the form of the "prayer of recollection." There was a virtual explosion of publication of books on spirituality and prayer, both by native authors writing in the vernacular and through translated contemporary and classical spiritual works. This stage ends roughly with the publication of the central works of Francisco de Osuna and Bernardino de Laredo and with the investigation and condemnation of the first groups of Alumbrados (a group of false mystics, to be discussed at length in the next chapter).

2. The Great Crisis (1525–1560)

The year 1525 is when the first group of misguided and heretical Alumbrados, often confused with the orthodox development of mysticism, was condemned by the Inquisition. In 1559, the first major Spanish Index of Forbidden Books was published as a response to the fear of the encroachment of heretical and dangerous mystical teaching and the effort to stem the arrival of Reformation ideas into Spain. Between these dates, we see growing resistance to promoting and teaching mystical prayer to ordinary

---

8. Andrés Martín, *Historia de la mística*, 66. Andrés Martín, in his other works on this topic (cited above), offers some minor variations in his identification of these stages of development.

people, suspicion of mystical experience, and growing concern about Erasmist and Reformation ideas.

3. Doctrinal and Lived Clarification (1560–1580)

During this stage, there is a greater consolidation of terms and concepts as well as a clearer differentiation from heretical developments. This is, of course, the time of Teresa's maturity and writing.

4. The Height and Full Unfolding (1580–1650)

This period was the height of the mystical writing among the various religious orders, coinciding with the flourishing of Spanish universities and theology. It was a rich period of theological discourse about human dignity and rights (in relationship especially with the dignity and rights of indigenous persons in the Americas), the moral foundation of early capitalism, and grace and freedom. Following the Council of Trent (1545–1563), we see a further consolidation of the reform movement within the church. Many new works of mysticism were published, not with great new insights, but with a high level of literary, theological, and experiential quality. John of the Cross was at his maturity in the first decade of this period.

5. Decline (1650–1725)

This was a period of increasingly dry and academic disputes about various distinctions and terms, the separation (rather than the mere distinction) of ascetical and mystical stages, and a focus on extraordinary phenomena and the criteria for distinguishing true from false.

Convergence of Elements

The movement outlined above seems to have emerged from the convergence of a number of different factors, some of them discussed in more detail in earlier chapters.[9] Among these elements are the general church reform movements throughout Europe, reform initiatives in Spain especially promoted by the crown, and the reform of religious orders that moved them toward a greater emphasis on prayer, simplicity, poverty, and contemplation. The movement in support of the prayer of recollection flows especially from the Franciscan reform, as we will see. And the various efforts to reform clergy and religious, together with the expansion of Spanish universities, brought a renewed flowering of preaching to feed the church.

Until the end of the fifteenth century, Spain had been inward looking, focused on slowly bringing into unity various smaller kingdom and slowly pushing back the Muslims who had ruled major parts of Spain since the middle of the eighth century. Efforts at reform coincided in Spain with the conclusion of this centuries-long "crusade" to win back the whole of the Iberian Peninsula from Muslim rule. Together with the discovery of the New World and its challenge of evangelization, this resulted in a missionary and evangelical zeal that permeated the spirit of the age. While mission and evangelization were its external face, the interior mission of a deeper spiritual "conquest" was its internal focus.[10]

The unification of the major kingdoms of Spain by Ferdinand and Isabella and the discovery of the New World gave Spain a new international outlook and involvement. Their

---

9. Andrés Martín, *Historia de la mística*, 72–89; Pacho, *Apogeo de la mística cristiana*, 125–212.

10. Andrés Martín, *Los recogidos*, 30.

grandson, Carlos V, inherited not only the Spanish crown but also territories throughout Europe, especially notably in this context, the modern-day Low Countries ("Flanders"). With this new international opening came the influx of people, exchange of students, and the importation of books.

Another important element to be mentioned here is not explicitly religious at all. It is the influence of Renaissance humanism—exemplified in one form by the ideas of Erasmus that entered Spain with some force in the second quarter of the sixteenth century. With it came a greater focus on the human person, the search for a deeper knowledge of self, and a greater sense of human interiority. Such ideas filled Spanish universities in the period and as such formed those who studied in them. A deeper appreciation of God at the depth of the person and the beauty of the person in the image of God is enhanced by this humanist influence and is evident in the Teresa's description of the soul in the first dwelling places in *The Interior Castle*.

But of special importance to the emergence of the distinctive mysticism of sixteenth-century Spain was the publication of numerous books of spirituality—in Latin (and many of the mystical writers were university educated and thus fluent in Latin) but also and especially translations into the vernacular and, as the century progressed, new spiritual works written in Castilian. We give special attention to this phenomena in the next section.

Books, Books, and More Books

Printing was still relatively new in the sixteenth century—invented around 1450—but with encouragement of Cardinal Cisneros, printing presses had multiplied in Spain: in Valencia in 1474, Zaragoza and Barcelona in 1475, Seville in 1477,

The Virgin of Carmel with Teresa of Ávila and John of the Cross by Juan Rodríguez Juárez (1675–1728) in Museo Nacional de Arte, Mexico City.

Portrait of Teresa of Jesus done during her lifetime by Friar Juan de la Miseria (1570).

The Vision of St. John of the Cross by Jacob van Oost the Younger (1639–1713) in Church of Saint-Maurice in Lille, France.

Carmelite Church and Monastery of St. Teresa on the site of her family home in Ávila.

Carmelite Church and Monastery of St. John of the Cross on the site of his family home in Fontiveros.

Carmelite Church and Monastery in Alba de Tormes, founded by St. Teresa, where she died, and where her remains are enshrined.

Carmelite Church and Monastery in Segovia where St. John of the Cross served as prior and where his remains are enshrined.

Monastery of the Incarnation in Ávila in which Teresa made her profession.

Photo by AdriPozuelo, 2012 / Wikimedia Commons

St. Albert presents the Rule to the Carmelites (1329) by Pietro Lorenzetti (ca. 1280–ca. 1348). From altarpiece in the former Church of the Carmelites, San Niccolo. Presently in the Pinacoteca di Siena, Italy.

View of Mount Carmel where the first Carmelite hermits gathered.

The first Carmelite hermits wore a striped mantle before coming to Europe. *Hermits at the Fountain of Elijah* by Pietro Lorenzetti (ca. 1280–ca. 1348) in Pinacoteca Nazionale di Siena, Italy.

Above: Columbus Before the Queen (1895) by Emanuel Leutze (1816–68) in Brooklyn Museum, Brooklyn, N.Y.

Right: Capitulation of Granada by Vicente Barneto y Vazquez (1836–1902). [*No specific date or physical location given*]

Below: Expulsion of the Jews by Joaquín Turina y Areal (1847–1903) in Centro de Interpretación de la Judería, Seville, Spain.

The Young Juan de Brocar Presents to Cardinal Cisneros the Final Page of the Polyglot Bible by José Méndez Andrés from *La Ilustración Española y Americana* 17 (1873): 57.

The Meeting of the Emperor Carlos V with Francisco Pizarro in the Palace in Toledo by Angel Lizcano Monedero and Eugenio Vela from *La Ilustración Española y Americana* 31 (1887): 40.

Philip II Presiding at an Auto de Fe (1871) by Domingo Valdivieso y Henarejos (1832–72). In Museo del Prado, Madrid, Spain.

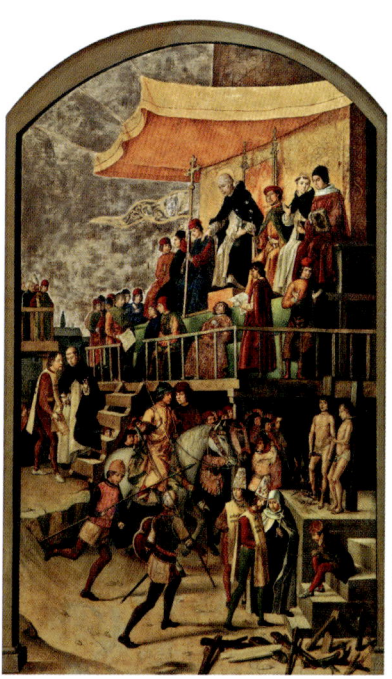

St. Dominic Presiding Over An Auto de Fe by Pedro Berruguette (ca.1450–1504) in Museo del Prado, Madrid, Spain (from the sacristy of the Dominican Church and Monastery of Santo Tomás in Ávila, the first headquarters of the Spanish Inquisition).

Dominions of Philip II of Spain in Europe and North Africa (1580) by Tyk, 2011.

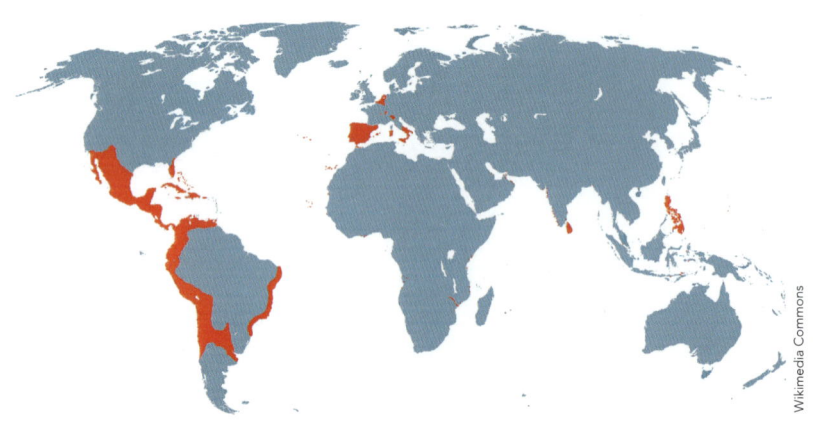

Spanish empire during the reign of Philip II (1580) by Ostiudo, 2014.

Above: Storming of the Teocalli by Cortez and His Troops (1520) by Emanuel Leutze (1816–68) in Wadsworth Atheneum Museum of Art, Hartford, Conn.

Right: Indigenous men working in the mines by Elisée Reclus (1830–1905) from *L'Homme et la* Terre, 1905.

Despite the obvious presence of baser motives, Christian evangelization of the New World was an important mission for many in Spain, including St. Teresa. *The First Mass Celebrated in Chile* (1904) by Pedro Subercaseaux Lustig in Chilean Museum of Fine Arts, Santiago, Chile.

Spanish Sixteenth Century Dress by Albert Kretschmer from *Costumes of All Nations*, 1882.

Classroom of Friar Luis de Leon (sixteenth century classroom, University of Salamanca, where John studied).

The nineteenth century artist's rather fanciful image of Teresa and Jerome Gratian who was actually some 25 years younger than Teresa. *St. Teresa Explains Her Reformed Foundations to Jerome Gratian* (1868) by Benito Mercadé (1831–97) in Museo del Prado, Madrid, Spain.

St. Peter of Alcántara Shows St. Teresa of Ávila the Way to Paradise (1765) by Francesco Fontebasso (1707–1769) in Chapel of San Francesco della Vigna, Venice, Italy.

Photo by Didier Descouens, 2016 / Wikimedia Commons

Jerome Gratian. [*See forthcoming "Pilgrimage of Anastasius" translated by Fr. Steven Watson OCD for further information*]

Above: Luis de León by Francisco Pacheco (1564-1644) from *El libro de descripción de verdaderos retratos, ilustres y memorables varones* (Seville, no date) in Real Academia de la Historia, Madrid, Spain.

Left: Although Luis de León was an admirer and the first editor of Teresa's complete works, he was also the author of a popular book promoting the idea of the inferiority of women. *The Perfect Wife* (1583) by Luis de León, in the private collection of Juan Fernandez.

St. Teresa "la Andariega" at the Monastery of the Incarnation, Ávila, Spain: bronze sculpture by Fernando Cruz Solis (1923–1991).

Photo © Lawrence Lew, O.P.; published with permission.

Monument of John of the Cross in a town square of Fontiveros where he was born.

Photo by Dahis 2010 / Wikimedia Commons

Valladolid in 1481, and around the same time in Salamanca.[11] Andrés Martín argues that the importance of this fact cannot be exaggerated for the unfolding of Spanish mysticism.[12] For Cisneros, it was a critical manner in which to promote reform through ensuring the availability of books to widen the mind and feed the soul. With this goal in mind, he promoted the importation of classic works of theology and spirituality, encouraging their translations from Latin and other European languages.

The proliferation of printing presses and of books coincides with the maturing of the Castilian language as a medium for quality literary works. The first grammar of the Castilian language had been published in 1492,[13] and increasingly writers had begun to seek to express themselves in the vernacular. In the sixteenth century, Spanish mystical writers intentionally began to write in Castilian in order to spread their invitation and teaching to a larger audience beyond the most educated class of persons. The poetry of John of the Cross fits in with the flowering of Castilian as a language of high literature. Teresa of Jesus wrote—both naturally and intentionally it seems—in the language and in the manner spoken "on the street" to attract and promote her teaching.

Translations of the classic works of Augustine, Jerome, John Climacus, Bernard of Clairvaux, Richard of St. Victor, and others appeared very early in the century. Recall that Teresa's "conversion" was prompted in part by reading Augustine's *Confessions*, only recently translated into Castilian (L 9.7).

The works of German-Flemish mysticism especially followed the arrival of Carlos V. And many of them were quickly translated

---

11. Ubarri, *Jan Van Ruusbroec*, 19.
12. Andrés Martín, *La teología española*, 1:251–52.
13. *Gramática de la lengua castellana* by Antonio Nebrija.

and published in Spain through the initiatives begun by Cardinal Cisneros.[14] These included works by saints Gertrude and Mechthild, Denis the Carthusian, and Ludolph of Saxony. Between 1530 and 1550, the works of the mystical writers Hendrik Herp, Henry Suso, John Tauler, John Ruysbroeck, and Meister Eckhart were made available.[15] Francisco de Osuna especially shows this influence, probably because of spending three years in Flanders.[16]

But external religious and spiritual influence did not come only from the Low Countries. The kingdom of Aragon had a longtime involvement in Italy, and the mendicant orders—especially again the Franciscans—had strong Italian roots and connections.[17] Works by Angela of Foligno, Clare of Assisi, Catherine of Siena, and other Italian spiritual writers were available in translation at the time. (Recall Teresa's devotion to St. Clare; L 33.13).

An aspect of this Italian influence, opposed by the Inquisition, were the works of the fiery apocalyptic Dominican preacher Girolamo Savonarola (d. 1498) who had been condemned for heresy. His works were nonetheless influential among Spanish Dominicans of the time, including Luis de Granada and probably at least Vicente Barrón, Teresa's early Dominican confessor. Although his works were circulating in translation, it is unlikely that Teresa herself read them; she most probably learned of him through her many Dominican contacts.[18] This apocalyptic spirit

---

14. On Flemish-Germanic influences, see Pacho, *Apogeo de la mística cristiana*, 140–85; and Ubarri, *Jan van Ruusbroec*, 67–86.

15. Andrés Martín, *Los recogidos*, 781.

16. Pacho, *Apogeo de la mística cristiana*, 152–53.

17. On Italian influences, see Pacho, *Apogeo de la mística cristiana*, 128–40.

18. Tomás Álvarez, "Santa Teresa y los movimientos espirituales de su tiempo," in *Estudios Teresianos I: Biografía e historia*, 405–46 (Burgos, Spain: Editorial Monte Carmelo, 1995), 413–15.

matched the sense of events converging by divine plan in a special way in Spain in the events that we have already mentioned: the union of the kingdoms of Spain under Ferdinand and Isabella and the subsequent unfolding of the Spanish empire in the sixteenth century; the conclusion of the centuries-long "crusade" to reclaim the whole of the Iberian Peninsula from the Muslims; the discovery of the Americas and the opening of the vast New World as ripe for evangelization; and the general and widespread sense and spirit of reform.[19]

The influence on Spanish mysticism of Jewish and Muslim sources, especially those available in Castilian, is possible but not clear. Certainly, the three religions had coexisted on the peninsula for centuries. Some parallels have been found in Christian, Jewish, and Muslim texts, though there is no proof that this is because of some direct influence. Still, there are scholars who argue for a significant Jewish influence,[20] and others for a Muslim influence,[21] though the preponderance of contemporary

---

19. Pérez, "Mística y realidad histórica en la Castilla del siglo XVI," in *Actas del Congreso Internaticional Sanjuanista*, ed. Teófanes Egido, 2:33–52 (Valladolid, Spain: Junta de Castilla y León. Consejería de Cultura y Turismo, 1993), 2:33–34.

20. See, for example, Catherine Swietlicki, *Spanish Christian Cabala: The Works of Luis de León, Santa Teresa de Jesús, and San Juan de la Cruz* (Columbia, Mo.: University of Missouri Press, 1986); and Michael McGaha, "Teresa of Ávila and the Question of Jewish Influence," in *Approaches to Teaching Teresa of Ávila and the Spanish Mystics*, ed. Alison Weber, 67–73, Approaches to Teaching World Literature series (New York.: Modern Language Association of America, 2009).

21. See, for example, William Childers, "Spanish Mysticism and the Islamic Tradition," in *Approaches to Teaching Teresa of Ávila and the Spanish Mystics*, ed. Alison Weber, 57–66, Approaches to Teaching World Literature series (New York.: Modern Language Association of America, 2009). For the opposing view, see, for example, Tapia, "El entorno morisco."

scholarship suggests that such claims have not been proven beyond establishing some of these parallels.[22]

Beyond translations of foreign books, there was a proliferation of ascetical and mystical publications in Castilian. E. Allison Peers recalls that in the nineteenth century, it had been suggested that close to 3,000 ascetical and mystical texts had been published in Spain during the sixteenth and seventeenth centuries. While that figure, he concludes, is exaggerated, they certainly number in the hundreds—many with multiple editions.[23] Melquíades Andrés Martín numbers the spiritual writers in Spain between 1470 and 1559 to be about seventy.[24] Perhaps even more amazing is his list of 1,200 spiritual books, listed in chronological order from 1485 through 1750—covering fifty pages—which he claims is still not exhaustive![25] His anthology of mystical writers of this period includes excerpts from 133 authors—which he claims does not exhaust the authors who could have been included.[26] There were many books about prayer and aids for meditating on biblical stories. But there was also a proliferation of texts to

---

22. Andrés Martín, *Historia de la mística*, 210–13. Elsewhere (*La teología española*, 405, 415–17), Andrés Martín argues that while Jewish influence might be possible, Muslim influence seems unlikely, despite some parallel use of images of ideas. Pacho, on the other hand, seems more open to the idea that some influence may have come from Jewish and Islamic sources available in Spanish at the time (Pacho, *Apogeo de la mística cristiana*, 127). See also Tyler, *Teresa of Avila*, 33n9.

23. E. Allison Peers, *The Mystics of Spain* (1951; repr., Maneola, NY: Dover, 2002), 15.

24. Melquíades Andrés Martín, "Pensamiento teológico y vivencia religiosa en la reforma española (1400–1600)," in *La Iglesia en la España de los siglos XV y XVI*, ed. José Luis González Novalín, part 2, 269–361, vol. 3 of *Historia de la Iglesia en España*, ed. Ricardo García-Villoslada (Madrid: Biblioteca de Autores Cristianos, 1980), 337.

25. Andrés Martín, *Historia de la mística*, 151–202.

26. Andrés Martín, *Los místicos*, xix.

promote the prayer of recollection and mystical prayer produced by authors from various religious orders.

Early in the century appeared important works in Castilian: *Carro de dos vidas* by García Gómez in 1500, *Ejercitatorio de la vida espiritual* by García de Cisneros (Benedictine abbot, cousin to the Franciscan Cardinal Cisneros) also in 1500, and *Teología mística* by Hugh of Balma in a Castilian translation titled *Sol de contemplativos* in 1514 that would have a major impact on the publications to follow.

The works of the Franciscans Francisco de Osuna (1497–1542), Bernardino de Laredo (1482–1540), and Bernabé de Palma (1482–1532) led the way in promoting in an explicit way the invitation to pursue quiet prayer and contemplation. Other Franciscan authors also contributed importantly to this body of literature, such as Antonio de Guevara (1480–1545), Alonso de Madrid (ca. 1480–1535), and Juan de los Angeles (1536–1609). Although more catechetical and ascetical, the works of John of Ávila, Doctor of the Church (1499–1569), played an important role in inviting ordinary Christians to enter into a life of deeper prayer. Among the Dominicans, the works of Luis de Granada (1504–1588), again more in the promotion of methods of meditation, stand out for their popularity and multiple editions. Alonso de Orozco (1500–1591), Pedro de Chaide (1539–1589), and Luis de León (1527–1591; the editor of the first published editions of St. Teresa's works) were Augustinian authors and promoters of deeper prayer. *The Spiritual Exercises* of Ignatius of Loyola (1491–1556), of course, is a classic from this same period—in structure, a book of meditation but no less an invitation to contemplative prayer. Among other Jesuits of the time stand out the works of Luis de Palma (1560–1641) and Pedro de Ribadeneyra (1529–1611). It is truly amazing to think that all of these spiritual writers—and many more—were contemporaries of the two greatest mystical writers of Spain's golden age, Teresa of Jesus (1515–1582) and John of the Cross (1542–1591).[27]

General Characteristics

While it can be traditional to organize the study of the history of Christian spirituality around major religious orders and their "schools" of spirituality, Andrés Martín suggests that the development of the key characteristics of the spirituality of sixteenth-century Spain is consistent across the religious orders. While recognizing distinct perspectives and emphases within different religious families, he sees more commonality than real differences in the characteristics outlined below. The principal distinction between writers of the period is whether their focus was basically at the earlier, more common phases of the spiritual journey (the "ascetical") or the more properly mystical.[28]

Andrés Martín very helpfully lists the general characteristics of the spirituality of this period in several of his works.[29] Some of these major elements are as follows:

---

27. In English, E. Allison Peers still provides one of the most thorough discussions of many of these writers in his two-volume work, cited above: *Studies of the Spanish Mystics*. See also Bernard McGinn, *Mysticism in the Golden Age of Spain (1500–1650)*, vol. 6, part 2 of *The Presence of God: A History of Western Christian Mysticism* (New York.: Herder and Herder, 2017). McGinn focuses most of his attention to the writings of Teresa, John, and Ignatius of Loyola. In Spanish, in addition to the works of Andrés Martín and Pacho, cited above, see Daniel de Pablo Maroto, *Espiritualidad Española del siglo XVI*, vols. 2 and 3 (Madrid: Editorial de Espiritualidad, 2014, 2015).

28. Andrés Martín, *Los místicos*, 5–6.

29. Andrés Martín, *Los recogidos*, 22–23; *La teología española*, 1:394–404. Citing the work of Andrés Martín, Peter Tyler offers a brief summary in English in *Return to the Mystical*, 109.

1. There was a general sense among these sixteenth-century Spanish writers of what we would today describe as *the universal call to holiness*, that is, the belief that all people (including the uneducated and women) should be invited to enter into deep and intimate prayer rather than seeing advanced prayer as a matter only for a spiritual elite of clergy and religious. Andrés Martín calls this the "democratizing" of serious prayer.[30] At the time, this was a controversial development since many thought that teaching deep prayer to those without a theological education could lead them to go astray (and to some degree, this seems to have been the case with misguided mystics of the time—at least for some groups of the so-called Alumbrados). This was certainly the opinion of the Inquisition and its supporters, as well as many of Teresa's opponents. Teresa herself, on the other hand, responds strongly to those who say that the nuns should be content with their Our Fathers and Hail Marys (W 21.2–5).

To some degree, this democratizing of spirituality became the foundation for the conflict between those with personal spiritual experience and others with academic learning. Osuna had taught that, despite the tension, the two perspectives could and should be held together for the benefit of both.[31] But as Andrés Martín notes, this was in practice difficult to do. The "learned" (*letrados* or *escolásticos*) emphasized the intellect, knowledge, learning, thought, and the "head." The so-called spirituals (*espirituales*, that is, those with personal spiritual experience), on the other hand, focused on the will, love, experience, desire/affect, and the

---

30. Andrés Martín, "Pensamiento teológico," 333.
31. Andrés Martín, 279–80.

"heart." Not long into the century, a serious antimystical spirit developed, often pitting especially (but not exclusively or always) Dominicans (the principal source of inquisitors) against reformed Franciscans.[32] Those drawn to the "new" spirituality accused the learned of promoting dry speculation, theology without life, and a restricted view of a God "contained" by dry doctrine. On the other hand, the learned warned of the danger of the uneducated drifting into heresy, and after the condemnation of the first Alumbrados in 1525, they had well-known examples to offer.[33] Central to the controversy was the issue of providing deep spiritual reading in the vernacular for the uneducated.[34] But this was not simply a matter of elite against elite. In fact, it appears that many ordinary people considered the promotion of mystical prayer to the "masses" to be a dangerous development—an idea promoted by the Inquisition but also a source of its support among common people.[35]

Teresa was caught up in this tension between "spirituals" and the "learned" and was confronted regularly by this antimystical movement. John of the Cross, of course, possessed both experience and learning, and so he would have felt the tension far less. In fact, many of the great mystical writers of the age, like John, were academically trained.[36] But Teresa, for her part, refused to choose between them. Recall

---

32. Andrés Martín, 280.

33. Pacho, *Apogeo de la mística cristiana*, 803–11.

34. Pacho, 789–96.

35. Pérez, "Mística y realidad," 47.

36. Andrés Martín ("Pensamiento teológico," 280) notes the examples of Osuna, Alonso de Madrid, John of Ávila, Luis de Granada, and Juan de los Angeles.

that she herself, even without academic training and yet with deep personal experience, always turned to "learned men." She was a friend of many of the most intellectual men of the time. And she recommended, as ideal, seeking out spiritual guides with both experience and learning (L 13.16–20). By doing so, she avoided what happened with the Alumbrados who came to make their own subjective experience of God the ultimate and only criteria by which to judge the faith and its practice. At the same time, Teresa took apparent delight in drawing *letrados* into deeper prayer—notably, the Dominicans García de Toledo (L 11.8; 20.21; 34.8) and Pedro Ibañez, who gave up his teaching and went to live in a reformed monastery in order to devote himself to prayer (L 38.13).

2. The writers of this period encouraged growth in a *methodical mental prayer*, that is, the spiritual discipline of a regular practice of active meditation, especially on the life of Christ. This meditation was conceived not primarily as an intellectual exercise in order to gain more knowledge but rather as a more affective effort, with God's help, to grow in more intimate personal knowledge of and relationship with Christ. The clearest example of this form of prayer is found in *The Spiritual Exercises* of Ignatius of Loyola,[37] though many books were published in this period as aids to growth in this kind of prayer. They would, for example, offer a paraphrase of a biblical story and then offer suggestions for specific points on which to ponder prayerfully. Often, these meditations were arranged very methodically with a plan for meditations on a specific progression of stories and mysteries of

---

37. Another notable example, though less well known today, is Alonso de Madrid's *Arte para server a Dios* (1521).

the faith spread over the weeks. Two significant periods of such meditation were normally recommended each day.

The introduction of this methodic meditation shows the likely influence of the so-called Devotio Moderna. It is probably the source of influence for the early manuals of this methodic meditation in Spain, including that of García de Cisneros.[38] This form of prayer began to be practiced regularly in reformed Benedictine and Franciscan houses in the middle of the fifteenth century. The first real manual published in Spain to teach the method more widely was the very influential *Exercitatorio de la vida espiritual* (The Practice of the Spiritual Life) by the Benedictine abbot García de Cisneros (cousin of the cardinal) in 1500—which Andrés Martín calls the "beginning" of the golden age of Spanish mysticism.[39] In the sixteenth century, this manual went through five Spanish editions, seven in Latin, two in Italian, and one in French.[40] This work may have influenced Ignatius of Loyola.[41] But perhaps the most popular manual of methodic prayer of the time was the *Libro de la oración y meditación* (Book of Prayer and Meditation) by the Dominican Luis de Granada. Both Cisneros and Granada recommend two daily periods of prayer, of about ninety minutes each, concentrating in the morning on meditation on the life of Christ and in the evening on critical self-knowledge (both on the great innate dignity of human nature as well as

---

38. McGinn, *Mysticism*, 6–8; Álvarez, "Santa Teresa y los movimientos espirituales," 407.

39. Andrés Martín, "Pensamiento teológico," 338.

40. Peers, *Mystics of Spain*, 16–17.

41. McGinn, *Mysticism*, 7.

its sinful state), on the reality of personal sin, and the making of good resolutions for change.[42]

John of the Cross (F 3.22) and Teresa presuppose the practice of such prayer. Recall that when Teresa teaches the types of prayer in second half of *The Way of Perfection*, she sees a normally necessary progression from vocal prayer into mental prayer, from active meditation into recollection, and from recollection into contemplation. But with many popular manuals already available, Teresa and John saw no need to say anything more about it at length. Such meditation was seen as the prelude to deeper and quieter prayer, that is, the prayer of recollection and then, God willing, into the gifted prayer of contemplation.

3. The invitation to seek "perfection" (human fulfillment through conformity to and union with God) was believed to initiate a *journey*—a path, an ascent, a way. While Spanish mystical writers, including Teresa and John, knew of and referred to the traditional manner of speaking of growth through the three ways (purgative, illuminative, and unitive), they often proposed a threefold movement through self-knowledge, meditation on the life and passion of Christ as well as more authentic imitation, and a deepening prayer through vocal prayer, meditation, recollection, and union with God.[43]

4. The spirituality of the period was notably *affective*, with a focus on spiritual desire and love for God. Manuals of prayer consistently urged their readers to meditate on the life and humanity of Christ and on his interpersonal interactions

---

42. Andrés Martín, "San Juan de la Cruz y los movimientos espirituales," 103.
43. Andrés Martín, *La teología española*, 2:132–33.

with Gospel characters and with the person in meditation. A special emphasis was given to prayerful and imaginative pondering on the passion. But "affect" in this context must be understood to mean both our ordinary experience of felt desire for God and a deeper consciousness of an existential sense of incompleteness and yearning for union with God.

5. The affective emphasis is related to a greater focus on the faculty or the power of the *human will*, which is the source of our ability and decision to *love*. We must strive to love, more than to understand God. Ultimately, it is love that will bring us to the deepest knowledge of God—not as an intellectual apprehension or grasping of God, and yet more profound and true.

6. Together with the general reform movements of the time, sixteenth-century spiritual writers encouraged reading and meditation on the *Bible*. In the first half of the century, there were a number of translations of the Bible into Castilian (though this was later halted by the Inquisition) as well as a plethora of books of meditation on scriptural stories that invited an affective response and a deepening relationship with the person of Christ. This development is related as well to the renewal of preaching.

7. The spirituality of this period was emphatically *Christocentric*, and Teresa of Jesus is a particularly good example of this. Recall that she even took to task those who said or implied that a person of deepening prayer would eventually arrive at a point that they could or should move beyond attention to the humanity of Christ (IC 6.7; L 22). This Christocentric focus, as we will see, distinguishes authentic developments in the period from heterodox deviations. Christ, in his humanity and in his divinity, must remain the focus, and

this coming together of divine and union in the incarnation was a particular focus of the age,[44] as we see in John of the Cross (C 5.3; 7.3; 23.1; 37.1–20).

8. The evolving spirituality of this period placed great emphasis on *interiority*—on self-knowledge, on interior prayer ("mental prayer"), and on finding God within. This contrasts with the medieval tendency, especially before the Devotio Moderna, to focus almost exclusively on the external—on ceremonies, rites, and vocal prayer. And so, we find the emphasis on God as dwelling within the inmost center of the soul in the works of Teresa of Jesus, especially in *The Interior Castle* but also in John of the Cross (F 1.9–13; 4.3; 2.8) as well as other mystical writers of the time.[45] This emphasis on the need to look inward toward the center finds its parallel in the emphasis of Flemish and German mystics on the "ground" (*grunt* or *grund*) of the soul. We must journey within to discover, encounter, and enter into union with this God, a journey that Teresa and others would insist includes both prayer and deepening self-knowledge (IC 1). Sometimes, with a different spatial image but with the same sense, authors spoke of the highest part of the soul rather than its center (recognizing that the soul, in fact, does not literally have "parts" or inner and outer).

9. But at the same time, contrary to one of the main errors of the heterodox Alumbrados (to be discussed in the next chapter), this focus on interiority did not negate the *importance to be given to the external*: to rites and ceremonies, sacraments and church authority, and external works and the

---

44. Andrés Martín, "Pensamiento teológico," 333.
45. Andrés Martín, *Los recogidos*, 14.

need to grow in virtue. In fact, writers of this period insisted on the need for what we would call asceticism—the graced work of overcoming vice, ordering our desires, and growing in virtue. Again, John and especially Teresa do not give a great deal of explicit attention to this aspect (at least as it is experienced by beginners in prayer), since they presumed that their readers would have been abundantly aware of other books to promote such practice.

10. Especially evident in the unfolding of the reformed religious orders, there was an accompanying focus on the *quiet and solitude* that deepening prayer and spiritual interiority normally requires. This coincided with the formation of houses of prayer and recollection and even, for periods of time, the embracing of an eremitical life by many in reformed orders.

11. With increasing interior quiet, the spiritual writers of this period emphasize the need for a deepening *detachment* (or as one might say today, "nonattachment") or "letting go" of everything that is less than God. This is the traditional "ascetical" preparation that must precede and accompany—and to some degree flow from—deepening prayer. This is especially evident in John of the Cross's rigorous teaching of *nada*, the ever-deepening letting go that is the path of the various nights described in *The Ascent of Mount Carmel* and *The Dark Night*. But this is the focus too of Teresa's insistence on the utter necessity of growing in the three necessary virtues of detachment, humility, and practical love of others (W 4.4).

12. Especially in the religious life, this emphasis on detachment is joined with the practice of penance as well as *simplicity and even austerity* in dress, buildings, and general manner of

living. This is clear in Teresa's early desire to found all of the monasteries of the reform in complete poverty.

13. But again contrary to the Alumbrados, this interiority and focus on solitude and silence did not in any way negate *the need for external works of love*. Again, Teresa is very clear about the need for "Martha and Mary to work together." The two are sisters, symbolizing the fact that the so-called active and contemplative lives must not be opposed or either of them left behind (IC 7.4.4; L 17.4; SS 7.3; ST 59.5; W 31.5). In fact, for Teresa, the intimate and essential relationship of prayer and external works of love becomes most apparent in the most interior dwelling places where the person united with God is affirmed in the need to be united in action with the divine love for others (IC 7.4.4).

14. As we mentioned above, the deepening union with God, though ultimately only by divine gift, brings a *profound knowledge of God*. But this is not an intellectual knowledge that can be expressed in doctrines and concepts, or even adequately in images. Rather, this is a loving knowledge, a "grasping" of God by love. John of the Cross speaks of mystical knowledge as a general, obscure, loving knowledge of God (A 2.24.4). It is general in that it does not involve concepts that could be adequately explained; it is obscure in that God remains hidden to the normal intellect, to our normal way of knowing through the senses; and it is a knowledge that is the fruit of love—of that love that is poured into our hearts by God and is God in the divine inflow of contemplation.

The characteristics just described are the context that formed the spirituality of Teresa of Jesus and John of the Cross, and we see it mirrored in their writings. The opposition that they—especially Teresa—experienced must also be understood in the context of the opposition experienced by proponents of the spirituality laid out above more generally.

Promotion of the "Prayer of Recollection"

In the context of these general antecedents of the spirituality of Teresa of Jesus and John of the Cross, we can now look more closely at their more immediate formation in the movement promoting the "prayer of recollection."[46] It is not separate from the characteristics that we described of the new direction of Spanish spirituality in the sixteenth century but really the principal manifestation or focus of it. Its promoters encouraged people of prayer to enter into quiet, into a deeper reflection on themselves as they are—that is, as graced and sinful, as blessed and as in constant need of the God's mercy and aid—and into an interior journey to enter into union with the God who dwells in the inmost center of every human person.

Teresa describes the prayer of recollection, as the word in English and in Spanish (*recogimiento*) suggests, as a drawing in, a regathering, or a re-collecting of the faculties or powers and, with them, the senses (W 28–29). It is a drawing together of our attention, our focus, our consciousness so we can enter into quiet, attentive prayer. She speaks of both "active" recollection (that is, this gathering in of our focus through own efforts) and of "passive" (infused or gifted) recollection, which is God's work in drawing in our attention (W 29). The latter is the first

---

46. McGinn offers a very good overview of the movement, focusing especially on a few major figures and their principal works (*Mysticism*, 24–45).

introduction of true contemplative prayer, though the passage from our own work of recollection to the priority of divine action can be very subtle.

While Teresa doesn't really provide a "method" for active recollection in any comprehensive way, she does provide some hints (W 26).[47] The active recollection of which she speaks has parallels in contemporary practices which seek to bring the praying person into an attentive quiet through the disciplined use of a prayer word or phrase, as well as in the "Jesus prayer" of Eastern Christianity and the "method" proposed by *The Cloud of Unknowing*.

But Teresa didn't originate the idea or the vocabulary for the prayer of recollection. She inherited it—or perhaps we can say she was immersed in it through her reading and in her conversations with some of her spiritual advisors. It is precisely the introduction that the reading of Osuna and Laredo provided for the early stages in her deeper spiritual journey.

The movement promoting the prayer of recollection began around 1470–1480 in the reformed houses of Franciscans. It became common across the reformed religious communities of the century. As the friars sought a deeper prayer, moving beyond the practice of active meditation, they began to invite laypeople to join them in this graced pursuit. This was a particularly staggering development considering the long history of elitism concerning the invitation to contemplation. Teachers of this form of prayer encouraged at least two lengthy periods of quiet prayer. We may recall Teresa's rather funny description of how she would force herself with

---

[47]. See the brief but helpful explanation of Teresa's "method" of active recollection in the ICS pamphlet *The Prayer of Recollection* (Washington, D.C.: ICS Publications, 2012).

a very determined determination to sit quietly through these lengthy prayer periods (L 8.7).

The earliest published works beginning to unfold the prayer of recollection include *Un brevísimo atajo* ("shortcut") in 1513, *Sol de contemplativos* also in 1513, *Caballería cristiana* in 1515, *Spill de la vida religiosa* also in 1515, and *Arte para servir a Dios* in 1521. But its three principal early expositors were Francisco de Osuna (*Third Spiritual Alphabet* in 1527),[48] Bernabé de Palma (*Via spiritus* in 1532–1534),[49] and Bernardino de Laredo (*Subida del Monte Sión* in 1529).[50] Certainly, it is Osuna's *Third Spiritual Alphabet* that is the key foundational work of the movement.[51] And in it, he offers a list of authors whom he considers historical exponents of the same type of prayer being promoted as recollection: Gregory Nazianzen, Pseudo-Dionysius ("San Dionisio"), Augustine, Gregory the Great, Bernard of Clairvaux, Hugh and Richard of St. Victor, Bonaventure, and others.[52]

Proponents of the prayer of recollection generally gave little attention to the ascetical preparation that, to some degree,

---

48. For information on Osuna and an overview of his *Third Spiritual Alphabet*, see especially, McGinn, *Mysticism*, 34–45. See also Peers, *Studies of the Spanish Mystics*, 1:77–131. In Spanish, see especially, Pacho, *Apogeo de la mística cristiana*, 408–85; Andrés Martín, *Los recogidos*, 107–67; and Andrés Martín, *La teología española*, 2:205–14.

49. On Bernabé de Palma, see Pacho, *Apogeo de la mística cristiana*, 556–96.

50. On Laredo, see McGinn, *Mysticism*, 27–33; and Peers, *Studies of the Spanish Mystics*, 2:39–76. In Spanish, see especially, Pacho, *Apogeo de la mística cristiana*, 485–556.

51. We recall though that Teresa reports it was Laredo's *Subida* that gave her the key vocabulary to understand her deepening spiritual experience in prayer (L 23.12).

52. Andrés Martín, *Los recogidos*, 778.

preceded but also accompanied growth in prayer. But as mentioned in the general characteristics above, they presupposed such work on the part of the person of prayer. Still, this appears to be a foundation of some of the aberrations of the Alumbrados. Recollection was being promoted as an art and as an *atajo* (a shortcut) to arrive at the deepest prayer and at "perfection," which is union with God.[53] And in fact, it was being proposed as a practice (more than as a specific method) by which a person of prayer could prepare the way to receive true contemplation from God. But some came erroneously to understand "shortcut" to mean they could practice the prayer of recollection and attain contemplation without the ascetical work of overcoming personal sin and growing in virtue, without the pursuit of critical self-knowledge, and without the aid of the sacramental life of the church. But this was not the intention of the principal promoters of the movement, nor would it have been characteristic or typical of the orthodox spirituality of the day, as we mentioned above.

From the literature on recollection emerged a number of images and analogies that would be taken up and used with the distinctive genius of Teresa of Jesus and John of the Cross: the soul as the silkworm (*gusano de seda*), as a glass window (*vidriera*), or as a garden (*huerto*); the need to travel in darkness, in nakedness of spirit, with the quieting of the intellect;

---

53. Both "*arte*" and "*atajo*" appear in the title of the work of an anonymous Franciscan published in 1513 (in the Spanish of the time): *Hun brevissimo atajo e arte de amor a Dios: con otra arte de contemplar e algunas reglas breves para ordenar la piensa en el amor de Dios* (my rough translation: A Very Brief Shortcut and the Art of Loving God: With Another Art of Contemplation and Some Brief Rules for Ordering the Mind in the Love of God). See Hamilton, *Heresy and Mysticism*, 14.

the use of water images and the idea of irrigating a garden to describe prayer; and deepening union in terms of betrothal and marriage.[54]

Teresa's Reading

We know very little of what John of the Cross read.[55] He quotes other authors very rarely. On the other hand, we know that he had a good education, and we can presume that he read many of the works mentioned above, both classic and contemporary texts. It is virtually unimaginable that he had not read the major works promoting the prayer of recollection. Teresa of Jesus, on the other hand, is more explicit about many of the books that she read and that therefore formed her thinking and shaped her experience. We know that she was an avid reader from her childhood, and again, we can presume that she read many of the same works—at least those written or translated into Spanish. She would have also absorbed a great deal from her many conversations with the educated men of her time as well as from preaching. She was certainly the beneficiary of the flurry of publication in the area of spirituality that had begun only shortly before her birth.[56] A review of what we know of her reading can help us better understand the influence on her of the tradition that she inherited and to which she and John of the Cross belonged.

---

54. Andrés Martín, *Los recogidos*, 56.

55. Probably the best source for information about St. Teresa's reading is provided by Daniel de Pablo Maroto, *Lecturas y maestros de Santa Teresa* (Madrid: Editorial de Espiritualidad, 2009).

56. Pérez, *Teresa de Ávila*, 191–210.

Knowledge of Biblical Stories

St. Teresa knew quite a bit about the Bible for a person of her time. In her works, she cites a total of twenty-three books of the Old Testament and eighteen of the New—many such citations from Genesis, Exodus, the Song of Songs, and the Gospels. And yet, it is quite possible that she did not own and perhaps had not even read the Bible directly at all.

Relatively few people in sixteenth-century Spain would have had access to the Bible, even the literate (already a minority in the population) and even nuns and priests. Translations of the Bible began to appear in the early part of the century, but the Inquisition put a stop to this because of fears of the encroachment of Reformation thinking. People could, however, pick up a great deal about the Bible and biblical narratives from reading popular lives of Christ or other books of meditation and devotion. Many of these offered summaries and even paraphrases of biblical stories, along with commentary and points for meditation. They could also pick up a lot from liturgical preaching over the cycles of the liturgical year.

Though it is quite possible that Teresa of Jesus never read the Bible directly, it seems certain that one of her principal sources for biblical stories was the *Vita Christi* by Ludolph the Carthusian.[57] A fourteenth-century work, it was one of the most popular and influential works of the late Middle Ages. It was published in Castilian in four volumes in 1502 and 1503.

---

57. Cistercian Publications has recently published the first volume of a four-volume translation of the work into English: *Life of Christ*, part 1, vol. 1, chaps. 1–40, trans. Milton T. Walsh (Athens, Ohio: Cistercian Publication/Liturgical Press, 2018). For a study of the document, see Mary Immaculate Bodenstedt, "The 'Vita Christi' of Ludolphus the Carthusian" (PhD diss., Catholic University of America Press, 1944).

It offers summaries of the Gospels, together with teachings of the Fathers and of medieval theologians concerning the texts of the life of Christ. It offers an invitation to the four steps of *lectio divina* (*lectio, meditatio, oratio, contemplatio*) taught by the twelfth-century Carthusian Guigo II. Teresa mentions the *Vita Christi* explicitly in the *Life* (L 38.9) and makes it the first recommendation for the nuns' reading in *The Constitutions* (Con 8). We know that Teresa was especially fond of three particular episodes in the life of Christ—the conversion of Mary Magdalene, the story of Martha and Mary, and the Samaritan woman at the well. The *Vita Christi* offers these three stories and their commentaries in three consecutive chapters. It also offers a lengthy commentary on the Our Father.

In addition to the Rule and Constitutions, Teresa most probably read or heard read at the Incarnation the *Institution of the First Monks*, which purported itself to be a document of the fifth century recounting the early history of the Carmelites. In fact, it was a fourteenth-century document translated into Castilian in the fifteenth century. It contained a collection of myths about the origins of the Carmelites. But even if much of its historical accuracy is doubtful, it would have conveyed to Teresa fundamental values of the order, such as its contemplative roots and values and its Marian piety.

Popular and Classic Religious Texts

Teresa had a great devotion to a number of saints, and we know that she read collections of the lives of saints called *Flos Santorum* (the title not of an individual work but of a type of work). Beyond just strict narratives of the saints' lives, such works also contained a wide range of biblical, catechetical, and doctrinal information. We don't know which particular of these works

Teresa may have read.[58] In addition to what she may have heard in preaching on the lives of saints on liturgical feasts, much of her later knowledge of stories of the saints probably came from this source. Such reading would have been a natural move from the stories of knightly chivalry (*libros de caballeria*) that she secretly read as a girl to the heroic lives of saints.

We know that Teresa had a special devotion to St. Augustine, and she probably had her first real contact with him while a young boarder with the Augustinian nuns at Santa María de Gracia in Ávila (L 9.7). She tells us further that her mature "conversion" was prompted in part by reading the *Confessions*, probably in a translation published only a few years earlier in 1554. In addition to this, she cites other works by Augustine or that were thought at the time to be his.

Teresa tells us that it was her reading of the letters of St. Jerome that helped her decide to enter the monastery (L 3.7). She also says that she read the moral reflections on Job (*Moralia in Job*) of Gregory the Great during her long recovery from the botched "cures" of the healer of Becedas (L 5.8). In fact, the Monastery of the Incarnation preserves a 1527 edition of the book with handwritten margin notes that have traditionally been believed to be those of Teresa herself. Although there are few other explicit references to the works of Gregory the Great in her writing, Daniel Maroto argues that his influence is nonetheless evident.[59]

---

58. Very popular in sixteenth-century Spain was the work of Dominican Pedro de la Vega: *Flos sanctorum: La vida de nuestro Señor Jesu Christo y de su santísima Madre y de los otros santos según la orden de sus fiestas*. It is divided into two parts. Part 1 includes commentaries on the liturgical seasons and major feasts as well as the life of Christ. Part 2 is a compendium of the lives of the saints as they appear in the annual liturgical calendar. See Pérez, *Teresa de Ávila*, 201.

59. Maroto, *Lecturas y maestros de Santa Teresa*, 106.

Above we noted the *Vita Christi* by Ludolph of Saxony as a probable source of much of Teresa's biblical knowledge, but it also probably served as a primer in basic doctrine and theology, particularly in a Christology grounded in patristic and medieval texts. And through it, she would have come into contact with such authors as Bernard of Clairvaux, Anselm of Canterbury, Bonaventure, and others commenting on Christological and theological topics.

In *The Constitutions* (Con 8), Teresa recommends several books or authors that we can therefore assume she had read: *The Imitation of Christ* by St. Thomas à Kempis (under the title *Contemptus mundi*) and works by the Dominican Luis de Granada (most likely including his popular *Book of Prayer and Meditation* published in 1554 with a new "corrected" edition in 1574 after the book had been placed on the Index of 1559—more because of the perceived danger of teaching deep prayer to the uneducated than for any doctrinal issues).[60]

Mystical Texts

Maroto organizes a major part of his study of the influences on and reading of Teresa of Jesus around the religious communities of her various advisors and confessors. Among the most influential were certainly Franciscans. We know that, in addition to recommending his works, Peter of Alcántara played an important early role in Teresa's mature spiritual development. Key to embracing fully the prayer of recollection, to deepening her prayer and giving her terms and concepts to understand and explain her experience, were Francisco de Osuna's *Third*

---

60. See *The Collected Works of St. Teresa of Ávila*, trans. Kieran Kavanaugh and Otilio Rodriguez (Washington, D.C.: ICS Publications, 1985), 3:495–96n7.

Spiritual Alphabet (L 4.7; probably the only of his many works that she read) and Bernardino de Laredo's *Ascent of Mount Sion* (L 23.11; also 12.6 and 17.5). There is no direct evidence that she read the works of Bernabé de Palma, but Maroto believes there are resonances of his work in her writing.[61] We have seen that these Franciscan works introduced Teresa especially to the Pseudo-Dionysian tradition and more specifically to the prayer of recollection.

We have noted Teresa's recommendation of the works of the great Dominican Luis de Granada. Though she does not recommend any other Dominican works, we know she was friends with and advised by as many as thirty-three Dominicans, many of them well-known theologians of their time. We can assume that, through them, she absorbed a great deal of what they were reading and teaching. Among them were her probable first Dominican confessor, Vicente Barrón; Domingo Báñez, who was one of her most constant guides and a defender at key moments (before the city council of Ávila on the foundation of St. Joseph's, before the Inquisition concerning the *Life*, and during her beatification process); Pedro Ibáñez; and García de Toledo.

The *Life* makes evident the important role played by a large number of Jesuits in Teresa's life, including many theologians. She was originally drawn to them because the Jesuits were a reformed order that had clearly embraced the current mystical trends, if not exactly the prayer of recollection as taught by the Franciscans. In general, they were both learned and experienced. In them Teresa found a number of key counselors. It seems likely that, through these Jesuit spiritual guides, Teresa was introduced

---

61. Maroto, *Lecturas y maestros de Santa Teresa*, 205–11.

to and perhaps even guided in the *Spiritual Exercises* of Ignatius of Loyola.[62]

Conclusion

To see the life and work of Teresa of Jesus and John of the Cross in the context of the spiritual movements of their time does not in any way detract from their distinctive genius. It is rather to acknowledge their humanity. They themselves were formed in movements and trends beyond themselves. Knowing this more ample background, for example, we can better understand what Teresa faced as a woman of the deepest experience confronted by people who sincerely doubted the truth—but, even more, the appropriateness of promoting such experience through her writing and teaching. We understand better what she means when she speaks of recollection, and we can appreciate more richly the importance of her earlier reading of Osuna and Laredo.

Teresa and John form the apex of the mysticism of sixteenth-century Spain described in the pages above. They were the high point, but they stood on the shoulders of those who went before. In a period of great change and even controversy, they maintained a balance and an equilibrium that allowed them to draw the best from what went before them, without falling into the errors that others embraced. It is to the main group of errant followers of the prayer of recollection that we now turn—the so-called Alumbrados (enlightened ones).

---

62. Maroto, 227.

SELECT BIBLIOGRAPHY

English

Hamilton, Alistair. *Heresy and Mysticism in Sixteenth-Century Spain: The Alumbrados*. Cambridge, UK: James Clarke and Co., 1992.

Kavanaugh, Kieran. "Spanish Sixteenth Century: Carmel and Surrounding Movements." In *Christian Spirituality*, 69–92. Vol. 3 of *High Middle Ages and Reformation*, edited by Louis Dupré and Don E. Saliers with John Meyendorff. Vol. 18 of *World Spirituality: An Encyclopedic History of the Religious Quest*. New York: Crossroad, 1991.

McGinn, Bernard. *Mysticism in the Golden Age of Spain (1500–1650)*. Vol. 6, part 2 of *The Presence of God: A History of Western Christian Mysticism*. New York, N.Y.: Herder and Herder, 2017.

Peers, E. Allison. *The Mystics of Spain*. 1951. Reprint, Maneola, N.Y.: Dover, 2002.

———. *Studies of the Spanish Mystics*. 2 vols. London: Sheldon Press, 1927, 1930.

Tyler, Peter. *The Return to the Mystical: Ludwig Wittgenstein, Teresa of Ávila, and the Christian Mystical Tradition*. New York: Continuum, 2011.

Spanish

Álvarez, Tomás. "Santa Teresa y los movimientos espirituales de su tiempo." In *Estudios Teresianos I: Biografía e historia*, 405–46. Burgos, Spain: Editorial Monte Carmelo, 1995.

Andrés Martín, Melquíades. *Historia de la mística de la Edad de Oro en España y América*. Madrid: Biblioteca de Autores Cristianos, 1994.

———. *La teología española en el siglo XVI*. 2 vols. Madrid: Biblioteca de Autores Cristianos, 1976–1977.

———. *Los místicos de la Edad de Oro en España y América: Antología*. Madrid: Biblioteca de Autores Cristianos, 1996.

———. *Los recogidos: Nueva visión de la mística española (1500–1700)*. Madrid: Fundación Universitaria Española, 1975.

———. "Pensamiento teológico y vivencia religiosa en la reforma española (1400–1600)." In *La Iglesia en la España de los siglos XV y XVI*, edited by José Luis González Novalín, part 2, 269–361. Vol. 3 of *Historia de la Iglesia en España*, edited by Ricardo García-Villoslada. Madrid: Biblioteca de Autores Cristianos, 1980.

———. "San Juan de la Cruz y los movimientos espirituales de su tiempo." In *Aspectos históricos de San Juan de la Cruz*, edited by Teófanes Egido, 99–115. Ávila, Spain: Institución Gran Duque de Alba de la Disputación Provincial de Ávila, 1990.

Balbino, Marcos. "Literatura religiosa en el siglo de oro español." In *La Iglesia en la España de los siglos XV y XVI*, edited by José Luis González Novalín, part 2, 443–552. Vol. 3 of *Historia de la Iglesia en España*, edited by Ricardo García-Villoslada. Madrid, Spain: Biblioteca de Autores Cristianos, 1980.

Maroto, Daniel de Pablo. *El Reinado de Felipe II*. Vol. 3 of *Espiritualidad Española del siglo XVI*. Madrid: Editorial de Espiritualidad, 2015.

———. *Época del emperador Carlos V (1519–1558)*. Vol. 2 of *Espiritualidad Española del siglo XVI*. Madrid: Editorial de Espiritualidad, 2014.

———. *Lecturas y maestros de Santa Teresa*. Madrid: Editorial de Espiritualidad, 2009.

Pacho, Eulogio. *Apogeo de la mística cristiana: Historia de la espiritualidad clásica española 1450–1650*. Burgos, Spain: Editorial Monte Carmelo, 2008.

Chapter 8

Alumbrados

In the previous chapter, we looked at the spirituality of recollection that so influenced the spirituality of Teresa of Jesus and John of the Cross. But now we must attend to a misshapen branch from the same tree. The so-called Alumbrados ("enlightened ones") or *dejados* ("abandoned ones," that is, completely abandoned to God) often shared many fundamental beliefs and perspectives with orthodox mystical teachers like Francisco de Osuna, Teresa, and John, but in various ways, they went astray, passing outside of orthodox Christian belief. As such, they became a particular focus of attention and investigation for the Inquisition.

Of particular relevance to the life of Teresa of Jesus, it is important to note that many of the central figures of the various groups of Alumbrados were conversos, women, and people who claimed extraordinary mystical experiences. Teresa was, of course, all three and thus even more likely to come under the gaze of the Inquisition and others who were suspicious of mystical teaching in general and of women who claimed mystical experience in particular. A number of widely known women from among the Alumbrados were processed and condemned by the Inquisition, and there were several very well-known misguided and even intentionally fraudulent women who claimed extraordinary experiences. This was true both of professed religious and of a group of women known as *beatas* (about which we will say more below). Successive decrees condemning the purported beliefs of the Alumbrados and public preaching against their errors does seem to have produced a popular reaction against them.[1]

Some understanding of the Alumbrados is important for a better appreciation of Teresa and John's mystical teaching, because they were often implicitly trying to distinguish themselves from their misguided brothers and sisters. It is likely that their insistence in their writings that they willingly submitted their writing to the teaching of the church is both utterly sincere and, at the same time, a pointed defense against claims of heterodox belief or practice. Furthermore, by highlighting how the Alumbrados went astray, we can attain a better understanding of what John and Teresa are—and aren't—saying. And by looking at how Christian mysticism can go astray, we can gain an even greater appreciation of the true and subtle genius of John and Teresa's mystical doctrine and theology.

An Umbrella Term

To speak of Alumbradism is not really to address a single, cohesive movement. It was never really a unified movement or system

---

1. Alvaro Huerga, *Temas y Personajes*, vol. 5 of *Historia de los alumbrados (1570–1630)* (Madrid: Fundación universitaria española, 1994), 45. The bibliography at the end of the chapter identifies several important studies of the Alumbrados. Certainly, the most thorough is Huerga's massive five-volume study. But even after four volumes, Huerga concludes that trying to define the Alumbrados is a very difficult and risky thing ("*cosa harto difícil y arriesgada*"; *Temas y Personajes*, 9). For a brief introduction in English, see McGinn, *Mysticism*, 45–50.

of belief or practice. In fact, the very term *alumbrado* is not what individual groups would have called themselves; rather, this came to be the pejorative term (that is, "those so-called enlightened ones") used by the Inquisition and others to describe them.[2] In the end, the term draws together several groups in sixteenth- and early seventeenth-century Spain that shared some central beliefs but could also be widely divergent in others. Its adherents left few writings of their own, and what we know of their beliefs comes down to us mostly from the edicts published against them by the Inquisition.[3]

After the 1520s, the inquisitors were looking for false mystics, Protestants, and to some degree Erasmists; but they could not always distinguish well among them. It seems clear that the inquisitors sometimes mistakenly attributed Protestant thought to the accused Alumbrados—beliefs they may or may not have held. In fact, the roots of the two were very different.[4] Even what might have looked like similar beliefs would have been grounded and understood in a different way by each. It also seems likely that the inquisitors did not always attend to the nuances of the actual beliefs held by the accused, basing the condemnations on what had been previously identified by the Inquisition as Alumbrado belief. Still, with all of that having been said, contemporary scholars believe we can arrive at a basic understanding of their belief and practice.

---

2. Hamilton, *Heresy and Mysticism*, 28.

3. Huerga includes in part 3 of the final volume of his extensive study, in Spanish, the principal extant decrees against and letters concerning the Alumbrados (*Temas y Personajes*, 391–441).

4. Huerga, 13.

Shared Roots

In general, the Alumbrados emerged in sixteenth-century Spain as part of the general movement of reform in Spain and across Europe, seeking to move beyond purely external manifestations of religion to a more personal experience of God.[5] And the Alumbrados would take both parts to their extreme—rejecting the need or even desirability for any external manifestation in sacrament or even works of charity while embracing a purely personal and subjective experience of God as utterly central to their religious life.

More particularly, the Alumbrados emerged from circles of Franciscan friars who were encouraging and teaching the prayer of recollection to other clergy, *beatas*, and laypeople.[6] Despite the fear of others that teaching such things to the "unlearned" was dangerous, these Franciscans downplayed such fears.[7] As we have seen, this was characteristic of this recollection movement: the belief in the universal call to deep prayer and thus a kind of "democratization" of spirituality. From our perspective

---

5. Melquíades Andrés Martín reviews the many shared beliefs of the Alumbrados and the general movement of recollection, as we saw in the previous chapter. Andrés Martín, *Los recogidos*, 360–61.

6. Huerga (*Temas y Personajes*, 48) views this connection as "indisputable." See also Antonio Márquez, *Los alumbrados: Orígenes y filosofía, 1525–1559* (Madrid: Taurus, 1972), 119–20.

7. As the divergence of the Alumbrado beliefs became clearer—and more widely known as a concern to the Inquisition—the Franciscans in Spain, in provincial chapters in 1524 (shortly before the condemnation of the first of group of Alumbrados in 1525) and again in 1528 condemned Alumbradism and sought to withdraw their friars from any involvement with the group. See Andrés Martín, *Los recogidos*, 360–66. Francisco de Osuna, whose writings seem to have been a special inspiration for these early Alumbrados—as they had been for St. Teresa— also condemned them, most clearly in his *Fourth Spiritual Alphabet*. See Maroto, *Teresa en oración*, 117.

today, this would be a very good development indeed. But many of these sincere persons did not have a basic theological or even catechetical formation, nor did they have sympathetic educated persons whom they could consult. It would be easy enough for them to go astray, trusting increasingly in their own personal, subjective experience without the "check" of biblical teaching or sound doctrine. Ultimately, they could weave their own doctrines without reference to more tried and true foundations.

This reality contrasts with what we know of John of the Cross who was firmly grounded in a sound theological formation and with Teresa of Jesus who read widely and consulted educated people with almost an obsession about her own experience and her understanding of it. It also makes clear why Teresa and John were so insistent that they would gladly submit their writings to the church's teaching and repudiate anything that was in conflict with it.

A critical point for us is that Alumbrados and orthodox mystics took divergent paths based on the same foundation in the Franciscan-inspired recollection movement. They shared much of the same vocabulary. The interviews of accused Alumbrados as well as extant records of some of their personal libraries reveal that many of them were reading the very same source materials as Teresa of Jesus and others: Francisco de Osuna, Alonso de Madrid, and others that we reviewed in the previous chapter.[8] In fact, the works of Teresa and John were found among later Alumbrados. All of this makes clear why the Inquisition sometimes found it difficult to distinguish the two branches from the same tree—and sometimes to distinguish authentic mystics like Teresa of Jesus from the misguided and fraudulent.

---

8. Huerga, *Temas y Personajes*, 75; Márquez, *Los alumbrados*, 122, 127–35.

Beyond the general connection with the Franciscan recollection movement and with the literature common to that movement, scholars have tried to discover some connection with particular heretical groups or movements outside of Spain. In short, were the Alumbrados simply a Spanish version of a heretical movement that had appeared in other parts of Europe? But it appears that the Alumbrados were, in fact, a distinctively Spanish phenomena, growing out of the particular context that we are investigating in the current work.[9] Certainly, we see in the Alumbrados what we also see in other Christian mystical movements that have gone astray: outside the checks and limits set by the Bible and some form of sure teaching, it is far too easy for intensely personal spiritual experience to lead even sincere people into developing highly subjective interpretations of that experience, of what constitutes an authentic relationship with God, and even who God is.

General Beliefs

As we have mentioned, several distinct groups of so-called Alumbrados emerged throughout the sixteenth century and early seventeenth century. They were not some kind of unified movement that simply "erupted" in different places and times.[10] In fact, there seems to be little or no direct relationship between or among them. Each of the first few, as we will see, had its own impact on the lives of Teresa of Jesus and John of the Cross. But despite the differences among these groups, scholars have identified some common elements to their apparent beliefs.[11]

---

9. Márquez, *Los alumbrados*, 98–99.

10. Hamilton, *Heresy and Mysticism*, 2–4.

11. Acknowledging the multivolume work of Huerga, Andrés Martín identifies fourteen beliefs held or at least alleged to the Alumbrados. See Andrés Martín, "San Juan de la Cruz y los movimientos espirituales," 107.

The Alumbrados came to believe that their deep personal encounter and union with God erased the distinction between Creator and creature. It created a union without distinction.[12] Because of this complete identification with God in union, the person who reached that level was no longer capable of sin. In fact, such people no longer possessed a will that could sin, mortally or even venially.[13] Implicitly, this was a denial of the retention of human liberty after the attainment of union.[14]

There is what may seem like a subtle but utterly critical difference between this Alumbrado belief and the teaching of John of the Cross and Teresa of Jesus. These orthodox mystical teachers, like those before and after them in the long tradition of the church, certainly promote a path that leads to union with God—a deep union in which the person enters into the divine life itself and "becomes" God by participation (but not by nature!). This is the meaning of "deification" or "divinization" in Christian mystical thought. It is a true union but with a continuing distinction between God and the person, between Creator and creature. There is not a complete identification with God in the sense of a loss of individual existence or in the resulting sense of a loss of human liberty. The person in this life—even in transforming union and even with the human will united with the divine will—remains at least theoretically capable of sin.

The Alumbrados believed that deep personal encounter and union with God made all external practices or devotions unnecessary—not sacraments or other rites or ceremonies,

---

12. This was especially and most explicitly true of the beliefs of the first group of Alumbrados condemned in 1525. Huerga, *Temas y Personajes*, 53.

13. Andrés Martín, *Los recogidos*, 361.

14. Román de la Inmaculada, "El fenómeno de los alumbrados y su interpretación," *Ephemerides Carmeliticae* 10 (1958): 61.

not priests or church hierarchy, not vocal or common liturgical prayer, and not even good works and growth in virtue.[15] In fact, such externals were not only unnecessary but even obstacles (*ataduras*) that held them back.[16] All that the Christian had to do was abandon self to God (*dejamiento*) in the deepening prayer of recollection—no need for asceticism, growth in virtue, or even works of charity. They might attend Mass to avoid the consequences of open rejection of the sacraments, but once present, many of them would simply not otherwise participate.[17]

Melquíades Andrés Martín draws some of the contrasts between the Alumbrados and their more orthodox counterparts in this way: The Alumbrados thought that vocal prayer was useless and even harmful; the others believed that vocal prayer is good, meditation on the life and passion of Christ is better, and the prayer of recollection is best. The Alumbrados believed that the "perfect" were free of every law; the others believed that the more prefect the Christian, the better the practice of the law of God and the church. The Alumbrados believed that the action of God in the person in divine union eliminated human freedom; the others believed that the action of God in the person ever more deeply illuminates and moves the person.[18]

The Alumbrados often shared a desire to engage the Bible, in keeping with the general spirit of reform of the age, but the key for them was that the Bible was not above their own experience of

---

15. In this denial of the need for such externals, the Alumbrados bore some resemblance to Reformation and Erasmian thought, but not for exactly the same reason or to the same extent. But it was enough for the Inquisition to lump them together.

16. Márquez, *Los alumbrados*, 190.

17. Márquez, 148.

18. Andrés Martín, *Los recogidos*, 360–61.

union.[19] They needed no further intermediary between God and themselves. In the end, in stark contrast to Reformation and Erasmian thought, the Alumbrados were not particularly Christocentric. In fact, ultimately, it appears that in their thought Christ really didn't have a very significant place at all. What was important was not faith in Christ; what was central was their personal experience of union.[20]

Individual Groups

Scholars have differed slightly on the exact grouping and dating of the various Alumbrado outbreaks, but we can take as reliable the five-part division of Alvaro Huerga in his massive five-volume study to the Alumbrados.[21] Only the first three are of interest to our study.

1. Toledo (1510–1530)
2. Extremadura (1570–1580)
3. Upper Andalusia (1570–1590)
4. New World (1570–1605)
5. Seville (1605–1630)

The Alumbrados of Extremadura and of Upper Andalusia bear the closest resemblance to one another. Otherwise, the differences between them can be significant, though all were lumped together by the Inquisition.[22]

---

19. Márquez, *Los alumbrados*, 125–26.
20. Márquez, 191.
21. Huerga, *Temas y Personajes*, 39–40. This is slightly different from his five-part division in an earlier work: *Predicadores, alumbrados e inquisición en el siglo XVI* (Madrid: Fundación Universitaria Española, 1973), 64–93.
22. Huerga, *Temas y Personajes*, 42.

The Alumbrados of Toledo and the Edict of 1525

The first group of what came to be known as Alumbrados emerged around 1512 in the area of Guadalajara, northeast of modern Madrid. They came to the attention of the Inquisition in 1519. This particular group has come to be known as the Alumbrados of 1525 (from the date of their condemnation) or the Alumbrados of Toledo, 1510–1530, (from the particular tribunal of the Inquisition that investigated and condemned them). The central figure was the Franciscan tertiary (in modern terms, a secular or third-order member) Isabel de la Cruz, together with her principal collaborator, the layman Pedro Ruiz de Alcaraz. Both were of humble origins. Isabel de la Cruz was a seamstress for local noble families; Alcaraz was an accountant to one of those families. As such, despite their modest backgrounds, they had access to prominent families. They, like many of those later associated with Alumbradism, were conversos, though it is not entirely clear why this coincidence exists.[23]

---

23. Márquez, *Los alumbrados*, 86–94. Some have argued that conversos were more likely to be drawn to Alumbradism because of some retained Jewish religious sensibilities that made Alumbradism seem to be a more natural form of Christian belief. Perhaps a more frequent suggestion is that, viewed suspiciously by Old Christians, conversos felt themselves to be marginalized in the church and thus more likely to embrace a more marginalized Christianity in which they could find full acceptance and take leadership. Angela Selke has argued, somewhat controversially, that the conversos were drawn to reform movements and reformed orders (for example, Franciscans and Jesuits) in general and to Alumbradism in particular to work out their active resentment against "Old Christians" and "their" externalized religion. Angela Selke, "El iluminismo de los conversos y la Inquisición. Cristianismo interior de los alumbrados: Resentimiento y sublimación," in *La Inquisición española: Nueva visión, nuevos horizontes*, ed. Joaquín Pérez Villanueva, 617–36 (Madrid: Siglo veintiuno, 1980), 618–19.

Consistent with what we mentioned above about the general beliefs of the Alumbrados, Isabel de la Cruz and her closest partners were accused of teaching a kind of quietism, that is, a belief that all that mattered was a complete abandonment (*dejamiento*) to God in prayer. Such *dejados* (abandoned ones), after surrendering to God's love, no longer needed sacraments or the externals of the faith. The union brought about by their surrender made it possible to desist from all external religious activity. It appears that the inquisitors may have confused this latter belief as the equivalent of what they believed to be the "faith alone" doctrine of Lutheran belief.[24]

The Edict of 1525 against the errors of these Alumbrados contains forty-eight false propositions the Inquisition believed it had identified—including explicit repudiation of the value of external devotions and ceremonies, the sacrament of confession, the value of vocal prayer, and the need for any form of church hierarchy.[25] Some of the propositions seem to indicate how the inquisitors lumped together Alumbrado thought with what they identified as Protestant and errant Erasmist thought.[26] No Inquisition record of the process against Isabel de la Cruz is extant, but an extant statement of Alcaraz's beliefs suggests he would not have seen himself accurately reflected in all forty-eight propositions.[27] In the end, despite the possible inaccuracies

---

24. Hamilton, *Heresy and Mysticism*, 1–4.
25. Huerga, *Temas y Personajes*, 46–57; Márquez, *Los alumbrados*, 273–83. Andrés Martín (*Los recogidos*, 363–67), in a chart covering four pages, draws the comparison/contrast between the Alumbrados as depicted by the forty-eight propositions against them in the Edict of 1525 and "orthodox" proponents of the prayer of recollection.
26. Márquez, *Los alumbrados*, 67–69.
27. Inmaculada, "El fenómeno de los alumbrados," 62.

or failure to catch important nuances of belief, Huerga concludes that, at the heart of its beliefs, the Alumbrados were profoundly heretical.[28]

Huerga argues that the key doctrine of these Alumbrados is identified by the edict's proposition nine, which condemns the belief that the love of God in the person is, in fact, God. Someone who abandons self (*se dejasen*) to this love of God enters into union with God—as a complete identity—and is therefore no longer capable of sin, neither mortal nor venial. Having arrived at this state, there is nothing more to do or be done. For Huerga, this is the quintessence or core of pure Alumbradism.[29] In this, Huerga distinguishes himself from the conclusion of Andrés Martín who views the Alumbrado idea of abandonment (*dejamiento*)—a kind of quietism that sees the necessity only of such surrender without further work or action on the person's part—as central.[30] In either case, the result is the lack of necessity for traditional externals of faith. In fact (according to condemned proposition twenty), as we have seen, such externals and vocal prayer were seen as an obstacle to true abandonment.[31]

Among the group investigated by the Inquisition were a number of Franciscan friars and members of prominent families in the area. But even with the involvement of friars and nobility, it was reported in the investigation of Alcaraz that a majority of those involved were uneducated (*personas idiotas y sin letras*)[32]—in terms that made evident the prejudice against

---

28. Huerga, *Temas y Personajes*, 53.
29. Huerga, 48–50.
30. Huerga, 54.
31. Huerga, 61.
32. Inmaculada, "El fenómeno de los alumbrados," 59–60.

the idea of encouraging deep prayer among "the masses" of uneducated Christians.

It was in response to these Alumbrados and the suspicions that followed—and in response to the threat of the infiltration of Protestant thought[33]—that the grand inquisitor published the Index of Forbidden Books of 1559, which dismayed Teresa of Jesus (and which we will address in the next chapter). Further, the investigation and condemnation of the Alumbrados of Toledo created—or significantly heightened—suspicions about all forms of mystical teaching. Coming from the same foundation and using similar resources and vocabulary, writers and teachers of prayer like John of the Cross and Teresa of Ávila thereafter had to be careful about the terms that they used in their writings (avoiding, for example, the word *dejamiento* [abandonment]), attentive to avoid even the appearance of the heresies of the Alumbrados, and ready to live under the cloud of suspicion and even opposition to writing about and encouraging mystical prayer, especially for laypeople—and, even more, women.

Alumbrados of Extremadura (1570-1580)

The Alumbrados of the region of Extremadura along Spain's modern border with Portugal (sometimes called the Alumbrados of Llerena for a city in that region) were not really related to the earlier Alumbrados of Toledo.[34] As we have said, they were not direct inheritors or disciples of the Alumbrados of Toledo. At heart, they do share many of the basic beliefs outlined above, but the first group of Alumbrados were more doctrinally focused, centered in their distinctive understanding

---

33. Inmaculada, 62.
34. Huerga, *Temas y Personajes*, 57–67.

of the nature of their union of identity with God and its consequences. They were not focused on extraordinary phenomena; there were no prominent reports of visions or ecstasies among them; and there was no implication of sexual excess. These later Alumbrados of Extremadura, on the other hand, were more focused on mystical experience itself, that is, the felt experience of approaching and attaining union with God. The Extremadura Alumbrados were much more focused on extraordinary experience—on visions, raptures, and ecstasies. And some of them passed from a kind of erotic spirituality (in itself not foreign to mystical writings that look to the biblical Song of Songs) into sexual behaviors that were seen as not contrary to their authentic experience of God but rather contributing to it.

These Alumbrados in Extremadura were rooted in the disciples of John of Ávila, the teacher of prayer and promoter of catechesis and evangelization. Some of them also seem to have been influenced by their encounter with Jesuits and with the *Spiritual Exercises* of Ignatius of Loyola. Works by John of Ávila and the Dominican Luis de Granada as well as the *Spiritual Exercises* featured prominently in the libraries of some of these Alumbrados.[35] Again, women featured also prominently in this group.[36]

The Alumbrados of Extremadura were condemned and their errors denounced in the Edict of 1574. An *auto de fe* (a public ceremony for their condemnation) in Llerena in 1579 was a fatal blow to the group.[37] Huerga judges that, in this case, the key proposition of the edict that defines the heart of this heretical movement is the tenth, which condemns the idea that certain

---

35. Huerga, 77–78.
36. Huerga, 59.
37. Huerga, *Predicadores*, 68–69.

feelings of spiritual ardor, trembling, and ecstasies are an indication of the presence of the love of God and through it individuals can know that they possess the Holy Spirit and are in grace.[38] Huerga describes this form of Alumbradism as "sensual pseudomysticism" and notes that, for some of its members, it devolved into a sexual licentiousness in which sexual ecstasy was seen as an aid to spiritual ecstasy and union.[39]

Though on slightly different grounds, these Alumbrados too concluded that they needed no intermediaries for their direct, unmediated encounter with God—not the sacraments, not the church, and not works of virtue. Their personal experience of personal ardor and their felt mystical experience gave them the assurance of attaining union with God without such helps—or really, for them, not helps but obstacles.[40]

The investigation and condemnation of these Alumbrados in the 1570s took place in the decade in which Teresa was present several times in southern Spain to found new monasteries of the reform. As a woman with widely known claims of extraordinary experience, it would have been difficult in that context for Teresa to avoid the attention and the suspicion of the Inquisition and of those opposed to mystical teaching. And it was in this setting, as we will see in our discussion of the Inquisition in the next chapter, that Teresa was falsely accused to the Inquisition. These accusations also included false reports of sexual impropriety in her monasteries—precisely in the time that the sensual mysticism of the Extremadura Alumbrados led some to sexual acting out.

---

38. Huerga, *Temas y Personajes*, 64.
39. Huerga, 65–66.
40. Huerga, 64.

As we know, Teresa of Jesus famously described many of her mystical experiences, which included ecstasies, raptures, and visions. (We might think in particular of Gian Lorenzo Bernini's famous statue in Rome of St. Teresa in ecstasy.) Characteristic in many ways of sixteenth-century Spanish spirituality in general and its mysticism in particular, hers was an affective, love-centered mysticism. This is also evident in poetry of John of the Cross. At the same time, John was insistent and consistent in urging his readers not to pay attention to feelings at any stage of prayer, not desiring extraordinary experiences, and not lingering on any particular experience, no matter how sublime. While Teresa is more descriptive and autobiographical, it must be noted that she did not believe that extraordinary experiences were necessary, nor that they were a clear indication of a greater holiness. Again, by seeing how the Alumbrados went astray and their mysticism became misguided, we see more clearly the orthodox and authentic path of Teresa and John.

The Extremadura Alumbrados would be relevant to the later history of St. Teresa in another way, because the Dominican friar, Alonso de la Fuente, who was the longtime, principal, and dogged investigator of those Alumbrados, became an equally insistent opponent of the posthumous publication of her works. After so many years of searching out and processing Alumbrados, he was certain that the works of St. Teresa were rampant with heresy. Ultimately, he failed to prevent their further publication—but not for lack of trying.[41]

---

41. Huerga (*Predicadores*, 39–63) offers a study of Alonso de la Fuente's activities as a prosecutor of the Extremadura Alumbrados and of his later challenge of Teresa's published works.

Alumbrados of Upper Andalusia (1570–1590)

These Alumbrados in southern Spain were more closely related to the Alumbrados in neighboring Extremadura. Like them, they placed a great value on felt experience in general and on extraordinary mystical phenomena. Their spirituality too could drift into sexual behaviors. Women featured prominently in the group. They were dealt their most serious blow in an *auto da fe* in 1590 in Córdoba.

Again both Teresa and John were in Andalusia during the 1570s and 1580s. They interacted with a number of people being investigated and later condemned by the Inquisition. John offered some spiritual advice to *beatas* in the area—who, as a group, were a particular object of Inquisition interest. Many *beatas* were condemned by the Inquisition for Alumbrado beliefs. The general atmosphere in Andalusia—heightened by the Inquisition processes in neighboring Extremadura—provided the more immediate context for the accusations made against Teresa herself and her communities. The Inquisition would be likely to take seriously accusations of misguided mystics among nuns and of sexual improprieties (accusations we will examine in the next chapter). Although John rejects Alumbrado beliefs in his writings (e.g., A 3.35–45 and F 3.43), without mentioning them by name, his works were denounced for Alumbradism after his death, thus delaying their wider publication. In fact, it seems evident that many Alumbrados in Andalusia read John's works, though interpreted according to their own understanding.[42]

---

42. Eulogio Pacho, "Alumbrados y Juan de la Cruz," in *Diccionario de San Juan de la Cruz*, ed. Eulogio Pacho, 56–59 (Burgos, Spain: Editorial Monte Carmelo, 2009).

Beatas and Alumbradism

Alvaro Huerga in particular focuses on the relationship of *beatas* and Alumbradism, that is, of the tendency of many of these women to embrace Alumbradism.[43] *Beatas* were lay women, single or widowed, who lived a type of devout religious life but without religious vows. We cannot know exactly how many *beatas* there were in Spain at the time because they were not organized and regulated, but there were certainly many of them especially in Extremadura and Andalusia. (One author estimated that as many as one to two thousand *beatas* may have been living in the environs of the Andalusian city of Baeza alone.)[44]

Such women might live together in a loosely organized community (*beaterios*). Others might live as individuals but sponsored by or directed by established religious orders. A third possibility is that they could live alone, without attachment to any order or other *beatas*. It is this last group that was most susceptible to going astray, since they lacked the opportunity for proper guidance and counsel.[45] Often, the *beatas* were illiterate—as we have seen was especially typical for women of the time—which meant their spiritual formation came orally from those who taught, guided, and confessed them. This could be especially problematic if those guiding them were themselves not well educated and formed, or were misguided or unscrupulous.

Some *beatas* might have pursued formal religious life but lacked the dowries required by some communities. Some chose the life because marriage did not seem to be a reasonable

---

43. Huerga (*Temas y Personajes*, 191–220) devotes an entire chapter to this connection.

44. Inmaculada, "El fenómeno de los alumbrados," 70.

45. Huerga, *Temas y Personajes*, 194, 220.

possibility with so many men off to fight wars or to seek fame and fortune in the New World or in other conflicts being waged by Spain throughout Europe. Some were very holy women; others were charlatans. Either could be given to a special fascination with extraordinary mystical experience. Especially in the later manifestations of Alumbradism, the experiences reported (and even sought) by many of these women were decidedly sensual—Huerga says "erotic."[46] He believes this is grounded in a sort of uncritical sexual drive in the absence of marriageable men that also made many of these *beatas* (especially those who might have chosen marriage if this had been possible) susceptible to unscrupulous confessors who took advantage of them.

Conclusion

Clearly among the Alumbrados could be found charlatans and the emotionally unstable. Some were probably deeply committed heretics, in the sense of consciously abandoning central, even creedal, beliefs of the Christian faith and of the Catholic tradition. But surely many were misguided. In an age of poor catechesis and widespread illiteracy and thus often with a lack of knowledge of sound, basic doctrine, it would be easy enough for sincere people to view their own deeply felt experience as the foundation of a misguided view of God and of the path to divine union. Unlike Teresa of Jesus who herself lacked formal theological training but who insistently turned to "learned men" to guide and even assess her ideas, surely many accused Alumbrados had neither the opportunity nor even the prudent idea that they could or should do so. In this, we must recall that Teresa

---

46. Huerga, 13–15.

was distinctively intelligent, an avid reader, and of a social class that would make "learned men" more willing to engage her at a serious spiritual level despite the misogyny of the era. How true would that have been for an illiterate *beata* of a lower social class?

In this light, perhaps the concerns of the Inquisition and its supporters—and those who were at least suspicious of teaching mystical doctrine to everyone and anyone—have some merit (without, of course, condoning its methods or its complete rejection of the very idea). We recall that both John of the Cross and Teresa of Jesus were insistent on the need for sound spiritual guidance, preferably by others who were both "learned" and "experienced" in the more advanced unfolding of the spiritual path. Without such guidance, they insisted, one could all too easily go astray—as they witnessed in the religious culture around them. In the next chapter, we will look more specifically at the Inquisition, especially in the ways it would have impacted the life and teaching of John and Teresa. But beyond that consideration, the sad experience of the Alumbrados and the prudent wisdom of Teresa and John can serve as a caution to us today to hold together our own deeply personal experience of God with a solid understanding of our faith concerning God, our relationship with the divine, and the authentic paths that lead us to union. Clearly, this is both the example and the insistent teaching of Teresa of Jesus and John of the Cross.

SELECT BIBLIOGRAPHY

English

Hamilton, Alistair. *Heresy and Mysticism in Sixteenth-Century Spain: The Alumbrados*. Cambridge: James Clarke and Co., 1992.

Kavanaugh, Kieran. "Spanish Sixteenth Century: Carmel and Surrounding Movements." In *Christian Spirituality*, 69–92, esp. 72–74. Vol. 3 of *High Middle Ages and Reformation*, edited by Louis Dupré and Don E. Saliers with John Meyendorff. Vol. 18 of *World Spirituality: An Encyclopedic History of the Religious Quest*. New York.: Crossroad, 1991.

Ruiz Salvador, Federico, ed. *God Speaks in the Night: The Life, Times, and Teaching of St. John of the Cross*. Translated by Kieran Kavanaugh. Washington, D.C.: ICS Publications, 1991, 2000. Pages 219–20.

Tyler, Peter. *Teresa of Avila: Doctor of the Soul*. New York.: Continuum, 2014. Pages 42–48.

Spanish

Andrés Martín, Melquíades. *Los recogidos: Nueva visión de la mística española (1500–1700)*. Madrid: Fundación Universitaria Española, 1975.

Huerga, Alvaro. *Temas y Personajes*. Vol. 5 of *Historia de los alumbrados (1570–1630)*. Madrid: Fundación universitaria española, 1994.

———. *Predicadores, alumbrados e inquisición en el siglo XVI*. Madrid: Fundación Universitaria Española, 1973.

Inmaculada, Román de la. "El fenómeno de los alumbrados y su interpretación." *Ephemerides Carmeliticae* 10 (1958): 49–80.

Márquez, Antonio. *Los alumbrados: Orígenes y filosofía, 1525–1559*. Madrid: Taurus, 1972.

Pacho, Eulogio. "Alumbrados y Juan de la Cruz." In *Diccionario de San Juan de la Cruz*, edited by Eulogio Pacho, 56–59. Burgos, Spain: Editorial Monte Carmelo, 2009.

Selke, Angela. "El iluminismo de los conversos y la Inquisición. Cristianismo interior de los alumbrados: Resentimiento y sublimación." In *La Inquisición española: Nueva visión. nuevos horizontes*, edited by Joaquín Pérez Villanueva, 617–36. Madrid: Siglo veintiuno, 1980.

Chapter 9

Jews, Conversos, and the Spanish Inquisition

Looking simply at what Teresa of Jesus says explicitly about the Inquisition in her writings might seem to suggest that it had little to no impact on her life, activity, and writing. But this would be inaccurate. The presence of the Inquisition loomed large in sixteenth-century Spain, and some of its principal concerns were conversos, mystics, and teachers of prayer. Teresa of Jesus was all three—and a woman besides, in an age that was especially prone to suspect the religious experience of women and certainly any teaching they might dare to offer to men, especially "learned" men. Further, she was surely aware of her own converso background, though it is not clear how widely it was known by others. In any case, she had many associations with prominent conversos. And as we shall see, conversos were a particular focus of attention for the inquisitors. In light of such factors, it would have been far more surprising if Teresa had not become a person of interest for the Inquisition or if she herself had paid it no mind. In fact, Teresa's brushes and encounters with the Inquisition were more significant than might be immediately apparent from her writings. The same can be said for its impact on her manner of writing.

Below in part 2 of this chapter, we will look more closely at these particular encounters, as well as offer a few words about John of the Cross and the Inquisition (though there is much, much less to say). But again it is the context of the history, purpose, and procedures of the Inquisition that will help us to fully understand why these encounters took place, their significance, and their possible impact on Teresa's attitudes and manner of activity. And so, the present chapter proceeds in two main parts: part 1 on the Spanish Inquisition in general and part 2 on Teresa of Jesus and the Inquisition.

Part 1: The Spanish Inquisition

The Spanish Inquisition was authorized by Pope Sixtus IV in 1478, and it continued in existence until its final abolishment in 1834 for a total of 356 years of operation.[1] Over the centuries since its beginnings, there have been many interpretations of its purposes and procedures.[2] Certainly, at least in the English-speaking world, the very word "Inquisition" is synonymous with cruelty and injustice—perceived as a kind of secret

---

1. This chapter's bibliography indicates the many principal works I have used to prepare this section on the history of the Spanish Inquisition. Of special note is the massive, three-volume, multiauthor work that discusses in detail (in Spanish) the history of interpretation, the origins and history, administration, procedures, finances, and virtually every other topic conceivable in relation to the Spanish Inquisition: Joaquín Pérez Villanueva and Bartolomé Escandell Bonet, eds., *Historia de la Inquisición en España y América*, 3 vols. (Madrid: Biblioteca de Autores Cristianos and Centro de Estudios Inquisitoriales, 1984, 1993, 2000).

2. For a view of the history of interpretation of the Spanish Inquisition, see Helen Rawlings, *The Spanish Inquisition* (Malden, Mass.: Blackwell, 2006), 2–20; and Henry Kamen, *The Spanish Inquisition: A Historical Revision*, 4th ed. (New Haven, Conn.: Yale University Press, 2014), 374–93.

police for whom torture and burning at the stake were the favored and predominant means of proceeding. Many of the published histories of this institution have continued this perception. Without suggesting that the Inquisition was, in fact, a model of justice and equanimity, more modern studies (notably the work of Henry Kamen)[3] have moderated the vehemence of this negative view. It is important to separate the facts from what became known as the "Black Legend" about Spanish cruelties in general and the savagery of its Inquisition in particular—a legend that grew up largely as a result of the propaganda of Reformation-day English, Dutch, and Spanish Protestants living in exile. Without attempting to justify religious intolerance and inhumane practices, we must understand the Inquisition in its context—a world in which many of its ideals and practices were common all over Europe. Otherwise we would misinterpret Teresa's encounters with it and her attitude toward it.

The Origins of the Spanish Inquisition

Spain was by no means the first or the only country to establish an inquisition. Nor were its practices particularly cruel, relative to the practices in both civil and ecclesiastical societies in Europe at the time. It was, however, unique in the extent of its intended outreach, its centralized authority, the elaborate nature of its structures and administration, the length of its existence, and the extent of its encouragement of denunciations.[4]

---

3. Kamen's book, cited above, was first published in 1965 and is currently in its fourth edition.

4. Joseph Pérez, *The Spanish Inquisition: A History*, trans. Janet Lloyd (New Haven, Conn.: Yale University Press, 2005), 174.

In the Middle Ages, accusations of heresy or heterodox practices were traditionally investigated and addressed in diocesan courts under the direction of a local bishop, with larger concerns about the spread of heretical thought addressed in local synods of bishops. But in the twelfth and early thirteenth century, popes began to appoint individuals with authority to investigate and punish heretics. This was largely a reaction to a failure or inability on the part of individual bishops to address especially the Albigensian heresy in southern France (and extending into the Spanish kingdom of Aragon, adjacent to France). Dominicans quickly became especially associated with this task—as they would with the Inquisition in Spain.[5] An inquisition was established in Rome itself around 1232.[6]

The Inquisition in Spain (that is, in particular, the kingdom of Castile and later Aragon) was especially, as we shall see, a response to concern about converted Jews (conversos) who, it was believed, were only feigning the appearance of Christian faith. Some have argued that beneath this presenting reason was a deeper anti-Semitism in society that simply extended to those with a Jewish heritage.[7] In any case, because the origins of the Spanish Inquisition are so closely associated with concern about conversos—and because Teresa of Jesus (and perhaps John of the Cross) belonged to this group—it is important to unfold this development more closely.

---

5. Stephen Haliczer, *Inquisition and Society in the Kingdom of Valencia, 1478–1834* (Berkeley: University of California Press, 1990), 9–10.

6. Kamen, *Spanish Inquisition*, 2.

7. Benzion Netanyahu argues strongly and in great detail that the origins of the Spanish Inquisition are found precisely in prevailing anti-Jewish sentiment and that conversos were persecuted principally for nothing other than sharing the Jewish race, even though many were sincerely Christian. See Benzion Netanyahu, *The Origins of the Inquisition in Fifteenth Century Spain* (New York: Random House, 1995).

Jews and Conversos

There is a modern perception that the three great religions of Christianity, Judaism, and Islam lived in harmony and mutual toleration—the so-called *Convivencia*, or "coexistence"—on the Iberian Peninsula until the advent of the Spanish Inquisition and the expulsion of the Jews. This view is not entirely accurate. While it is true that Jews and Christians generally lived in relative peace in the Muslim kingdoms of southern Spain and that Muslims lived in relative peace in Christian areas as the reconquest of the peninsula progressed over the centuries, this does not exactly equate to toleration and harmony as we would understand it today. Persecutions did break out from time to time, depending on the rulers at any particular time; the nondominant religionists were not entirely free to proselytize and practice their religion in public without restriction; and the minority religionists could be taxed more heavily and suffer other forms of discrimination in possibilities of advancement, possible occupations, and places to live. Still, this might be called relative toleration in light of the times and the culture.[8]

Jews had lived on the Iberian Peninsula certainly since at least Roman times. In general, they were tolerated and in some periods and times could thrive as individuals and as a community. But there was an undercurrent of anti-Jewish sentiment that erupted from time to time in violent local persecutions of Jewish populations. This was true in the mid- and late fourteenth century in Spain. These persecutions coincided especially with periods of particular economic hardship when resentment over the perception of Jewish affluence and ascendance in Spanish society made them easy scapegoats who could be blamed for the hard times.

---

8. Pérez, *Spanish Inquisition*, 1–4.

We must recall again the hardships and economic distress caused by the Black Death in the middle of the fourteenth century. Typically, the upper classes almost always fare better in the face of plague and economic hardship, and so it is not unlikely that more prosperous Jews did fare better than many of their Christian neighbors. In the summer of 1391, serious anti-Jewish riots and attacks against local Jewish communities broke out across Spain. Many Jews were forced to convert or converted out of fear of further reprisals (perhaps as many as half of the 200,000 Jews estimated to have lived in the kingdoms of Castile and Aragon). We have here, then, the beginning of the group of people called "*conversos*" (converted ones)—as distinguished from "Old Christians" (those whose families had been Christian for as long as could be remembered). Here too we have the roots of concerns for "purity of blood" (*pureza de sangre*, that is, "purity" from the "taint" of Jewish or Moorish blood) so detested by Teresa of Jesus. Such persecutions continued to arise from time to time, and economic distress in 1447–1449 and again in 1465–1473 brought similar riots and attacks on conversos who were suspected of being Christian only in name and perceived to have advanced at the expense of "Old Christians."

Many (perhaps most) conversos had, of course, become sincere, believing, and practicing Christians—as Catholic as any of their neighbors. But suspicions continued, generations after the conversion of the Jews, that in reality many of these conversos were "judaizing," that is, secretly continuing in Jewish belief and practice. There is no way to know, of course, how common this might have been. Surely, there were many conversos who were Christian only in name. There were others who lived a sort of in-between existence, trying to believe and practice both faiths.

But there seems to have been many conversos, later processed by the Inquisition, who continued Jewish dietary and other practices simply as a kind of cultural inheritance from their parents without any sense of practicing the Jewish religion in any way—though for the Inquisition, such practices (like reading and speaking Hebrew, not eating pork, eating unleavened bread, or maintaining certain family Sabbath customs) were sure proof of judaizing.

Conversos could also find themselves unable to defend themselves effectively because they could not give proof of their knowledge of basic doctrines of the Christian faith. But this may have been not for actual lack of Christian belief but rather because of poor catechesis. Mass forced baptisms without catechetical follow-up would not serve as a good basis for establishing knowledge of basic doctrines for the first generation or their descendants. Add to this the reality of the sad state of religious catechesis across Spain at the time. It seems evident that the vast majority of Christians were in fact poorly or little catechized. One of the tests introduced by the Inquisition to give evidence of the presence of true Christian faith in those brought before its tribunal was to test the accused in the most basic of Christian prayers and beliefs. Inquisition records show that initial results were dismal (though more concentrated efforts to improve catechesis throughout the sixteenth century, especially in line with the concerns of the Council of Trent, resulted in growing evidence of improvement).[9] Accused conversos, therefore, could be seriously disadvantaged, sharing in the general ignorance of doctrine of the wider population while bearing the prior suspicion of judaizing simply because they belonged to families that had been Jewish in someone's memory.

---

9. Kamen, *Spanish Inquisition*, 48, 77; Payne, *Spanish Catholicism*, 44–45.

Despite some interpretations to the contrary, there is no reason to believe that the establishment of the Spanish Inquisition was the result of anti-Semitism on the part of King Ferdinand and Queen Isabella. Spanish monarchs had traditionally been protectors of Jewish communities in the face of the kinds of persecutions mentioned above. Jews and later especially conversos could and did advance in royal, civil, and ecclesiastical administration. But the monarchs were not immune to the suspicions of many of their subjects in regard to the conversos. Both of them, deeply committed to the Catholic faith and seeking unity at every level in their recently united kingdoms of Castile, Aragon, and later Granada, were apparently convinced that supposed judaizing by large numbers of conversos represented a threat to that unity. And so, they petitioned the pope for the authority to establish the Inquisition in Spain under their immediate authority. This was granted in 1478, though the first inquisitors were not appointed for a couple of years. In fact, some prominent churchmen were counseling restraint, arguing that what was needed was better catechesis, not an inquisition. And as a result, this period saw the publication of a number of new catechisms, manuals on prayer, commentaries on the Gospels, and even Gospels in simplified language in the vernacular,[10] though some of these later came under the scrutiny of the Inquisition. Paradoxically, it appears that the establishment of the Spanish Inquisition was actively supported by a number of prominent conversos who apparently hoped it would root out true judaizers and free conversos like themselves of the perception of being anything less than sincere and committed Christians.

---

10. Hamilton, *Heresy and Mysticism*, 9–10.

All of this becomes part of the context to understand the royal decision to expel the Jews in 1492. While the expulsion of the Jews does not bear directly on the life of Teresa of Jesus, it does further broaden our sense of the converso "issue" because, again, fear of judaizing by conversos was one of the principal reasons for the expulsion. A brief discussion of that decision will explain why.

The Expulsion or Forced Baptism of the Jews

Over the centuries of interpretation, the royal decision to expel the Jews from Spain (or compel their baptism) has been interpreted in varying degrees as anti-Semitism, as the desire to seize Jewish assets for financial gain for the crown, or as a purely political scheme to bring a multilevel unity to the kingdom.[11] But these interpretations do not adequately weigh the lack of previous evidence of anti-Semitism on the part of Ferdinand and Isabella, the fact that they did not gain financially from the expulsion (in fact, the opposite is the case for the crown itself), and their deeply held religious convictions.

We have already glimpsed the presence of anti-Semitism in Spanish society. Neither this reality nor the tendency to scapegoat the Jews was in any way exclusive to Spain in that period. But there is no sign that Ferdinand and Isabella shared in this prejudice. Like previous Spanish monarchs, they had begun their reign as protectors of Jewish communities from violence and persecution. They personally had Jewish physicians and financial advisors.[12]

---

11. A summary of these various interpretations is provided by Pérez, *Spanish Inquisition*, 21–25; and Antonio Domínguez Ortiz, "Las presuntas 'razones' de la Inquisición," in Pérez Villanueva and Bonet, *Historia de la Inquisición* (2000), 3:58–82.

12. Kamen, *Spanish Inquisition*, 21–22.

The fact is that the decision to expel the Jews caused financial harm rather than benefit to the crown. The sad reality is that the expelled Jews were not permitted to maintain ownership of property if they chose to leave rather than be baptized, nor were they allowed to take large sums of money out of the country with them. But such property and money did not simply become forfeit to the crown. Part of the human tragedy is that as the deadline for leaving was looming, Jews most often had to sell their property at ridiculously low prices to their Christian neighbors. (Financially, such so-called Christians did in fact benefit from the expulsion.) As for the crown, the Jews had traditionally provided proportionately more tax revenue than their numbers might warrant. It is estimated that in 1480, a third of the royal tax income in the kingdom of Castile came from Jewish sources, even though their total population in the kingdom was probably only about 80,000—greatly reduced after the persecutions in the late fourteenth and earlier in the fifteenth century.[13] And Jewish lenders had been critical to providing the substantial resources necessary to conquer the remaining Muslim kingdoms. The expulsion was, financially, a hardship to the royal government.

It is true that expulsion of the Jews served in part the goal of a religious unity to match and bolster a relatively new and even hard-won political unity. But this must not be understood in a purely secular political manner. We must recall that the Reconquista (reconquest) that was finally accomplished with the fall of Granada after seven hundred years of Muslim rule in large swaths of the peninsula was viewed as a kind of Christian crusade. Obviously, political fame and riches could be amassed by the victorious, but more deeply, while other Europeans had turned their

---

13. Kamen, 17–20.

eyes to "liberating" the Holy Land in the Crusades, the Spanish had pursued their own crusade on their own territory. And Ferdinand and Isabella seemed to have embraced very intensely the title the "Catholic kings" (*los reyes Católicos*), which the popes had proclaimed them to be upon the conquest of Granada. As we have seen, they had a sense of divine mission about reforming the church and its religious orders within Spain and defending the Catholic faith. And in that age, the modern separation between political and religious realms and aims was not so clearly demarcated as it is today.[14] Yes, the expulsion of the Jews was part of the goal of attaining a firmer political unity—but based on a foundational sense of the sacral nature of the royal mission.

In the end, the principal reason for the expulsion—as stated in the royal decree that mandated it[15]—was the perceived need to separate converted Jews from their still-Jewish counterparts. It was reasoned by those who influenced the monarchs—an idea supported by the Inquisition[16]—that the presence of Jewish communities and the continued interaction of conversos with still-Jewish relatives, friends, and associates merely provided an attraction to the conversos to secretly leave the Christian faith or fail to embrace it wholeheartedly and completely. Henry Kamen concludes unequivocally that the decision to expel the Jews was exclusively religious.[17]

It may be that Ferdinand and Isabella had expected more Jews to accept baptism. Perhaps as many as half did so. Others went into exile, only to move from tragedy to tragedy. Many who fled to northern Africa were enslaved upon arrival. In other European countries, they were taken advantage of and faced further

---

14. Domínguez Ortiz, "Las presuntas," 58–69.
15. Kamen, *Spanish Inquisition*, 24.
16. Kamen, 25.
17. Kamen, 24.

discrimination. Those who fled to Portugal were expelled from that country only a few years later. In the end, it is estimated that well over half of the Jews expelled from Spain ended up returning and accepting baptism (and were able to reclaim at least some of their property)—only further exacerbating the converso "problem." No matter the reason for the expulsion or the circumstances of the historical context, the human toll and tragedy was immense.[18]

Like so many parts of this story, the expulsion of Jews was not unique or original to Spain. In 1290, England had expelled its small population of Jews. France followed in 1306 and other states throughout the fourteenth century. The Italian duchies of Parma and Milan did so in 1488 and 1490, the city of Warsaw in 1483. The Spanish kingdoms did not do so at that time, though as early as the 1480s many Spanish cities did at least partially expel their Jewish populations precisely to minimize contact with conversos. But at the same time, it must be said that these other countries did not have Jewish populations of the same size, nor, at least in many places, did the Jews have such an integral and long-standing place in society as they did in Spain.[19]

From Conversos to Alumbrados and "Lutherans"

In the first decades of the Inquisition's existence until the 1520s, its focus was suspected judaizing among conversos. These were also its most savage years, not yet having clear, established guidelines for the manner of proceeding and without gathered experience, resulting in the most inhumane practices with the maximum number of executions. Perhaps as many as 2,000

---

18. Kamen, 30.
19. Kamen, 15–27.

people were executed in that period—75 percent of the total of those executed by the Spanish Inquisition during its existence—with another 15,000 processed and "reconciled" (that is, disciplined or penalized in some form).[20] In fact, more than half of those processed by the Inquisition in its entire history were processed in that period. But beginning in the 1520s, and through the sixteenth century, the Inquisition's focus moved to concern for false mystics and the encroachment of Reformation ideas into Spain. (And toward the end of that century and thereafter, its attention moved more to superstition, witchcraft, blasphemous statements, and moral misbehaviors.)[21]

We have previously addressed the reality of the Alumbrados, the followers of Erasmus, and the presence (or relative lack of presence) of Protestants in sixteenth-century Spain. We need not review that material here. Here it must simply be noted that neither the Inquisition as an institution nor individual inquisitors were necessarily opposed to church reform, nor would they have doubted the possibility of mystical prayer and experience. Their concern involved what was viewed as unacceptable and even heretical notions of reform and the perception (and reality) of false (misguided or fraudulent) mystics and the aberrations from true doctrine that could result. But at the same time, neither those who denounced others to the Inquisition nor the inquisitors

---

20. Pérez notes that earlier estimates grossly overestimated those impacted by the Inquisition. This earlier data suggests that during the entire existence of the Spanish Inquisition, 340,592 people were tried; 31,913 were burned; 17,659 were burned in effigy; and 291,021 were reconciled or given lesser penalties (though "lesser" does not mean "light" or "insignificant"). In more recent estimates, Pérez reports, for the period between 1540 and 1700 (that it is, after its most harsh period), there were 125,000 trials; 49,082 arrests; and 810 executions (again, after the most harsh, first decades of the Spanish Inquisition's existence). Pérez, *Spanish Inquisition*, 170–73.

21. Rawlings, *Spanish Inquisition*, 14–20.

themselves may have been always equipped to distinguish Protestant, Erasmian, and authentic reform or authentic mystical doctrine and aberrations from it. The Inquisition's zeal to protect the true faith, together with a lack of confidence in ordinary people to be able to distinguish right belief from heresy (a lack of confidence not without some justification, given the state of basic catechesis and low of level of literacy), made the inquisitors hypersensitive and vigilant. In short, they were ready to "throw the baby out with the bathwater." The inclusion of so many sound and orthodox books on prayer in the Index of 1559 makes this hyperconcern abundantly clear. Especially since at least that particular index played an important role in Teresa's development, the subject of censorship and indexes of forbidden books merits brief comment.

Censorship and Indexes of Books

The discovery of groups of Protestants in the major cities of Valladolid and Seville,[22] including individuals of prominent families, in 1558 set off an intense round of inquisitorial activity in 1559–1560.[23] Another result was the Index of Forbidden Books of 1559—the so-called Valdés Index—which Teresa mentions in the *Life* (L 26.5). It included 701 items including works of Erasmus, translations of the Bible into the vernacular, catechisms, and

---

22. For a detailed discussion of the various indexes of prohibited books as well as the effort to control the import and publication of books, see Virgilio Pinto Crespo, *Inquisición y control ideológico en la España del siglo XVI* (Madrid: Taurus Ediciones, 1983).

23. Eighty-three people were executed between 1559 and 1563 in the height of this Protestant scare—though about four times more people were executed in England and three times more in France in the same period. In short, it was a time of religious intolerance all over Europe. By 1560, Spain had the lowest rate of execution for religious reasons. See Kamen, *Spanish Inquisition*, 107, 253.

books on prayer and spirituality in Latin but especially in the vernacular. It was obviously meant to address the threat of both Protestantism and false mysticism. Included in the index were works that were found to be not in doctrinal error but rather dangerous for the ordinary Christian to read. This was especially true of vernacular spiritual works, since the ability to read Latin usually meant that the reader had advanced studies. The Index of 1559 was followed in 1583 with an even more extensive index.

In another response to the Protestant scare, King Philip II banned Spanish students from studying in foreign universities with the exception of three approved universities in Italy and one in Portugal. But this was hard to enforce, and the royal decree applied only to the kingdom of Castile—not the kingdom of Aragon, where another legal mechanism would have been required for royal action.[24]

Previous to these indexes, there had been prohibitions of the import or publication of individual works or of the works of individual persons; for example, the works of Martin Luther were prohibited in 1521 and some of the works of Erasmus in 1536. In 1502, the monarchs mandated prior censorship before any book could be published or imported into Spain (though this was virtually impossible to enforce in light of porous borders and constant travel by Spaniards and foreigners for trade or study). Between 1521 and 1551, the Spanish Inquisition prohibited seventy-one particular books as well as all of the works of sixteen particular individuals.[25] In light of the fact that the presses in Calvinist Geneva alone were estimated to be producing 300,000 volumes a year in the mid-sixteenth century, the objectives of the Inquisition faced immense challenges.[26]

---

24. Kamen, 119–20.

25. Kamen, 125–28. See also Pinto Crespo, *Inquisición y control*, 150–57.

26. Pinto Crespo, *Inquisición y control*, 23.

Again, like so much of what we have said in relation to the Spanish Inquisition, the indexes of forbidden books were not exclusive to Spain. Beginning in 1487, the popes began to give approval of individual efforts in different parts of Europe to censor or prohibit the publication of particular books.[27] In 1544, the University of the Sorbonne in Paris issued an index, followed in 1546 by the University of Louvain in present-day Belgium (which in the sixteenth century was part of the Spanish realm), in 1549 in the Republic of Venice in Italy, and in 1551 in Rome. The Spanish indexes were based on these earlier lists, thus including works in other languages and not likely widely available in Spain at all.[28] In 1564, the Council of Trent issued its own index.

The Inquisitorial Procedure and Teresa's Paternal Grandfather

Generally, in the first decades of the Inquisition, beyond specific accusations that could be made and received at any time, the Inquisition would begin activity in a particular area by arranging for a reading of an "edict of faith" at Masses in local churches in which was listed various forms of heresy and judaizing behaviors.[29] The people were then given a "period of grace" of about thirty to forty days, either to confess their own fault (with relatively minimal subsequent consequence in most cases) or to denounce others for one or more of the listed heresies or behaviors. It was generally

---

27. Martínez de Bujanda, "Indices de libros prohibidos del siglo XVI," in Pérez Villanueva and Bonet, *Historia de la Inquisición* (2000), 3:773–75.

28. Pérez, *Spanish Inquisition*, 181–83.

29. Helen Rawlings offers a nice summary of the Inquisition's procedures (*Spanish Inquisition*, 30–41) with a concise summary on page 36. See also Joseph Pérez's two chapters (*Spanish Inquisition*, 101–75) on the structure, organization, and procedures of the Inquisition. And Kamen's two chapters on the same topic (*Spanish Inquisition*, 181–259).

safer to confess than to be denounced by others. And so, a converso who was a sincere Christian but whose family still observed certain Jewish customs in their homes might prudently ponder if these practices had become known to others (for example, Old Christian neighbors, servants, or other employees). In that case, it might have been wise to "confess" and be "reconciled" with minor penalty rather than wait to be accused.

Contrary to our modern sense of justice, such accusations could be made and accepted with no accompanying proof or evidence. Even hearsay could be accepted as the foundation of a denunciation (that is, "I heard that he said . . . or did . . ." or "they say his father used to . . ."). And contrary even to the practice of civil courts at the time, the accuser could remain anonymous. The invitation to take vengeance on someone without consequence to the accuser is obvious here—a fact that was not lost, at least in some cases, on the inquisitors themselves as they considered the accusations and interviewed the accused (which may have been a factor in Teresa's encounters with Inquisition, to be discussed below). In fact, it appears that many accusations had their roots in interpersonal, familial, and social hostility rather than in heresy. Perhaps paradoxically, it seems that many Jews—before the expulsion and after its enforcement became lax—were not reluctant to accuse those who chose to feign Christian belief while secretly trying straddle both worlds and maintain their Jewish practice.[30] (The Inquisition had no jurisdiction over Jews.)

Specifically in regard to the prosecution for judaizing, neither the accusers nor in many cases the inquisitors could separate out clearly which traditional Jewish practices might signify

---

30. Kamen, *Spanish Inquisition*, 22–23.

a lack of true adherence to Catholic faith (that is, "I noticed that he doesn't eat pork . . ."). Such cultural practices could be taken as proof of remaining a Jew by religion.

Not every denunciation resulted in questioning or an arrest. But if the charge seemed plausible, the person would be arrested and encouraged to confess, to speculate on why he or she had been accused and told to lay out the details of their life, without knowing at first the exact nature of the accusation. If there was no confession, a formal procedure and trial would be initiated in which the accused could read or be told the accusation (but not the accuser), present collaborating witnesses, and offer extenuating circumstances. Such procedures could drag on for a considerable time—even years. And with each passing day, the accused's reputation was further sullied.

Torture could be used in this process (as was practiced in civil procedures throughout Europe at the time), though this occurred substantially less after the first few decades. The most typical forms of torture were stretching on the rack, being suspended by pulleys while weighted, and what we would now call "water boarding." Confessions obtained by torture had to be confirmed by the accused twenty-four hours later. Inquisitors came to see rather early that torture rarely revealed the truth, since someone under torture could easily confess to anything, whether true or not. In fact, both torture and executions were relatively rare after the first two decades of the existence of the Spanish Inquisition. Between 1560 and 1614, it is calculated that about 2.25 percent of accused were condemned to death in person (though others who had escaped the hands of the Inquisition through escape or death could be burned in effigy).[31] Many other countries—including

---

31. Rawlings, *Spanish Inquisition*, 30–41.

England, France, and parts of Germany—continued to burn heretics (and witches) well into the seventeenth century.[32]

Judgment was issued by a tribunal consisting of inquisitors, advisers, and a representative of the local bishop. Even if acquitted, the accused's reputation might well be ruined, even more in more protracted proceedings. Punishments for the condemned could consist of a wide range of penalties depending on the charge, the weight of the evidence, and whether the accused had confessed or not—from merely spiritual penances of saying mandated prayers or a period of fasting, forms of public penance (as in the case of Teresa's grandfather), time in a monastery or convent, prohibition of preaching for clergy, exile for a period, forfeiture of property, flogging, a period of arduous service on naval galleys, or execution.

Those arrested by the Inquisition would be maintained in special Inquisition prisons until sentence was given, but there was no prison system to maintain prisoners for longer periods as punishment after judgment. In fact, Inquisition prisons could be relatively humane by the standards of the time. The accused could be visited by doctors and clergy. These prisons were inspected several times a year to ensure they were maintained in a humane state (again, according to the standards of the time). In fact, there are stories of people being kept in civil and other ecclesiastical prisons who tried to find a reason to be transferred to an Inquisition prison.[33]

One of the public manifestations of the work of the Inquisition were periodic *autos de fe* (acts of faith) that have become synonymous with burnings at the stake though they were much

---

32. Rawlings, 2.
33. Kamen, *Spanish Inquisition*, 235.

broader than the executions that sometimes followed. In fact, they could be rather small, simple affairs in which only a few of the accused were publicly "reconciled" and "penanced" without any executions. Or at least periodically, they could be grand (and costly), sometimes daylong spectacles, in a public square with crowds of local dignitaries and masses of people, beginning with long processions of the city's clergy and religious, public preaching, the parading of the condemned, the reading of the sentences, and the acceptance of the public penances and penalties. The executions followed in a separate location, since they were handled not by the church itself but civil authorities. Those condemned for serious crimes but who had confessed were "mercifully" strangled before their bodies were burned at the stake. Such spectacles were meant to serve as a warning to those who might be tempted to drift from orthodox doctrine or practice.[34]

It is in this context that we can understand the experience of Teresa's paternal grandfather, Juan Sánchez of Toledo. We know from the documents discovered in 1947 that he was publicly "reconciled" on July 20, 1485, for having lapsed into Judaism. (Recall that this was during the early and most harsh years of the Inquisition.) It is not known if he was accused or if he himself confessed during a "period of grace." As we have seen, it is entirely possible that he and his family were sincere Christians but that the family practiced some Jewish customs in their home. Any public knowledge of this fact alone would have made him susceptible to accusation by anyone envious of his success or whom he had angered in some previous interpersonal or economic encounter. In fact,

---

34. In the thirty-five years between 1575 and 1610, for example, the tribunal of the city of Toledo held twelve public autos de fe in which 386 of the condemned appeared. During the same period, 786 of the condemned were processed in small ceremonies. See Rawlings, *Spanish Inquisition*, 37.

in 1486, when the Inquisition began in Toledo, 2,400 conversos came forward to "confess" and be "reconciled"—a total of 4,300 in the two-year period between 1486 and 1487.[35]

Since he and his family were subsequently able to resettle elsewhere and resume their business suggests that, whatever was at the heart of the "relapse," the penalty had not involved confiscation of goods. Rather, he and perhaps his sons were subject to one of the common forms of public penance and humiliation.[36] For several Fridays, he and others who had been "reconciled" would have been paraded through the streets of Toledo—to the mockery and jeers of the crowds—carrying candles and wearing the *sanbenito*.[37] This was typically a full cloth scapular in yellow fabric, "decorated" with crosses and upside-down flames (to show that the reconciled had been spared the flames). After the specified period of public humiliation, the sanbenito would then be hung in the parish church of the condemned as a permanent reminder of their humiliation and of the consequences of judaizing.[38] It is no wonder that Juan Sánchez would have chosen to move his family and business elsewhere.

It is difficult to imagine that Teresa would not have been aware of her family's converso background. But she never mentioned it in writing. It remains unknown if she knew the details of her grandfather's "reconciliation" before the Inquisition. It may well

---

35. Kamen, *Spanish Inquisition*, 66–67.

36. There is some question about whether Juan's sons (i.e., Teresa's father and uncles) were publicly "reconciled" along with Teresa's grandfather. Egido is convinced that only Juan himself, and not his sons, endured this public humiliation. See Egido, *El linaje judeoconverso*, 24–26.

37. Egido, 250.

38. All of this is described in a general way by Pérez, *Spanish Inquisition*, 162–63.

be that her father and uncles would have been only too happy to forget it altogether. Teresa was a young girl when the matter came to light during the brothers' effort to get their status as hidalgos recognized, and it is at least plausible that she did not learn of the details of the procedure and the testimony given.[39]

Fear and Trembling in the Face of the Spanish Inquisition?

Henry Kamen in one of the later chapters of his classic work on the Spanish Inquisition (in a chapter titled "The Image and Reality of Power")[40] concludes that it is by no means obvious that the Inquisition spread fear and terror in the hearts of Spaniards, though he notes that the Inquisition functioned more intensely in some locales than others and, as we have seen, with focus on some groups more than others. In fact, it is possible that the Inquisition was simultaneously feared and generally popular at the same time.[41] The Spanish church in general and the Inquisition in particular in its published edicts and in public preaching regularly decried the dangers of the encroachment of Reformation thought and the spread of Alumbradism. And it appears that many of the faithful did in fact come to embrace their concerns as genuine threats to the faith.[42] Together with the widespread, if largely unjustified, suspicion of judaizing by conversos, many ordinary people may well have accepted the necessity of the Inquisition and viewed its methods as not uncommon of the administration of justice in general at the time.

---

39. Pérez, *Teresa de Ávila*, 26–27.
40. Kamen, *Spanish Inquisition*, 261–80.
41. Egido, "Ambiente histórico," 72.
42. Pérez, "Mística y realidad histórica," in Egido, *Actas del Congreso*, 47.

Further, as Helen Rawlings notes, the Inquisition was not as powerful as once thought. In fact, it had regularly to contend with jurisdictional disputes—with the crown and the church—as well as internal disagreements about proceedings.[43] Certainly, Teresa of Jesus belonged simultaneously to a number of groups that were in fact a special focus of the Inquisition, and she was a well-known figure. But the conclusions of Kamen and Rawlings, among other contemporary interpreters of the Spanish Inquisition, should make us pause before concluding that she lived in constant fear before the threat of the Inquisition. And it is to Teresa's own attitudes toward and encounters with the Inquisition that we now turn.

Part 2: Teresa of Jesus and the Spanish Inquisition

A number of contemporary authors have argued that we must understand some of the tone and emphases of Teresa's writings—for example, her explicit statements of submission to church authority and acknowledging her status as an uneducated woman (and perhaps even some of her emphasis on humility)—as a reaction to the presence and threat of the Inquisition. In order to assess the weight of this claim, we must try to understand her attitude toward that institution and her actual encounters with it.

Teresa's Attitude toward the Inquisition

But before entering into those topics more deeply, let's begin with the following question: did Teresa fear the Inquisition? Perhaps we might immediately respond affirmatively, especially if we know

---

43. Rawlings, *Spanish Inquisition*, 2.

anything about the reputation of the Spanish Inquisition; any sensible person would! But the actual response is not so clear. Certainly, many of Teresa's supporters feared for her sake and told her so. There is no doubt that Teresa of Jesus was intelligent, prudent, and even shrewd (in a good way). One would have been a fool not to take note of the Inquisition and its specific concerns, mold one's writings in particular ways to avoid suspicion as much as possible in those areas of concern, and even foster relationships with influential people who could attest to one's orthodoxy, sanity, honesty, and special gifts. Teresa clearly did all of those things, whether in a fully conscious and calculated way or not. Contemporary feminist interpreters and others have looked particularly at her style and rhetorical devices as a likely response to inquisitorial interest, and we will examine those interpretations later. But we cannot ignore her own comments or the witness of those who interacted with her in her own time.

One of the most explicit and interesting comments by Teresa herself about her reaction to the Inquisition appears in the *Life* (33.5):

> Likewise the devil began striving here through one person and another to make known that I had received some revelation about this work. *Some persons came to me with great fear to tell me we were in trouble*[44] and that it could happen that others might accuse me of something and report me to the Inquisitors. This amused me and made me laugh, for I never

---

44. Emphasis added in order to note that in the original Spanish text, Teresa famously refers to the "difficult" or "hard" times (*los tiempos recios*) in which the fear of the Inquisition would cause such disquiet: "También comenzó aquí el demonio, de una persona en otra, procurar se entendiese que había yo visto alguna revelación en este negocio, e iban *a mí con mucho miedo a decirme que andaban los tiempos recios* y que podría ser me levantasen algo y fuesen a los inquisidores."

> had any fear of such a possibility. If anyone were to see that I went against the slightest ceremony of the Church in a matter of faith, I myself knew well that I would die a thousand deaths for the faith or for any truth of Sacred Scripture. And I said they shouldn't be afraid about these possible accusations; that it would be pretty bad for my soul if there were something in it of the sort that I should have to fear the Inquisition; that I thought that if I did have something to fear I'd go myself to seek out the Inquisitors; and that if I were accused, the Lord would free me, and I would be the one to gain.

So according to her own statement, Teresa was amused at the idea that she had reason to be concerned about the Inquisition. (See also Teresa's ironical reference in her *Critique*, a response to Francisco de Salcedo [also in the introduction of the same], written after her being denounced to the Inquisition in Córdoba, to be discussed below.) This does not necessarily suggest that she was not, at the very same time, shrewd enough to be careful especially in her writings. But a number of factors offer reasons that Teresa can be taken largely at her word here. Although there were many reasons to fear the Inquisition, it must be noted that the fact of its existence, its proposed mission to ensure right faith and practice, and even much of its methodology (common in that age and culture) were generally accepted and even supported by the general populace, even if we might rightly find some of the methods abhorrent today. In that age, they were common in civil and ecclesiastical societies across Europe. To begin with the idea that the Inquisition was perceived as the enemy or as the purveyor of injustice to be feared by all is to read back into history certain subsequent interpretations. One factor in Teresa's lack of fear may be that she did not begin with such a negative view of the Inquisition and its intentions. And Teresa, as she notes above, was deeply committed to adhere completely to the teaching and authority of the church. On that, we have no reason to doubt in the least her sincerity.

Moreover, all of Teresa's major works were written after she had already attained great mystical advances.[45] She had already experienced much in her deep encounters with God. It's true that she had passed through an early period of uncertainty and even fear about her experiences and her understanding of them. But by the time that she wrote and that her writing and experiences became more widely known, she had arrived at deep security about divine action in her life and activity. In fact, her explicit encounters with the Inquisition—beyond the fear expressed by friends—occurred after she had attained the spiritual marriage in 1572. In that light, it would actually be more surprising if she had taken a more fearful attitude toward the Inquisition. This is not to suggest that she no longer felt normal human emotions, but it does offer support to her stated lack of deep concern even as the actual events unfolded. It appears that she was more concerned that any action by the Inquisition against her personally might jeopardize the reputation and thus the growth of the reform in its still delicate flowering.

The fact is that, though she had her share of detractors and doubters, Teresa also had a very positive reputation for her reform and for her mystical experiences. Teresa had supporters at many levels of civil and ecclesiastical society. Undoubtedly, even the high nobility and bishops were not exempt from the inquiries of the inquisitors, but Teresa had a very wide circle of friends and supporters in many walks of life and social class.

---

45. Enrique Llamas Martínez, *Santa Teresa de Jesús y la Inquisición Española* (Madrid: Consejo Superior de Investigaciones Científicas, Instituto "Francisco Suarez," 1972), xv; 97–105.

There is no reason to doubt that such support was a help to her in the face of Inquisition concern.[46] She could report—as she did (ST 58)—that she had tested her experiences, ideas, and writings with some of the most respected theologians of her time. These, in turn, could offer testimony of her behalf.

In fact, Teresa had prominent supporters associated with the Inquisition itself. It was the inquisitor Francisco de Soto y Salazar (who had known her family and later became bishop of Salamanca) who suggested that she send the *Life* to the highly regarded John of Ávila (proclaimed Doctor of the Church in 2012) for a critical review of its content. It was one of her most trusted counselors, the Dominican Domingo Bañéz who offered the official—and positive—assessment of the *Life* for the Inquisition. And when the inquisitor general, Cardinal Gaspar de Quiroga, read it around 1574–1575, he was impressed by it and thereafter remained a supporter. In the same way, other inquisitors changed their views of her or at least softened them after they had read the *Life* or encountered her personally. It may be that the relative speed with which later procedures moved was due to the fact that some within the Inquisition did not want to harm her reform by any damage to her reputation.[47]

Rather than express fear of the Inquisition in her writings—not denying that she was shrewd enough to write in a way to deflect the suspicion of inquisitors and others—Teresa could be critical of the Inquisition, subtly but nonetheless evident.[48]

---

46. Enrique Llamas Martínez, "Teresa de Jesús y los alumbrados: Hacia una revisión del 'alumbradismo' español," in *Congreso Internacional Teresiano (4–7 octubre, 1982)*, ed. Teófanes Egido et al., 1:137–67 (Salamanca, Spain: Universidad de Salamanca, 1983), 138–39.

47. Llamas Martínez, *Santa Teresa de Jesús*, xii.

48. Egido, "Ambiente histórico," 135.

In fact, some of the sympathetic censors of her writings felt the need to restrain the bite in some of her remarks (L 26.5).

Teresa's Encounters with the Inquisition

Previously, we discussed the encounter of Teresa's paternal grandfather with the Inquisition.[49] This must have been deeply traumatic for him and for his young sons. It is likely that Teresa had some knowledge of this history—at least enough to be fully aware of the presence of the Inquisition and the possible consequences of running afoul of it. In fact, no one in Spanish society could have been ignorant of this reality, even if it had not touched their own families.

We have already mentioned the concern expressed to Teresa by friends, supporters, and confessors. It is evident in Teresa's own account in the *Life* that as she began to seek counsel in regard to her first mystical experiences, her confessors and advisors were concerned both about demonic activity and about unwanted attention by the Inquisition. A number of well-known purported women mystics had been investigated and condemned by the Inquisition. Well known at the time were the cases of the Dominican María de Santo Domingo who had claimed—falsely, it was later proved—to experience prophecies, ecstasies, and raptures, as well as the Poor Clare Magdalena de la Cruz who had fraudulently claimed to have received the stigmata. (We know that the

---

49. In Spanish, the most thorough discussion of Teresa's encounters with the Inquisition is provided by Enrique Llamas Martínez (*Santa Teresa de Jesús* cited above). See also: Francisco Ruiz de Pablos, *Santa Teresa y la Inquisición: homenaje V centenario* (Ávila, Spain: Taller Gráficas E&D, 2014). A much briefer but still thorough discussion is offered by Pérez, *Teresa de Ávila*, 259–67. See also Alberto Pacho, "Inquisición," in *Diccionario de Santa Teresa: Doctrina e historia*, ed. Tomás Álvarez, 942–48, 2nd ed. (Burgos, Spain: Editorial Monte Carmelo, 2006).

comparison with Magdalena de la Cruz was made explicitly before the city council of Medina del Campo when Teresa was in the city to found her Carmel in 1567.)[50]

There seems to have been rumors of heresy and misguided mysticism in Ávila itself at the time that Teresa was receiving her first mystical experiences. It may be that Doña Guiomar de Ulloa, Teresa's great friend and supporter, was suspected by some of Alumbrado leanings. In 1559, Agustín Cazalla was condemned by the Inquisition in Valladolid for seeking to spread Protestant thought. He and his followers had been in Ávila between 1556 and 1559, and they may have tried unsuccessfully to engage Teresa in their movement. All of this was probably part of the reason others were concerned for Teresa.

Although it did not touch directly on any of her own later writings, the Valdés Index of Prohibited Books of 1559 concerned her deeply, as she describes in the *Life*. Any subsequent authors of books about prayer, especially mystical prayer, would have been foolish not to be concerned in light of the many highly respected books on prayer that had been placed on the index.

As we pass now to Teresa's actual encounters with Inquisition, we can say at the outset that, though she was denounced to the Inquisition—falsely, as we shall see—she was never formally processed or judged by it. In the same way, it is true that the Inquisition requested and held the *Life* until after her death, but it was never placed on an index, nor was it or any of its parts condemned. Teresa's final words that she died a daughter of the church may reflect her sense of vindication—and possibly relief—that she did not die under a cloud of

---

50. Llamas Martínez, *Santa Teresa de Jesús*, 16.

condemnation or long inquisitorial procedures or even under a cloud of suspicion.[51]

Teresa's first actual encounter with the Inquisition did not involve any interpersonal contact but rather involved *The Book of Her Life*.[52] It appears that the princess of Eboli, following the disastrous foundation and abandonment of a monastery of the reform under her patronage in Pastrana, denounced Teresa and the *Life* to the Inquisition around 1574. This appears to be the copy that the grand inquisitor Cardinal Quiroga read and valued. This nearly coincided with a request for information and specifically for a copy of the *Life* by the tribunal of the Inquisition in Córdoba.

The Inquiries of the Tribunal of Córdoba

The Inquisition had been active in investigating the presence of Alumbrados in the region around the city of Córdoba in Andalusia (southern Spain) since about 1552. There was a great deal of spiritual fervor in the area, due in large measure to the evangelical and catechetical activity of John of Ávila (d. 1569) and the circle of priests influenced by him and their supporters. But the Inquisition was concerned that some of the fervor had drifted into heresy and Alumbradism. John of Ávila himself was prosecuted by the Inquisition for suspicions of Alumbradism in 1531–1533, and spent some time in an Inquisition prison.[53] Although he was ultimately cleared, his principal followers were under suspicion. Of particular concern was the large number of *beatas* in the area, among whom there was a particular

---

51. Llamas Martínez, *Santa Teresa de Jesús*, xv; Egido, "Ambiente histórico," 74.
52. See Álvarez, *St. Teresa of Ávila*, 295–98.
53. Pérez, *Teresa de Ávila*, 259.

fascination with mystical and extraordinary experience. Teresa herself had not been in the south of Spain since 1568, but while there she had been in contact with many of those associated with John of Ávila's circle, some of whom were under investigation in the 1570s. And some of them may have been familiar with the *Life*, identified with her experience and reputation, and perhaps even mentioned it in interviews before the Inquisition.

It was in this context that Teresa's name first appeared in a report from the tribunal in Córdoba to the Consejo (General Council of the Inquisition or the "Suprema") in Madrid. The exact content of the tribunal's concerns is not known, but Teresa was not called in to be interviewed, nor was there any public action against her. The Inquisition, with its web of activities, was investigating numerous things throughout the country, and it would not be unusual for someone to be part of an active investigation without any knowledge of it. It appears that the tribunal principally wanted to obtain a copy of the *Life*. The Consejo in Madrid instructed the tribunal of Valladolid to obtain a copy of the book, which it did through Teresa's friend, the bishop of Ávila, Alvaro de Mendoza, to whom Teresa had given a copy. It was then reviewed officially on behalf of the Inquisition by Teresa's longtime supporter and advisor, the Dominican Domingo Bañéz, who gave a favorable report dated July 7, 1575. (A second Dominican, Hernando del Castillo, offered a similar judgment to the tribunal.) The content of his critique suggests that the focus of the Inquisition's inquiry was not so much its doctrinal points but rather as a kind of cross-check of the sincerity of her claims of mystical experience, her solid spirit, and life of virtue. Bañéz, although expressing a general caution about women mystics and their visions and spiritual teaching, attested to Teresa's authenticity.

Throughout this process, Teresa shows no evidence of having been aware of the Inquisition's inquiries, though we know she encountered Bañéz face-to-face during 1575. Again, the bishop of Ávila was a longtime friend. In any case, if she was aware, there is no evidence that she was in any way concerned about it.

Accusations before the Tribunal of Seville: The First Phase

Teresa was again in Andalusia in 1575 to found a Carmel at Beas (a city the Inquisition considered a hotbed of Alumbradism) from where Jerome Gratian directed her to found in Seville. Though officially established in May 1575, this was a foundation surrounded with many difficulties and involved another, more direct encounter with the Inquisition. This contact involved two phases, 1575–1576 and 1578–1579.

The phase 1575–1576 seems to have been a particularly inauspicious time for Teresa to appear on the Inquisition's "radar." We know that also in 1575, the Inquisition was actively investigating a group of purported Alumbrados in Toledo, a movement with distinctively apocalyptic overtones. A principal figure was the *beata* Francisca de los Apostoles who was linked with other *beatas*, priests, and laypeople in the area. Also in that same year, the Inquisition was looking into a case of an Augustinian nun in Ávila, an example we will look at a little more closely below in relation to John of the Cross who acted on behalf of the Inquisition in that case. At the same time, Ignatius of Loyola and his *Spiritual Exercises* were also a focus of investigation.

The first phase began with one of the Seville community's early novices, María del Corro, who at about forty years old was a widow and had been a well-known *beata* in the city. But it appears that she found her status as just one of the novices in a poor and struggling community different than what she had expected. She left after only about four months. Perhaps because of chagrin at the implicit rejection of her presumed sanctity or perhaps to serve, whether consciously or not, as a cover for her embarrassment at her failure as a Carmelite, she and her confessor accused the nuns of Alumbradism in their teachings about prayer, inappropriate manners of governance, unhealthy devotional practices, and immorality.

Teresa was still present in Seville as this unfolded. The inquisitors came to the monastery a number of times—unannounced, apparently trying to catch the nuns off guard. The nuns, including Teresa herself, were interviewed. It is not clear if they were required to leave the cloister to be interviewed at the tribunal itself. The inquisitors in Seville sent the materials to the Consejo in Madrid, which ordered the investigation to focus attention on only one of the nuns mentioned in the accusation (who it apparently later judged to be emotionally unstable but not guilty of anything worthy of further investigation). Apparently, with the *Life* already in hand and with the Córdoba investigation recently concluded, the Consejo felt there was no need for further investigation. Moreover, the accusations themselves may have seemed outlandish to the inquisitors, and they would have been aware that accusations could come forward because of vindictiveness rather than for just cause. And again, Teresa had supporters and admirers in Seville, some with close relations with the Inquisition, and by this time, the head of the Inquisition, Cardinal Quiroga, would have read the *Life* and, with other inquisitors, come away with a positive sense of Teresa.

It is believed that *Spiritual Testimony* 58 (Seville, 1575) is Teresa's account of her life written for the Seville tribunal. *Spiritual Testimony* 53 (Seville, November 8, 1575) contains a reference to the "false accusation" and reports a vision that she received during the octave of All Saints, which offered her assurance in the face of false accusation and persecution. In a letter of December 30, 1575 (Ltr 98), she makes no reference to the process. A letter of April 29, 1576 (Ltr 105) makes a brief reference to the accusation. Gratian, who himself was worried about the situation, found Teresa undisturbed, and others who had contact with her at the time later testified that she seemed tranquil and patient throughout the process.[54]

The final sentence of the Inquisition is not extant, but it must have been in favor of Teresa and the nuns, probably for the lack of evidence. She herself left the city in June 1576, and the case was most likely settled by then.

Seville: The Second Phase

The second phase of involvement with the Seville Inquisition involved unbalanced nuns, given to extraordinary phenomena; an inexperienced and unwise confessor; a young and capable but inexperienced prioress; and the ongoing dispute between Calced and Discalced[55]—in short, a recipe for trouble. The problems

---

54. Llamas Martínez, *Santa Teresa de Jesús*, 86–87, 97–105; Llamas Martínez, "Teresa de Jesús y los alumbrados," 142.

55. Llamas Martínez ("Teresa de Jesús y los alumbrados," 143) believes that the conflict between Calced and Discalced in Andalusia and animosity toward Gratian in his role as apostolic visitator for Andalusia—in the jumble of jurisdictions mentioned in a previous chapter of this work—played an important role in the unfolding of this phase of the Teresa's encounters with the Inquisition.

began to unfold shortly after Teresa left Seville, and she was forced to attempt to address the situation with Gratian and the prioress by mail—a difficult undertaking, given the state of the postal service at the time.

The problems began when one of the young nuns felt herself particularly endowed with mystical gifts and thus in need of special and regular spiritual counsel. This, she received from the monastery's young confessor, a priest who had been helpful to the community during its founding. But as the nun began to seek special, frequent, and long confessions and spiritual talks with the priest, the prioress and the other nuns became concerned. It must be noted that the Inquisition had investigated a number of cases in which priests had become sexually involved with young nuns and *beatas* in relationships that seemed to have begun innocently enough. (Eight priests in Extremadura had been prosecuted for seducing *beatas* under the pretense of offering spiritual guidance.)[56] But when the prioress tried to restrict contact between the nun and priest, he began to speak out publicly against her. When the prioress arranged his removal as confessor altogether, the priest appealed to the Calced provincial. He in turn intervened, restored the confessor against the prioress's wishes, threatened to remove the prioress, and to impose other penalties. (We have here another manifestation of the jurisdictional problems that plagued the Discalced until the separation: Gratian at the time was the visitator for Andalusia by appointment of the nuncio.)

The priest, two of the community's nuns, and the Calced provincial accused the prioress, Teresa, and Gratian to the Inquisition. It appears that Teresa received word as well as the content

---

56. Pérez, *Teresa de Ávila*, 261–64.

of these accusations late in 1578 or early in 1579. Teresa's Letter 284 (January 31, 1579) is directed to the community. Letter 294 (May 3, 1579) is addressed to the two nun-accusers. Teresa wrote to her friend and supporter, Hernando de Pantoja, prior of the Carthusians in Seville (Letter 283 of January 31, 1579), asking him to be a support and help to the nuns.

We do not have an extant copy of the accusations, but later reports by those present at the time and other documents—including the later retractions written by the two nuns[57]—reveal their basic sordid content. These included ugly suggestions of an amorous relationship between Gratian and Teresa, as well as accusations that Gratian embraced and kissed the nuns and that he spent several nights in the Seville cloister. The claim was made that Teresa had, on occasion, slipped out of the cloister wearing secular clothes to meet Gratian. (Recall that Teresa would have been in her midsixties at the time; Gratian, in his midthirties!). It was even reported that Teresa may have born children by her own brother and then subsequently had them sent to the Americas!

But the local Inquisition, having just completed an inquiry into the community that included unannounced visits to the monastery and interviews of the nuns as well as Teresa herself, seems to have given little serious consideration of the accusations. The charges seemed outlandish, and Teresa's many supporters came forward to intervene with the Inquisition and even to accost the Calced provincial. The whole matter was settled by March 1579. The monastery was officially removed from the

---

57. Llamas Martínez (*Santa Teresa de Jesús*, 194–220) includes copies of the extant declaration of the prioress and the retractions of the two nun-accusers in an appendix to his book.

authority of the Calced provincial, the priest was removed from any further involvement with the monastery by the archbishop, and the two nuns came to their senses.

In the end, having reviewed these incidents, Joseph Pérez concludes that it would be inaccurate to say that Teresa of Jesus had been pursued by the Inquisition in any focused way. Her explicit brushes with it were more the result of false accusations brought out of a desire for vengeance. There is no evidence that the Inquisition ever weighed heavily the possibility of pursuing a more active and formal investigation and procedures against her. Her supporters were concerned for her in a time when such concern was certainly justified. But the actual activity of the Inquisition in her regard would not have warranted it, and Teresa was right in not allowing herself to be too bothered by it.[58]

Posthumous Inquiries concerning Her Works (1589-1598)

Perhaps Teresa's most serious encounters with the Inquisition—or at least with her works—began with the posthumous publication of her works in 1588. Alonso de la Fuente, for twenty years a zealous and energetic inquisitor of Alumbradism in the region of Extremadura, pursued a vigorous campaign to discredit her works as tainted with Alumbrado thought. A special focus of attention in Extremadura had been misguided and fraudulent women claiming mystical experiences. For a time, in the 1590s, it appeared that such accusations against Teresa's books would prevail, but they were never condemned and were ultimately completely vindicated.

---

58. Pérez, *Teresa de Ávila*, 265–67.

Enrique Llamas Martínez concludes his study of Teresa, the Alumbrados, and the Inquisition by asking the following provocative and even disturbing question: if Alonso de la Fuente and others accusers of St. Teresa were so insistently wrong about her teaching and orthodoxy, were they also wrong in the cases of many of those who were in fact condemned as Alumbrados?[59]

John and the Inquisition

There are just a few words to be offered about the encounters of John of the Cross with the Inquisition, because there is no evidence or suggestion that, in his lifetime, any formal case was ever pursued against him. Still, it appears possible that he may have been accused to the Inquisition for suspicion of being an Alumbrado during his time in Andalusia. If so, it probably occurred in Baeza where he had founded a house of the reform. This would not have been surprising since the Inquisition was very active in that area and at that time, and John was known to have had conversations with a number of people who were later processed as Alumbrados. But in the end, if there had been any investigation concerning John, it did not yield sufficient evidence to continue with a formal process.[60]

Although there is some conjecture that his father may have had a converso background and his mother a Morisco background, many factors would have shielded him from the inquisitors' gaze: he was, first of all, a man; educated; and not describing his own experience but rather offering guidance in a formal and even scholastic way. Further, although he was a

---

59. Llamas Martínez, "Teresa de Jesús y los alumbrados," 164.
60. Rodríguez, *100 fichas sobre San Juan de la Cruz*, 396–98.

principal collaborator in the reform of the male as well as the female Carmelites, he was not so public or well known. Still, John was prudent, and his attestations in his writings to submit everything to the judgment of the church were both entirely sincere and most probably calculated.

In fact, John was at least once called upon to serve as an active consultor by the Inquisition in the case of María de Olivares, an Augustinian nun of the monastery of Santa María de Gracia in Ávila while he was chaplain at the Incarnation. This was the very monastery in which the young Teresa had been a boarding student, and she may have known the nun in question. Ultimately, after interviewing the nun and despite the approval and admiration of many learned men of Ávila, John exposed her deception and exorcised her on several occasions in 1572–1573.

While in life he avoided the brushes with the Inquisition endured by Teresa, in death his works faced even more difficult challenges. In fact, his mystical doctrine came under close scrutiny by the Inquisition, and concerns about the presence of Alumbradism—later proven completely false—not only kept his books from being published quickly and widely but also likely delayed the process of his beatification. A number of external factors were probably at play in the ability of Teresa's work to more easily clear the obstacles put up by the Inquisition: as we have seen, in life, she had been investigated and cleared on a few occasions (and the Inquisition kept careful records); she had a much wider public reputation for sanctity (and mystical experience) and far more—and more influential—admirers to support her cause; and as the founder of the reform, the Discalced promoted her cause with more focused zeal.

SELECT BIBLIOGRAPHY

Part 1: The Spanish Inquisition

English

Haliczer, Stephen. *Inquisition and Society in the Kingdom of Valencia, 1478–1834*. Berkeley: University of California Press, 1990.

Kamen, Henry. *The Spanish Inquisition: A Historical Revision*. 4th ed. New Haven, Conn.: Yale University Press, 2014 (first edition, 1965).

Netanyahu, Benzion. *The Origins of the Inquisition in Fifteenth Century Spain*. New York.: Random House, 1995.

Pérez, Joseph. *The Spanish Inquisition: A History*. Translated by Janet Lloyd. New Haven, Conn.: Yale University Press, 2005.

Rawlings, Helen. *The Spanish Inquisition*. Malden, Mass.: Blackwell, 2006.

Spanish

Domínguez Ortiz, Antonio. "Las presuntas 'razones' de la Inquisición." In *Historia de la Inquisición en España y América*, edited by Joaquín Pérez Villanueva and Bartolomé Escandell Bonet, 58–82. Vol. 3. Madrid: Biblioteca de Autores Cristianos and Centro de Estudios Inquisitoriales, 2000.

García Cárcel, Ricardo. *La Inquisición*. Madrid: Anaya, 1991.

González Novalín, Jose Luis. "La Inquisición Española." In *La Iglesia en la España de los siglos XV y XVI*, edited by José Luis González Novalín, part 2, 107–268. Vol. 3 of *Historia de la Iglesia en España*, edited by Ricardo García-Villoslada. Madrid: Biblioteca de Autores Cristianos, 1980.

Pérez Villanueva, Joaquín, and Bartolomé Escandell Bonet, eds. *Historia de la Inquisición en España y América*. 3 vols. Madrid: Biblioteca de Autores Cristianos and Centro de Estudios Inquisitoriales, 1984, 1993, 2000.

Pinto Crespo, Virgilio. *Inquisición y control ideológico en la España del siglo XVI*. Madrid: Taurus Ediciones, 1983.

Part 2: Teresa of Jesus and the Spanish Inquisition

English

Álvarez, Tomás. *St. Teresa of Avila: 100 Themes on Her Life and Work*. Translated by Kieran Kavanaugh. Washington, D.C.: ICS Publications, 2011. (See pp. 295–98.)

Spanish

Llamas Martínez, Enrique. *Santa Teresa de Jesús y la Inquisición Española*. Madrid, Spain: Consejo Superior de Investigaciones Científicas, Instituto "Francisco Suarez," 1972.

———. "Teresa de Jesús y los alumbrados: Hacia una revisión del 'alumbradismo' español." In *Congreso Internacional Teresiano (4–7 octubre, 1982)*, edited by Teófanes Egido et al., 137–67. Vol. 1. Salamanca, Spain: Universidad de Salamanca, 1983.

Pacho, Alberto. "Inquisición." In *Diccionario de Santa Teresa: Doctrina e historia*, edited by Tomás Álvarez, 942–48. 2nd ed. Burgos, Spain: Editorial Monte Carmelo, 2006.

Ruiz de Pablos, Francisco. *Santa Teresa y la Inquisición: homenaje V centenario*. Ávila, Spain: Taller Gráficas E&D, 2014.

Chapter 10

Teresa of Jesus: A Woman in Sixteenth-Century Spain

Teresa of Jesus was a truly extraordinary person. Her spiritual gifts and experiences, her exceptional ability to explain and teach the path that leads to the deepest prayer, her leadership in the Carmelite Reform against great odds, and her remarkable personal qualities make her a truly extraordinary person of the sixteenth century and, more broadly, in the history of the church. It is no wonder that she was declared the first woman Doctor of the Church. In an age in which women were generally discounted as too weak, too emotional, and too susceptible to the passions to be trusted with teaching in the church, with the path of mystical prayer, and with a vision of reform, Teresa of Jesus was a woman—a person—ahead of her times.

But Teresa was also, and inevitably, a woman of her culture and of her time. No one can completely rise above the world in which they are formed and with which they daily interact. Teresa was exceptional, but she was no exception to this fundamental truth. This fact is the very reason for a book like this one that seeks to provide a sense of the context in which Teresa and John of the Cross lived and wrote.

Teresa of Jesus lived in a time when being a woman meant being disparaged just for the fact of not being a man. It was the world in which she was formed. To think otherwise—to try to cast her as a modern-day woman with a contemporary feminist perspective—is to do her and her teaching a disservice since it refuses to see her as she was and therefore to truly see her greatness as a woman precisely within her own world and context. But this is not at all to deny that she was a woman whose natural and supernatural gifts enabled her to see beyond the stereotypes in which her world tried uncritically to envelop her. It is to say that this extraordinary human being was, in the end, a *human* being who was extraordinary.

A superficial reading of Teresa's work might lead one to believe that she bought into the misogyny of the time. She speaks frequently of her "wretched" state and her lack of learning in an age in which any form of advanced education for a woman would be rare indeed. She acknowledges the boldness of a woman writing on the topics on which she writes, while professing and teaching the importance of humility. She submits her writings to educated men and to the teaching of the church.

But in our day, there have been a number of very valuable and insightful interpretations of Teresa's writings that suggest that much of her self-deprecatory language was a "rhetorical strategy" by which she sought to circumvent the prejudices of her time. To acknowledge the genuine insight of these interpretations is to acknowledge the prudence and shrewdness of this remarkable woman who was able to accomplish what otherwise would have seemed impossible in the culture in which she prayed, taught, wrote, and lead. But at the same time, to deny the basic sincerity of her own statements is to refuse to see her as a sixteenth-century woman standing in a long cultural and spiritual tradition, for good or for ill.

The Misogyny of Sixteenth-Century Spain

The misogyny—if not actual "hatred of women," certainly "strong prejudice against women"—was characteristic of Spanish culture of the 1500s. In this culture in which Teresa of Jesus was formed, women were largely viewed and treated as inferior to men—basically, as perpetual minors. This viewpoint was believed to be simply grounded in the reality of things and made evident by the science of the time. According to doctors and textbooks, women suffered from the physiological effects of a nature that left them more susceptible to the control of emotion and passion rather than reason. This "fact" made them prone to fickleness, less adept at reasoning, and thus more susceptible to and less gifted to resist the temptations of the devil.[1] All of this was viewed as evident in the first woman: Eve who was first to fall to the seductions of the devil in the Garden of Eden.

---

1. Stephen Haliczer, *Between Exaltation and Infamy: Female Mystics in the Golden Age of Spain* (New York.: Oxford University Press, 2002), 48; Gillian T. W. Ahlgren, *Teresa of Avila and the Politics of Sanctity* (Ithaca, N.Y.: Cornell University Press, 1996), 7–8; Joan Cammarata, "El discurso femenino de Santa Teresa de Ávila, defensora de la mujer renacentista," in *Actas Irvine* 92, 58–65, Asociación Internacional de Hispanistas. (Irvine.: University of California Irvine, 1994), 58. In Spanish, Ulrich Dobhan offers many quotes from authors of sixteenth-century Spain, manifesting their view of women as inherently inferior and better suited to enclosure in home or cloister. See Ulrich Dobhan, "Teresa de Jesús y la emancipación de la mujer," in *Congreso Internacional Teresiano (4–7 octubre, 1982)*, ed. Teófanes Egido et al., 1:121–36 (Salamanca, Spain: Universidad de Salamanca, 1983), 123–27.

In a society in which few people were literate and could afford books, women were even less likely to be taught to read, much less have access to real learning, even in families of financial means and social status. The boarding school for young women at the Augustinian convent of Santa María de Gracia in Ávila to which the young Teresa was briefly sent provided all of the education to which a young woman of her social class might normally aspire: some basic reading, catechesis, and the skills to maintain a home. It was unusual that Teresa's father had made it a point to have his daughters taught to read, that he himself maintained a library, and that Teresa's mother encouraged her in reading. Teresa of Jesus, the reformer, would later seek this for all of her nuns (Con 6.1).

Contemporary treatises on the proper virtues of women encouraged both men and women to think of women as less capable to function in the world of leadership, finance, and learning. Often referring to women by such diminutive terms such as *mujercillas* or *mujercitas* (little women), such texts perpetuated the idea that women were intellectually and emotionally much like children, best kept to home or cloister under the benign supervision and guidance of supposedly more intellectually gifted and emotionally stable men. While such diminutives might be used in a more positive sense to describe a truly humble, virtuous woman, increasingly they implied the prejudged silliness, innate ignorance, and even presumption of the women of the time.[2] The mature Teresa's leadership in the reform and her financial astuteness in the work of founding monasteries across Spain stands out all the more in this context of devaluing women and their gifts.

---

2. Ahlgren, *Teresa of Avila*, 8; Alison Weber, *Teresa of Avila and the Rhetoric of Femininity* (Princeton, N.J.: Princeton University Press, 1990), 32–33.

In regard to prayer, the prevailing view was that women lacked the inherent intellectual focus for real meditation. Their emotional nature directed them more properly to the life of devotion.[3] The same culture that largely denied women access to real theological learning also judged that the practice of deeper forms of prayer would be dangerous to them and those they might presume teach, since they would be more easily confused and led into serious error. This view seemed amply confirmed in the well-known cases of women in early sixteenth-century Spain who were accused of being deluded or false mystics after reports of ecstasies and visions. This fact caused Teresa serious concern in regard to her own experience as her mystical journey first began to unfold (L 23.2). In this context, it is all the more noteworthy that the early advocates of the prayer of recollection—while holding many of their culture's prejudices against women—were encouraging both women and men to embrace this path to still deeper prayer. Teresa herself would later laugh at the idea that women were not suited to such prayer and even went so far as to suggest that they were in fact more suited to it than men (L 40.8).

The few women who did come to be recognized as true mystics of this period by their confessors and others were often thought of as having miraculously circumvented or "overcome" their gender. God had somehow made these women "manly." In her beatification and canonization processes, Teresa was frequently and positively referred to as possessing "manly" qualities. One of Teresa's confessors, during her canonization process, responded to the question "What do you think of Teresa of Jesus?" by saying, "Oh, you fooled me by saying that she was a woman; by faith she isn't, but rather a masculine man and of

---

3. Cammarata, "El discurso femenino," 63.

the most manly [bearded]."[4] In fact, Teresa herself urged her nuns to be "manly" (IC 2.1.6). In *The Way of Perfection*, she cautioned the nuns against referring to one another by what she considered to be silly feminine terms such as "my life," "my soul," "my only good." "They are," she concludes, "very womanish, and I would not want you, my daughters, to be womanish in anything, nor would I want you to be like women but like strong men. For if you do what lies in your power, the Lord will make you so strong that you will astonish men" (W 7.8). In a letter to one of her prioresses, she says, "You and the other nuns are more obliged to behave as valiant men and not as worthless little women" (Ltr 451.9).

Still, Teresa would have known several examples of strong and saintly women, recognized as such by the broader society (though perhaps also viewed as either "manly" or specially gifted by God).[5] Queen Isabella (d. 1504) was already esteemed as a strong, determined leader as well as a devout and loving spouse and mother. In Ávila, Jimena Blázquez was a legendary figure who was said to have successfully defended the city against Muslim attack while the men of the city were away—by organizing their wives and daughters to dress as warriors and parade on the city walls. The *beata* Maridíaz was a contemporary of Teresa who was renowned for holiness in the city of Ávila, and to whom many came for counsel and prayers. Teresa met her through

---

4. Quoted in Gillian T. W. Ahlgren, "Negotiating Sanctity: Holy Women in Sixteenth-Century Spain," *Church History* 64, no. 3 (September 1995), 381.

5. Bernard McGinn provides an overview of the phenomena of *beatas* and widely known women visionaries in the time immediately prior to Teresa's public life. See McGinn, *Mysticism*, 12–24. See also Tomás Álvarez, "Santa Teresa: Perfil histórico e itinerario espiritual," in *Estudios Teresianos I: Biografía e historia* (Burgos, Spain: Editorial Monte Carmelo, 1995), 26.

her friend and benefactor Doña Guiomar de Ulloa. Teresa also mentions María de Jesús, who independently founded a Carmel a year after the foundation of St. Joseph's and who convinced Teresa of the need to establish her monasteries without a fixed income from lands and endowments (L 35). Teresa also mentions the eccentric Catalina de Cardona, from a noble family, but who famously embraced a rigorous ascetical and eremitical life (F 28). In fact, Spanish historians of the period have identified as many as thirty women of the time who were writers and humanists (though probably not widely recognized even in that time).[6]

At the beginning of the sixteenth century, there were some voices among the new Christian humanists such as Erasmus who began to reject this negative view of women. Women, it was argued, were not inherently intellectually inferior and thus should be taught to read and allowed access to real learning about the faith and Sacred Scripture.[7] In fact, it was among the heretical Alumbrados—in which the writings of Erasmus were most influential through their studies at the new university of Alcalá—that women gained prominent leadership roles, taught, and even preached. And herein lies a problem for Teresa of Jesus. The Inquisition found that many women (and conversos) played a central role in what they judged to be false mysticism and heretical doctrine. Perhaps it was inevitable that this was the lens through which many would at least initially come to view Teresa: the conversa woman who presumed to suggest that she had authentic mystical experience and could teach a path to deeper prayer to other women (and to men!). Her critics were quick to recall that St. Paul had taught that women should

---

6. Álvarez, *Cultura de mujer en el siglo XVI*, 8–10.
7. Weber, *Teresa of Avila*, 20–21.

remain silent in church and be content to learn from their husbands (1 Cor 14:33–36; see also 1 Tim 3:11).[8] Nonetheless, Teresa firmly believed that her writing and teaching was a mission conferred on her by God.[9]

As we saw earlier, Teresa lived and wrote within a larger tension in the spirituality of the time, between those with academic theological learning with its concepts and vocabulary (*letrados*) and those who believed they had deeper spiritual experience that gave them a deeper knowledge of God and the divine ways (*experimentados*).[10] The two need not always be in conflict. John of the Cross was both, and Teresa was adamant about the need to seek out the learned. But Teresa, like other women of the time, lacked the academic training and vocabulary to explain their experiences and aspirations in a way that could seem entirely beyond suspicion to those with a focus on careful scholastic, academic terms and distinctions. Many women of the time got into trouble, but Teresa was both shrewd and humble enough to remain in dialogue with her more academically learned confessors, counselors, and friends.

The misogyny of the culture of sixteenth-century Spain becomes perhaps most evident and focused in regard to Teresa in the controversy surrounding the posthumous publication of her works.[11] Although there were prominent supporters—notably the famed Augustinian Luis de Leon who was chosen to collect

---

8. Weber, 22–28. Teresa mentions this Pauline teaching (W 15.6). But elsewhere she tells us that God told her that scriptural passages from St. Paul must be read in the context of other scriptural texts (ST 15).

9. Egido, "Ambiente histórico," 127.

10. Ahlgren, "Negotiating Sanctity," 376–77.

11. See, especially, Ahlgren, *Teresa of Avila*, 114–43; and Weber, *Teresa of Avila*, 158–65.

and edit her works—even these men often noted the exceptional nature of the woman who was their author. Again, it was supposedly her "manly" qualities that made it possible, together with a special intervention by God, for a woman to experience and then to teach such doctrine. The opponents were adamant, however, focusing on the inappropriateness of publishing the works of a woman, especially on such sublime and delicate topics. The Dominican Alonso de la Fuente argued that it was positively against the nature (*praeter naturam*) of women and beyond their capacity to be able to rise to such a task![12]

Teresa's Seemingly Ambiguous Response

Teresa's response to the prevailing view of women in her society appears ambiguous or at least complex. On one hand, it might appear that Teresa simply and fully embraced the prevailing view of women in the society of her time. She regularly speaks of her own unworthiness, her lack of learning, and her wretched state (she refers to herself as *ruin* about thirty times in the *Life* alone). She refers to herself and her nuns in the diminutive form as a *mujercillas* (L 28.18; F 2.4, 15.11, 28.18; Ltr 107, 249.2) and *mujercitas* (L 11.14, 36.19; F 4.5, 12.10). She cautions her confessor not to make known the part of the *Life* that deals with mystical experiences especially because they are written and experienced by a woman—and a wretched one at that (L 10.8). She acknowledges that women, because of their greater weakness (F 4.2), are especially quick to believe they are experiencing

---

12. Elias Rivers, "The Vernacular Mind of St. Teresa," in *Centenary of St. Teresa*, ed. John Sullivan, 113–29, vol. 3 of *Carmelite Studies* (Washington, D.C.: ICS Publications, 1984), 114.

genuinely mystical ecstasies (IC 6.42, 4.3.11; F 8.6) and more susceptible to the deceptions of the devil (L 23.13). "But everything," she warns, "can be harmful to those as weak as we women are" (W Prol 3). Perhaps with a touch of irony, she urges the Carmelite general to be patient: "And even though we women are not good for giving counsel, we sometimes hit the mark" (Ltr 102.8).

As we will see, a number of authors today understand such remarks as part of Teresa's rhetorical strategy. In any case, and on the other hand, she offers instances of bold defense of women in the face of contemporary stereotypes and prejudices. She bemoans the sad state of many married women subjected to their husbands at great cost to themselves. Even women of high social status, she says, can feel unable to tell their husbands that they are seriously ill or heavily burdened in other ways simply for fear of annoying them (W 11.3). She urges her nuns to see their good fortune in being called by God to the religious life in which they could be free of such subordination: "They say that for a woman to be a good wife toward her husband she must be sad when he is sad, and joyful when he is joyful, even though she may not be so. (See what subjection you have been freed from, sisters!)" (W 26.4). The nuns should see "the great favor God has granted them in choosing them for Himself and freeing them from being subject to a man who is often the death of them and who could also be, God forbid, the death of their souls" (F 31.46).

It is in sections of the original text of *The Way of Perfection* in which Teresa speaks most emphatically in defense of women embracing the path of recollection and deepening prayer. She scoffs at the typical objections raised (by men) in regard to encouraging women to embrace the prayer of recollection and the path to still deeper prayer: "It's not for women, for they will be susceptible to illusions'; 'it's better they stick to their sewing'; 'they don't need these delicacies'; 'the Our Father and the Hail Mary are sufficient'" (W 21.2). And she goes on then to teach the path to mystical prayer precisely by offering a commentary on the Our Father. Sadly, many of these bolder statements were edited out at the urging of her first censors who considered them too dangerous for publication (though they are now restored in contemporary editions of her works). After noting in the censored text that Jesus did not despise women while he walked on earth, Teresa went on to offer the following bold statement:

> And You found as much love and more faith in them than You did in men. Among them was Your most blessed Mother, and through her merits—and because we wear her habit—we merit what, because of our offenses, we do not deserve. Is it not enough, Lord, that the world has intimidated us . . . so that we may not do anything worthwhile for You in public or dare speak some truths that we lament over in secret, without Your also failing to hear so just a petition? I do not believe, Lord, that this could be true of Your goodness and justice, for You are a just judge and not like those of the world. Since the world's judges are sons of Adam and all of them men, there is no virtue in women that they do not hold suspect. Yes, indeed, the day will come, my King, when everyone will be known for what he is. I do not speak for myself, because the world already knows my wickedness—and I have rejoiced that this wickedness is known publicly—but because I see that these are times in which it would be wrong to undervalue virtuous and strong souls, even though they are women. (W 3.7)

More strongly still, Teresa states her belief that it is women who are more disposed toward and more frequently found on the path of mystical prayer: "There are many more women than men to whom the Lord grants these favors. This I heard from the saintly Friar Peter of Alcántara—and I too have observed it—who said that women make much more progress along this path than men do. He gave excellent reasons for this, all in favor of women; but there's no need to mention them here" (L 40.8).

Teresa's "Rhetorical Strategy"

Contemporary feminist authors—most notably Alison Weber and Gillian Ahlgren—have argued that Teresa of Jesus consciously and shrewdly employed "rhetorical strategies" in her writing as a defense against criticism and to avert dire action by the Inquisition.[13] She was, after all, a woman writing about mystical experiences, recommending a spiritual path, dialoguing with and even advising learned men, and effectively leading a reform movement. These were bold moves for a woman of that time and culture—sure not only to raise eyebrows but even to invite critical scrutiny and even formal investigation by the Inquisition. In order to defend herself and to "fly under the radar," it is argued that Teresa regularly used the language of humility, female subordination, and obedience as a kind of cover or diversion. Her writing style was, it is said, decidedly colloquial and conversational in order to convey a message that she, an "unlearned" woman, was not presuming to teach spiritual doctrine. She protested that she wrote only out of obedience to her confessors, rather than presumptuously choosing on her own to take up the pen. She claimed that she was writing for her cloistered nuns, not for a wider audience. She uses diminutive terms in reference to herself, acknowledges regularly her lack of

---

13. Weber, *Teresa of Ávila*; Ahlgren, *Teresa of Ávila*.

learning, and frequently begins explanations of key points with the equivalent of "it seems to me." She explicitly and prominently expressed the submission of her writings to the authority of the church. With all of these devices, it is believed Teresa was able consciously to avoid the fate of many of her contemporaries, men and women, who ended up facing the Inquisition, being arrested and imprisoned, or having their works placed on the Index of Prohibited Books.

Both Weber and Ahlgren highlight grave dangers facing Teresa as a mystic, a writer, and a reformer in the context of her times. Weber concludes that Teresa's situation was "so precarious" that she was forced to take on such defensive rhetorical strategies.[14] For Ahlgren, Teresa was engaged in a "quest" or "struggle" for survival.[15] Her interactions with the Inquisition were, Ahlgren believes, "the most significant influence in her career as a writer."[16] Because of the threat posed by the Inquisition and of other potential and real critics, for Teresa, "remaining a 'daughter of the church' [Teresa's deathbed affirmation] was perhaps the single most difficult thing Teresa accomplished."[17] The last is a very strong claim.

There is no doubt that Teresa of Jesus was a shrewd (in the best sense of the word), prudent, and insightful person. She was quite aware of the prevailing view of women in her society, the presence of the Inquisition, the prominent women mystics and Alumbrados who had fallen afoul of the inquisitors, and the immediate skepticism and even hostility that her writing might provoke. That she would craft her writing to the reality of this

---

14. Weber, *Teresa of Avila*, 50.
15. Ahlgren, *Teresa of Avila*, 4, 33.
16. Ahlgren, 33.
17. Ahlgren, 1.

situation would be no surprise. Time after time, she was able to convince wary and suspicious prelates and professors to come around to her way of thinking. She was a master and convincing communicator. Bárbara Mujica points out that Teresa uses the self-deprecating style in her letters addressed to aristocracy and to potential benefactors, but it is lacking in her other correspondence, confirming its use as a chosen strategy.[18] But perhaps Teresa's sense of being in a precarious situation and the suggestion that all or many of the characteristics of her writing mentioned above were mostly a chosen strategy are overstated.[19]

The active presence of the Inquisition was certainly a cause for concern—as many of Teresa's supporters cautioned her. But she tells us in the *Life* that, at least in one instance, her response to a particular warning was, "This amused me and made me laugh, for I never had any fear of such a possibility" (L 33.5). Surely, to some degree, we must take her at her word. In the last chapter, we looked at Teresa's encounters with the Inquisition. Based on that discussion, it may be that, while cautious, she did not view herself in a "struggle for survival" or in a "precarious" situation. Her lack of deep concern—which, again, is not to say she was without prudence or caution—was also (as we shall see) attested in reports of those who knew her. Teresa had friends within the Inquisition and in the upper echelons of church and society. She was in constant dialogue with learned theologians, as she attests in one of her spiritual testimonies (written, it seems, for the Seville tribunal of the Inquisition in 1576) in which she mentions many of her learned counselors by name (ST 58).

---

18. Mujica, *Teresa de Ávila*, 66–67.

19. Elena Carrera, *Teresa of Avila's Autobiography: Authority, Power and the Self in Mid-Sixteenth Century Spain* (London: Legenda/Modern Humanities Research Association and Maney Publishing, 2005), 7.

But most importantly, as we have said, by the time Teresa wrote the *Life*, she was already very advanced in her mystical journey. Her later, and more significant, encounters with the Inquisition occurred after she had attained the spiritual marriage. This surely would have given her an inner freedom—not immune from mundane concerns and ordinary emotions (as her letters show) but free of an abiding and life-directing fear of anything around her.[20] Immersed in the realities of her time, Teresa of Jesus was, at the same time, a woman who was profoundly free and thus unimpeded in any serious way from expressing her feelings and her personal experience of prayer.[21]

Mujica, while acknowledging Teresa's use of some of the rhetorical strategies described above, challenges us not to interpret Teresa's expressions of humility as a ploy or mere subterfuge. Humility is a time-honored virtue in the Christian tradition (even if today we must more clearly distinguish it from passivity and the uncritical acceptance of injustice and subordination). Most importantly, it was a virtue extolled by all of the spiritual literature that formed Teresa—notably the Franciscans who were the principal promoters of the prayer of recollection and the Jesuits among whom were Teresa's principal confessors.[22] Teresa does not just demonstrate her own humility; in *The Way of Perfection*, she teaches that it is one of the three essential virtues without which deep prayer simply cannot be attained. Throughout her writings, self-knowledge is seen to be critical, as both a knowledge of the profound beauty of the human created in the image of God and a constant awareness of how we have marred this image by sin.

---

20. Dobhan, "Teresa de Jesús," 1:127–35.
21. Maroto, *Teresa en oración*, 105–8.
22. Mujica, *Teresa de Ávila*, 56–57.

Self-knowledge was thus intimately related to an attitude of genuine humility. In fact, Teresa's humility—by which she placed herself and her plans into the hands of God—made her bold and confident. She could better trust God to accomplish everything according to the divine will.

Juan Antonio Marcos in a recent study of Teresa's rhetorical strategies—aware of the work of Ahlgren and Weber—argues that these strategies were not primarily "strategies for survival" but rather strategies to convince.[23] Facing a readership likely to be suspicious and even hostile, this master at bringing people around to her way of thinking engaged at least some of the characteristics mentioned above in a conscious way to disarm and persuade.

At the same time, as well read and bright as she was, the truth is that Teresa lacked the advanced education to write in an academic way and even to think in many of the complex Scholastic categories. She probably did write in a colloquial style in order to disarm and draw in her readers, but it was a style that was an expression of her personality. Further, contemporary Spanish humanists were advocating a more colloquial style rather than writing in an "affected way."[24] Even today, people are drawn to the evident humanity and warmth of Teresa's style.

Teresa of Jesus was an extraordinary person. But she was human and thus inevitably a person of her time and formed—and thus limited, to some degree—by the culture around her. That she would have internalized some of the cultural prejudices about women would be unavoidable. Certainly, she could not avoid being formed by the spirituality of the time and its

---

23. Juan Antonio Marcos, *Mística y subversiva: Teresa de Jesús. Las estrategias retóricas del discurso místico* (Madrid: Editorial de Espiritualidad, 2001).

24. Tyler, *Teresa of Avila*, 25–26.

principal themes. She was a woman specially gifted by God with the deepest of prayer and was wise enough to avoid the error of other mystics who had failed to test their spiritual experience against the theological learning provided by others. She was too shrewd to miss how others had gone astray.

But extraordinary, Teresa was. She saw the false prejudices and unjust discrimination against the women of her time. She herself felt their constraints. And she knew how to live, to teach, to write, and to lead even in that context. And she knew how to charm and to persuade, even those who had been merely curious or intrigued, suspicious, or even doubtful. Ultimately, she was a woman who had deep experiences of God and possessed the God-given ability to teach, and she found the most effective ways to communicate what she wanted to those who were at least open to hear.

Mujica raises the question, "Was Teresa of Ávila a Feminist?" At the conclusion of a study of the question, she writes,

> I would say this: Teresa was a product of her times and undoubtedly believed women were flawed in some areas, but she turned women's supposed imperfections into a defense of their special spiritual aptitude. Furthermore, as a reformer who saw women as whole beings with spiritual needs, a foe of abusive convent confessors, a promoter of women's education, a model of leadership who provided women with the tools and experience they needed to achieve administrative excellence, Teresa was most certainly a champion of her sex—a true feminist.[25]

---

25. Bárbara Mujica, "Was Teresa of Ávila a Feminist?" in *Approaches to Teaching Teresa of Ávila and the Spanish Mystics*, ed. Alison Weber, 74–82, Approaches to Teaching World Literature series (New York.: Modern Language Association of America, 2009), 81.

SELECT BIBLIOGRAPHY

English

Ahlgren, Gillian T. W. "Negotiating Sanctity: Holy Women in Sixteenth-Century Spain." *Church History* 64, no. 3 (September 1995): 373–88.

———. *Teresa of Avila and the Politics of Sanctity*. Ithaca, N.Y.: Cornell University Press, 1996.

Carrera, Elena. *Teresa of Avila's Autobiography: Authority, Power and the Self in Mid-Sixteenth Century Spain*. London: Legenda/Modern Humanities Research Association and Maney Publishing, 2005.

Lehfeldt, Elizabeth A. *Religious Women in Golden Age Spain: The Permeable Cloister*. Aldershot, England: Ashgate, 2005.

Mujica, Bárbara. *Teresa de Ávila: Lettered Woman*. Nashville.: Vanderbilt University Press, 2009.

———. "Was Teresa of Ávila a Feminist?" In *Approaches to Teaching Teresa of Ávila and the Spanish Mystics*, edited by Alison Weber, 74–82. Approaches to Teaching World Literature series. New York: Modern Language Association of America, 2009.

Slade, Carole. "St. Teresa of Avila as a Social Reformer." In *Mysticism and Social Transformation*, edited by Janet K. Ruffing, 91–103. Syracuse, N.Y.: Syracuse University Press, 2001.

Weber, Alison. *Teresa of Avila and the Rhetoric of Femininity*. Princeton, N.J.: Princeton University Press, 1990.

Spanish

Cammarata, Joan. "El discurso femenino de Santa Teresa de Ávila, defensora de la mujer renacentista." In *Actas Irvine* 92, 58–65. Asociación Internacional de Hispanistas. Irvine: University of California Irvine, 1994.

Dobhan, Ulrich. "Teresa de Jesús y la emancipación de la mujer." In *Congreso Internacional Teresiano (4–7 octubre, 1982)*, edited by Teófanes Egido et al., 121–36. Vol. 1. Salamanca, Spain: Universidad de Salamanca, 1983.

Marcos, Juan Antonio. *Mística y subversiva: Teresa de Jesús. Las estrategias retóricas del discurso místico*. Madrid: Editorial de Espiritualidad, 2001.

Vigil, Mariló. *La vida de las mujeres en los siglos XVI y XVI*. Madrid: Siglo Veintiuno Editores, 1986.

CONCLUSION

Each human person *has* a history—the culmination of what they have done and what has been done to them over the years of their lives. In some form, each event has contributed, for good or ill, to the formation of the person that we are in the present moment. Each person *has* a history . . . *and* every human being exists *within* a history—not only the unfolding of world events, societies, and cultures in general but also the often random and countless happenings and interactions that ultimately have their effect on us and form us as the unique persons we are. And so, we can also say that each person *is* a history, the distinctive convergence of their own acts and interactions, together with the larger world unfolding around them.

Great Christian mystics, like Teresa of Jesus and John of the Cross, are not less human, even for all their extraordinary experiences, encounters with God, spiritual wisdom, and sage guidance. In fact, the great Christian mystics, like Teresa and John, are arguably more human. In their communion with God, they become more of what all of us are meant to be as human beings, while the rest of us, in varying degrees and ways, remain marred by sin and thus less than what we are meant to be and to become.

John of the Cross and Teresa of Jesus, Doctors of the Church and mystical writers, were—for all their greatness—flesh and blood. They had a history; they were immersed in a history; and they were key actors in the subsequent unfolding of the history of the church and of Christian spirituality. For those who have read their works and have felt the power of their spiritual wisdom, they are now part of the personal histories of their readers and followers.

We do John and Teresa a disservice—and more, we fail to understand them and their wisdom as we might—if we fail to see them in the context in which they lived, encountered God, and wrote. It is true that, in so many ways, they stood apart from their contemporaries and their predecessors. But they were inescapably formed by them, shaped by their interaction with them, and able to profoundly affect others precisely because they spoke the same language, with the same vocabulary and concepts, and shared a history with them.

In this book, we have examined the context of Teresa and John's lives and writings from a number of different perspectives: historical, social and cultural, economic, spiritual, and ecclesiastical. So much more could be said about each of the topics addressed, and other lenses applied. But it is my hope that the reader has gained a better sense of the context in which Teresa and John lived and wrote. The footnote and bibliographical references have attempted to point to further and more detailed reading.

John of the Cross and Teresa of Jesus can be profitably read and reread over and over again. This is one of the things that make their writings truly classics. With a deeper or broader knowledge of their world, I encourage the reader to take up their works again—both to gain new insights and to ask new questions. With each rereading, their wisdom can become clearer to us and their guidance more profitable. And it will become more evident why they are considered true masters and sure guides in the spiritual path—not because they were somehow angelic but rather precisely in their flesh-and-blood humanity. Teresa of Ávila and John of the Cross were a woman and a man of their particular world, and it is only with that distinctive context in mind that we can gain a fuller and more authentic understanding and appreciation of their lives, their works, and their achievements.

GENERAL BIBLIOGRAPHY

English

Ahlgren, Gillian T. W. *Enkindling Love: The Legacy of Teresa of Avila and John of the Cross*. Mapping the Tradition. Minneapolis: Fortress Press, 2016.

———. "Negotiating Sanctity: Holy Women in Sixteenth-Century Spain." *Church History* 64, no. 3 (September 1995): 373–88.

———. *Teresa of Avila and the Politics of Sanctity*. Ithaca, N.Y.: Cornell University Press, 1996.

Álvarez, Tomás. *St. Teresa of Avila: 100 Themes on Her Life and Work*. Translated by Kieran Kavanaugh. Washington, D.C.: ICS Publications, 2011.

Barden, William, "St. Teresa and the Dominicans." In *St. Teresa of Avila: Studies in Her Life, Doctrine, and Times*, edited by Fr. Thomas and Fr. Gabriel, 206–21. Westminster, Md.: Newman Press, 1963.

A Benedictine of Stanbrook Abbey. *Medieval Mystical Tradition and Saint John of the Cross*. Westminster, Md.: Newman Press, 1954.

Bilinkoff, Jodi. *The Avila of Saint Teresa: Religious Reform in a Sixteenth Century City*. Ithaca, N.Y.: Cornell University Press, 1989.

———. "St. Teresa of Avila and the Avila of St. Teresa." In *Centenary of St. Teresa*, edited by John Sullivan, 53–68. Vol. 3 of *Carmelite Studies*. Washington, D.C.: ICS Publications, 1984.

———. "Teresa of Jesus and the Carmelite Reform." In *Religious Orders of the Catholic Reformation: Essays in Honor of John C. Olin on His Seventy-Fifth Birthday*, edited by Richard L. De Molen, 165–86. New York: Fordham University Press, 1994.

Bodenstedt, Mary Immaculate. "The 'Vita Christi' of Ludolphus the Carthusian." PhD diss., Catholic University of America Press, 1944.

Brodrick, James. "St. Teresa and the Jesuits." In *St. Teresa of Avila: Studies in Her Life, Doctrine, and Times*, edited by Fr. Thomas and Fr. Gabriel, 222–35. Westminster, Md.: Newman Press, 1963.

Carrera, Elena. *Teresa of Avila's Autobiography: Authority, Power and the Self in Mid-Sixteenth Century Spain*. London: Legenda/Modern Humanities Research Association and Maney Publishing, 2005.

Childers, William. "Spanish Mysticism and the Islamic Tradition." In *Approaches to Teaching Teresa of Ávila and the Spanish Mystics*, edited by Alison Weber, 57–66. Approaches to Teaching World Literature series. New York.: Modern Language Association of America, 2009.

Chorpenning, Joseph. "St. Teresa's Presentation of Her Religious Experience." In *Centenary of St. Teresa*, edited by John Sullivan, 152–88. Vol. 3 of *Carmelite Studies*. Washington, D.C.: ICS Publications, 1984.

Edwards, John. *The Spain of the Catholic Monarchs, 1474–1520*. Oxford: Blackwell, 2000.

Egan, Keith J. "The Spirituality of the Carmelites." In *High Middle Ages and Reformation*, edited by Jill Raitt with Bernard McGinn and John Meyendorff, 50–62. Vol. 2 of *Christian Spirituality*. New York: Crossroad, 1989.

Egido, Teófanes. "The Economic Concerns of Madre Teresa." In *Carmelite Studies IV: Edith Stein Symposium, Teresian Culture*, edited by John Sullivan, translated by Michael Dodd and Steven Payne, 151–72. Washington, D.C.: ICS Publications, 1987.

———. "The Historical Setting of St. Teresa's Life." In *Spiritual Direction*, edited by John Sullivan, translated by Michael Dodd and Steven Payne, 122–82. Vol. 1 of *Carmelite Studies*. Washington, D.C.: ICS Publications, 1980.

Friedman, Elias. *The Latin Hermits of Mount Carmel: A Study of Carmelite Origins*. Rome: Institutum Historicum Teresianum, 1979.

Garrido, Pablo María. *St. Teresa, St. John of the Cross, and the Spanish Carmelites*. Translated by Joseph Chalmers. Darien, Ill.: Carmelite Media, 2015.

Haliczer, Stephen. *Between Exaltation and Infamy: Female Mystics in the Golden Age of Spain*. New York: Oxford University Press, 2002.

———. *Inquisition and Society in the Kingdom of Valencia, 1478–1834.* Berkeley: University of California Press, 1990.

Hamilton, Alistair. *Heresy and Mysticism in Sixteenth-Century Spain: The Alumbrados.* Cambridge: James Clarke and Co., 1992.

Kamen, Henry. *The Spanish Inquisition: A Historical Revision.* 4th ed. New Haven, Conn.: Yale University Press, 2014 (first edition, 1965).

Kavanaugh, Kieran. "Faith and the Experience of God in the University Town of Baeza." In *John of the Cross*, edited by Steven Payne, 48–64. Vol. 6 of *Carmelite Studies.* Washington, D.C.: ICS Publications, 1992.

———. "Spanish Sixteenth Century: Carmel and Surrounding Movements." In *Christian Spirituality*, 69–92, esp. 72–74. Vol. 3 of *High Middle Ages and Reformation*, edited by Louis Dupré and Don E. Saliers with John Meyendorff. Vol. 18 of *World Spirituality: An Encyclopedic History of the Religious Quest.* New York: Crossroad, 1991.

Lehfeldt, Elizabeth A. *Religious Women in Golden Age Spain: The Permeable Cloister.* Aldershot, England: Ashgate, 2005.

Lovett, A. W. *Early Habsburg Spain, 1517–1598.* Oxford: Oxford University Press, 1986.

McGaha, Michael. "Teresa of Ávila and the Question of Jewish Influence." In *Approaches to Teaching Teresa of Ávila and the Spanish Mystics*, edited by Alison Weber, 67–73. Approaches to Teaching World Literature series. New York: Modern Language Association of America, 2009.

McGinn, Bernard. *Mysticism in the Golden Age of Spain (1500–1650).* Vol. 6, part 2 of *The Presence of God: A History of Western Christian Mysticism.* New York: Herder and Herder, 2017.

———. "The Role of the Carmelites in the History of Western Mysticism." In *Carmel and Contemplation: Transforming Human Consciousness*, edited by Kevin Culligan and Regis Jordan, 25–50. Vol. 8 of *Carmelite Studies.* Washington, D.C.: ICS Publications, 2000.

McGreal, Wilfrid. *The Fountain of Elijah: The Carmelite Tradition.* Traditions of Christian Spirituality. Series edited by Philip Sheldrake. London: Darton, Longman and Todd, 1999.

Mujica, Bárbara. *Teresa de Ávila: Lettered Woman.* Nashville, Tenn.: Vanderbilt University Press, 2009.

———. "Was Teresa of Ávila a Feminist?" In *Approaches to Teaching Teresa of Ávila and the Spanish Mystics*, edited by Alison Weber, 74–82. Approaches to Teaching World Literature series. New York: Modern Language Association of America, 2009.

Mulhall, Michael, ed. *Albert's Way: The First North American Congress on the Carmelite Rule.* Barrington, Ill.: Province of the Most Pure Heart of Mary, 1989.

Mullins, Patrick. *St. Albert of Jerusalem and the Roots of Carmelite Spirituality.* Volume 34 of Institutum Carmelitanum, *Textus et Studia Historical Carmelitana.* Rome: Edizioni Carmelitane, 2012.

Netanyahu, Benzion. *The Origins of the Inquisition in Fifteenth Century Spain.* New York: Random House, 1995.

O'Reilly, Terence, and Colin P. Thompson and Lesley Twomey, eds. *St. Teresa of Ávila: Her Writings and Life.* Studies in Hispanic and Lusophone Cultures, 19. Cambridge: Legenda (Modern Humanities Research Association), 2018.

Payne, Stanley G. *Spanish Catholicism: An Historical Overview.* Madison, Wisc.: University of Wisconsin Press, 1984.

Payne, Steven. *The Carmelite Tradition.* Spirituality in History series. Series edited by Phyllis Zagano. Collegeville, Minn.: Liturgical Press, 2011.

Peers, E. Allison. *The Mystics of Spain.* 1951. Reprint, Maneola, N.Y.: Dover, 2002.

———. *Studies of the Spanish Mystics.* 2 vols. London: Sheldon Press, 1927, 1930.

Pérez, Joseph. *The Spanish Inquisition: A History.* Translated by Janet Lloyd. New Haven, Conn.: Yale University Press, 2005.

Quitslund, Sonya A. "Elements of a Feminist Spirituality in St. Teresa." In *Centenary of St. Teresa*, edited by John Sullivan, 19–50. Vol. 3 of *Carmelite Studies.* Washington, D.C.: ICS Publications, 1984.

Rawlings, Helen. *Church, Religion, and Society in Early Modern Spain.* New York: Palgrave, 2002.

———. *The Spanish Inquisition.* Malden, Mass.: Blackwell, 2006.

Rivers, Elias. "The Vernacular Mind of St. Teresa." In *Centenary of St. Teresa*, edited by John Sullivan, 113–29. Vol. 3 of *Carmelite Studies*. Washington, D.C.: ICS Publications, 1984.

Rohrbach, Peter-Thomas. *Journey to Carith: The Story of the Carmelite Order*. 1966. Reprint, Washington, D.C.: ICS Publication, 2015.

Ruiz Salvador, Federico, ed. *God Speaks in the Night: The Life, Times, and Teaching of St. John of the Cross*. Translated by Kieran Kavanaugh. Washington, D.C.: ICS Publications, 1991.

Sauer, Michelle M. and Kevin J. Alban, eds. *Celebrating St. Albert and His Rule: Rules, Devotion, Orthodoxy and Dissent*. Volume 44 of Institutum Carmelitanum, *Textus et Studia Historica Carmelitana*. Rome: Edizioni Carmelitane, 2017.

Slade, Carole. "St. Teresa of Avila as a Social Reformer." In *Mysticism and Social Transformation*, edited by Janet K. Ruffing, 91–103. Syracuse, N.Y.: Syracuse University Press, 2001.

Smet, Joachim. *The Carmelites: A History of the Brothers of Our Lady of Mount Carmel*. 4 vols. (in 5 bindings; vol. 3 has separate part 1 and part 2). Darien, Ill.: Carmelite Spiritual Center, 1976–1988.

———. *The Mirror of Carmel: A Brief History of the Carmelite Order*. Darien, Ill.: Carmelite Media, 2011. [This text is a "digest" of the preceding text.]

Surtz, Ronald. *Writing Women in Late Medieval and Early Modern Spain: The Mothers of Saint Teresa of Avila*. Philadelphia: University of Pennsylvania Press, 1995.

Swietlicki, Catherine. *Spanish Christian Cabala: The Works of Luis de León, Santa Teresa de Jesús, and San Juan de la Cruz*. Columbia, Mo.: University of Missouri Press, 1986.

Tyler, Peter. *The Return to the Mystical: Ludwig Wittgenstein, Teresa of Ávila, and the Christian Mystical Tradition*. New York: Continuum, 2011.

———. *Teresa of Avila: Doctor of the Soul*. New York: Continuum, 2014.

Weber, Alison, ed. *Approaches to Teaching Teresa of Ávila and the Spanish Mystics*. Approaches to Teaching World Literature series. New York: Modern Language Association of America, 2009.

———. *Teresa of Avila and the Rhetoric of Femininity*. Princeton, N.J.: Princeton University Press, 1990.

Welch, John. *The Carmelite Way: An Ancient Path for Today's Pilgrim*. Mahwah, N.J.: Paulist Press, 1996.

———. "To Renew a Tradition: The Reforms of Carmel." In *Carmel and Contemplation: Transforming Human Consciousness*, edited by Kevin Culligan and Regis Jordan, 3–23. Vol. 8 of *Carmelite Studies*. Washington, D.C.: ICS Publications, 2000.

Spanish

Álvarez, Tomás. *Cultura de mujer en el siglo XVI: El caso de Santa Teresa*. Burgos, Spain: Editorial Monte Carmelo, 2006.

———, ed. *Diccionario de Santa Teresa: Doctrina e historia*. 2nd ed. Burgos, Spain: Editorial Monte Carmelo, 2006.

———. *Estudios Teresianos I: Biografía e historia*. Burgos, Spain: Editorial Monte Carmelo, 1995.

———. *100 fichas sobre Teresa de Jesús*. Para Aprender y Enseñar. 2nd ed. Burgos, Spain: Editorial Monte Carmelo, 2010.

Álvarez Vázquez, José Antonio. *Trabajos, dineros, y negocios: Teresa de Jesús y la economía del siglo XVI (1562–1582)*. Madrid: Editorial Trotta, 2000.

Andrés Martín, Melquíades. "Erasmismo y tradición en las 'Cuentas de Conciencia.'" In *Perfil histórico de Santa Teresa*, edited by Teófanes Egido, 95–117. 3rd ed. Madrid: Editorial de Espiritualidad, 2012.

———. *Historia de la mística de la Edad de Oro en España y América*. Madrid: Biblioteca de Autores Cristianos, 1994.

———. *La teología española en el siglo XVI*. 2 vols. Madrid: Biblioteca de Autores Cristianos, 1976–1977.

———. *Los místicos de la Edad de Oro en España y América: Antología*. Madrid: Biblioteca de Autores Cristianos, 1996.

———. *Los recogidos: Nueva visión de la mística española (1500–1700)*. Madrid: Fundación Universitaria Española, 1975.

———. "Pensamiento teológico y vivencia religiosa en la reforma española (1400–1600)." In *La Iglesia en la España de los siglos XV y XVI*, edited by José Luis González Novalín, part 2, 269–361. Vol. 3 of

Historia de la Iglesia en España, edited by Ricardo García-Villoslada. Madrid: Biblioteca de Autores Cristianos, 1980.

———. "San Juan de la Cruz y los movimientos espirituales de su tiempo." In *Aspectos históricos de San Juan de la Cruz*, edited by Teófanes Egido, 99–115. Ávila, Spain: Institución Gran Duque de Alba de la Disputación Provincial de Ávila, 1990.

Avilés Fernández, Miguel. "San Juan de la Cruz y el erasmiso." In *Historia*, edited Teófanes Egido, 53–97. Vol. 2 of *Actas del Congreso Internaticional Sanjuanista*. Valladolid, Spain: Consejería de Cultura y Turismo de la Junta de Castilla y León, 1993.

Balbino, Marcos. "Literatura religiosa en el siglo de oro español." In *La Iglesia en la España de los siglos XV y XVI*, edited by José Luis González Novalín, part 2, 443–552. Vol. 3 of *Historia de la Iglesia en España*, edited by Ricardo García-Villoslada. Madrid: Biblioteca de Autores Cristianos, 1980.

Cammarata, Joan. "El discurso femenino de Santa Teresa de Ávila, defensora de la mujer renacentista." In *Actas Irvine* 92, 58–65. Asociación Internacional de Hispanistas. Irvine, Calif.: University of California Irvine, 1994.

Cancelo García, José Luis. *Santa Teresa y los Agustinos: El agustinismo de Santa Teresa y la defensa agustiniana del espíritu teresiano*. Burgos, Spain: Editorial Monte Carmelo, 2016.

Cátedra, María. *Un santo para una ciudad: ensayo de antropología urbana*. Barcelona, Spain: Editorial Ariel, 1997.

Chevalier, Maxime. *Lectura y lectores en la España de los siglos XVI y XVII*. Madrid: Ediciones Turner, 1976.

Diego, Sánchez, Manuel. *Bibliografía de San Juan de la Cruz*. Madrid: Editorial de Espiritualidad, 2000.

———. *Bibliografía de Santa Teresa de Jesús*. Madrid: Editorial de Espiritualidad, 2008.

Dobhan, Ulrich. "Teresa de Jesús y la emancipación de la mujer." In *Congreso Internacional Teresiano (4–7 octubre, 1982)*, edited by Teófanes Egido et al., 121–36. Vol. 1. Salamanca, Spain: Universidad de Salamanca, 1983.

Domínguez Ortiz, Antonio. "Las presuntas 'razones' de la Inquisición." In *Historia de la Inquisición en España y América*, edited by Joaquín Pérez Villanueva and Bartolomé Escandell Bonet, 58–82. Vol. 3. Madrid: Biblioteca de Autores Cristianos and Centro de Estudios Inquisitoriales, 2000.

Egido, Teófanes. "Ambiente histórico." In *Introducción a la lectura de Santa Teresa*, edited by Alberto Barrientos, 63–155. 2nd ed. Madrid: Editorial de Espiritualidad, 2002.

———. "Claves históricos para la comprensión de San Juan de la Cruz." In *Introducción a le lectura de San Juan de la Cruz*, edited by Salvador Ros García, 59–124. Salamanca, Spain: Junta de Castilla y León, Consejería de Cultura y Turismo, 1993.

———. *El linaje judeoconverso de Santa Teresa: Pleito de hidalguía de los Cepeda*. Madrid: Editorial de Espiritualidad, 1986.

———. "El tratamiento historiográfico de Santa Teresa: Inercias y revisiones." In *Perfil histórico de Santa Teresa*, edited by Teófanes Egido, 13–31. 3rd ed. Madrid: Editorial de Espiritualidad, 2012.

———. "La infancia de un santo del barocco." *San Juan de la Cruz* 47, no. 1 (2013–2014): 43–84.

———. "Los Yepes, una familia de pobres." In *Aspectos históricos de San Juan de la Cruz*, edited by Teófanes Egido, 25–41. Ávila, Spain: Institución Gran Duque de Alba de la Diputación Provincial de Ávila, 1990.

———. "Significado eclesial y social de la fundación del Monasterio de San José." In *Vivir en Ávila cuando Santa Teresa escribe el libro de su "Vida,"* edited by Rómulo Cuartas Lodoño and Francisco Javier Sancho Fermín, 169–207. Colección Claves. Burgos, Spain: Editorial Monte Carmelo, 2011.

Elizalde, Ignacio. "Teresa de Jesús y los Jesuitas." In *Teresa de Jesús: Estudios histórico-literarios*, 151–75. Rome: Teresianum, 1982.

Fernández Álvarez, Manuel. "El entorno social de Santa Teresa." In *Congreso Internacional Teresiano (4–7 octubre, 1982)*, edited by Teófanes Egido et al., 91–101. Vol. 1. Salamanca, Spain: Universidad de Salamanca, 1983.

García Cárcel, Ricardo. *La Inquisición*. Madrid: Anaya, 1991.

García Oro, José. "La vida monástica feminina en la España de Santa Teresa." In *Congreso Internacional Teresiano (4–7 octubre, 1982)*, edited by Teófanes Egido et al., 331–49. Vol. 1. Salamanca, Spain: Universidad de Salamanca, 1983.

———. "Observantes, recolectos, descalzos: La monarquía católica y el reformismo religioso del siglo XVI." In *Historia*, edited Teófanes Egido, 53–97. Vol. 2 of *Actas del Congreso Internaticional Sanjuanista*. Valladolid, Spain: Consejería de Cultura y Turismo de la Junta de Castilla y León, 1993.

———. "Reformas y Observancias: Crisis y renovación de la vida religiosa española durante el Renacimiento." In *Perfil histórico de Santa Teresa*, edited by Teófanes Egido, 33–55. 3rd ed. Madrid: Editorial de Espiritualidad, 2012.

Garrido, Pablo María. "El Carmelo español en tiempo de Santa Teresa." In *Congreso Internacional Teresiano (4–7 octubre, 1982)*, edited by Teófanes Egido et al., 407–29. Vol. 1. Salamanca, Spain: Universidad de Salamanca, 1983.

González y González, Nicolás. "El ambiente religioso del Monasterio de la Encarnación en los tiempos de Santa Teresa." In *Vivir en Ávila cuando Santa Teresa escribe el libro de su "Vida,"* edited by Rómulo Cuartas Lodoño and Francisco Javier Sancho Fermín, 135–68. Colección Claves. Burgos, Spain: Editorial Monte Carmelo, 2011.

———. *La ciudad de las Carmelitas en tiempos de Doña Teresa de Ahumada: Documentación histórica y gráfica del monasterio de la Encarnación de Ávila en el periodo de treinta años, en el que vivió santa Teresa de Jesús (1535–1562 y 1571–1574)*. Ávila, Spain: Institución Gran Duque de Alba de la Diputación Provincial de Ávila, 2011.

———. *Historia del monasterio de la Encarnación de Ávila*. Madrid: Editorial de Espiritualidad, 1995. This is the one-volume update of an earlier two-volume work: *El Monasterio de la Encarnación de Ávila*. 2 vols. Ávila, Spain: Obra Social y Cultural de la Caja Central de Ahorros y Prestamos de Ávila, 1976.

González Novalín, Jose Luis. "La Inquisición Española." In *La Iglesia en la España de los siglos XV y XVI*, edited by José Luis González Novalín, part

2, 107–268. Vol. 3 of *Historia de la Iglesia en España*, edited by Ricardo García-Villoslada. Madrid: Biblioteca de Autores Cristianos, 1980.

Gutierrez Nieto, Juan Ignacio. "El proceso de encastamiento social de la Castilla del siglo XVI. La respuesta conversa." In *Congreso Internacional Teresiano (4–7 octubre, 1982)*, edited by Teófanes Egido et al., 103–20. Vol. 1. Salamanca, Spain: Universidad de Salamanca, 1983.

Huerga, Alvaro. *Predicadores, alumbrados e inquisición en el siglo XVI*. Madrid: Fundación Universitaria Española, 1973.

———. *Temas y Personajes*. Vol. 5 of *Historia de los alumbrados (1570–1630)*. Madrid: Fundación universitaria española, 1994.

Inmaculada, Román de la. "El fenómeno de los alumbrados y su interpretación." *Ephemerides Carmeliticae* 10 (1958): 49–80.

Llamas Martínez, Enrique. *Santa Teresa de Jesús y la Inquisición Española*. Madrid: Consejo Superior de Investigaciones Científicas, Instituto "Francisco Suarez," 1972.

———. "Teresa de Jesús y los alumbrados: Hacia una revisión del 'alumbradismo' español." In *Congreso Internacional Teresiano (4–7 octubre, 1982)*, edited by Teófanes Egido et al., 137–67. Vol. 1. Salamanca, Spain: Universidad de Salamanca, 1983.

Marcano, Mercedes de Lara. "Hermanos de Santa Teresa de Jesús en el nuevo mundo." In *Santa Teresa y la literatura mística hispánica*. Actas del I congreso internacional sobre Santa Teresa y la mística hispánica, edited by Manuel Criado de Val, 245–51. Madrid: EDI-6, 1984.

Marcos, Juan Antonio. *Mística y subversiva: Teresa de Jesús. Las estrategias retóricas del discurso místico*. Madrid: Editorial de Espiritualidad, 2001.

Marcos Martín, Alberto. "San Juan de la Cruz y su ambiente de pobreza." In *Historia*, edited by Teófanes Egido, 143–84. Vol. 2 of *Actas del Congreso Internacional Sanjuanista*. Valladolid, Spain: Consejería de Cultura y Turismo de la Junta de Castilla y León, 1993.

Maroto, Daniel de Pablo. *Época del emperador Carlos V (1519–1558)*. Vol. 2 of *Espiritualidad Española del siglo XVI*. Madrid: Editorial de Espiritualidad, 2014.

———. *Lecturas y maestros de Santa Teresa*. Madrid: Editorial de Espiritualidad, 2009.

———. "Resonancias históricos del *Camino de Perfección*." In *Congreso Internacional Teresiano (4–7 octubre, 1982)*, edited by Teófanes Egido et al., 41–64. Vol. 1. Salamanca, Spain: Universidad de Salamanca, 1983.

———. *Santa Teresa de Jesús: Nueva biografía (escritora, fundadora, maestra)*. Madrid: Editorial de Espiritualidad, 2014.

———. "Santa Teresa y el protestantismo español." In *Perfil histórico de Santa Teresa*, 3rd ed., edited by Teófanes Egido,119–51. Madrid: Editorial de Espiritualidad, 2012.

———. *Ser y misión del Carmelo Teresiano: Historia de un carisma*. Madrid: Editorial de Espiritualidad, 2011.

———. *Teresa en oración: Historia-experiencia-doctrina*. Madrid: Editorial de Espiritualidad, 2004.

Márquez, Antonio. *Los alumbrados: Orígenes y filosofía, 1525–1559*. Madrid: Taurus, 1972.

[Montalva], Efrén de la Madre de Dios, and Otger Steggink. *Tiempo y vida de San Juan de la Cruz*. Madrid: Biblioteca de Autores Cristianos (BAC), 1992.

———. *Tiempo y vida de Santa Teresa*. 3rd ed. Madrid: Biblioteca de Autores Cristianos (BAC), 1996.

Pacho, Alberto. "Inquisición." In *Diccionario de Santa Teresa: Doctrina e historia*, edited by Tomás Álvarez, 942–48. 2nd ed. Burgos, Spain: Editorial Monte Carmelo, 2006.

Pacho, Eulogio. "Alumbrados y Juan de la Cruz." In *Diccionario de San Juan de la Cruz*, edited by Eulogio Pacho, 56–59. Burgos, Spain: Editorial Monte Carmelo, 2009.

———. *Apogeo de la mística cristiana: Historia de la espiritualidad clásica española 1450–1650*. Burgos, Spain: Editorial Monte Carmelo, 2008.

———. *Historia, textos, hermenéutica*. Vol. 1 of *Estudios sanjuanistas*. Burgos, Spain: Editorial Monte Carmelo, 1997.

Pérez, Joseph. "Cultura y sociedad en tiempos de Santa Teresa." In *Congreso Internacional Teresiano (4–7 octubre, 1982)*, edited by Teófanes Egido et al., 31–40. Vol. 1. Salamanca, Spain: Universidad de Salamanca, 1983.

———. "Mística y realidad histórica en la Castilla del siglo XVI." In *Vivir en Ávila cuando Santa Teresa escribe el libro de su "Vida,"* edited by Rómulo Cuartas Lodoño and Francisco Javier Sancho Fermín, 39–68. Burgos, Spain: Editorial Monte Carmelo, 2011.

———. *Teresa de Ávila y la España de su tiempo*. 3rd ed. Madrid: Editorial EDAF, 2015.

Pérez Villanueva, Joaquín, and Bartolomé Escandell Bonet, eds. *Historia de la Inquisición en España y América*. 3 vols. Madrid: Biblioteca de Autores Cristianos and Centro de Estudios Inquisitoriales, 1984, 1993, 2000.

Pinto Crespo, Virgilio. *Inquisición y control ideológico en la España del siglo XVI*. Madrid: Taurus Ediciones, 1983.

Rodríguez, Carmen. "Infraestructura del epistolario de Santa Teresa: Los correos del siglo XVI." In *Congreso Internacional Teresiano (4–7 octubre, 1982)*, edited by Teófanes Egido et al. 65–90. Vol. 1. Salamanca, Spain: Universidad de Salamanca, 1983.

Rodríguez, José Vicente, ed. *Aspectos históricos de San Juan de la Cruz*. Ávila, Spain: Institución Gran Duque de Alba de la Disputación Provincial de Ávila, 1990.

———. *100 fichas sobre San Juan de la Cruz: Para aprender y enseñar*. Burgos, Spain: Editorial Monte Carmelo, 2008.

———. *San Juan de la Cruz: La biografía*. Madrid: San Pablo, 2012.

Rodríguez-San Pedro Bezares, Luis Enrique. "La formación universitaria de San Juan de la Cruz." In *Historia*, edited Teófanes Egido, 220–49. Vol. 2 of *Actas del Congreso Internaticional Sanjuanista*. Valladolid, Spain: Consejería de Cultura y Turismo de la Junta de Castilla y León, 1993.

———. "Libros y lecturas para el hogar de don Alonso Sánchez de Cepeda." *Salmaticensis* 34 (1987), 169–88.

Ruiz de Pablos, Francisco. *Santa Teresa y la Inquisición: homenaje V centenario*. Ávila, Spain: Taller Gráficas E&D, 2014.

Ruiz Salvador, Federico. *Dios habla en la noche: Vida, palabra, ambiente de San Juan de la Cruz*. Madrid: Editorial de Espiritualidad, 1990.

Selke, Angela. "El iluminismo de los conversos y la Inquisición. Cristianismo interior de los alumbrados: Resentimiento y sublimación." In *La Inquisición española: Nueva visión. nuevos horizontes*, edited by Joaquín Pérez Villanueva, 617–36. Madrid: Siglo veintiuno, 1980.

Sobrino Chomón, Tomás. *San José de Ávila: historia de su fundación*. Ávila, Spain: Institución Gran Duque de Alba de la Diputación Provincial de Ávila, 1997.

Steggink, Otger. "Arraigo carmelitano de Santa Teresa de Jesús." In *The Land of Carmel: Essays in Honor of Joachim Smet, O.Carm*, edited by Paul Chandler and Keith J. Egan, 247–84. Rome: Institutum Carmelitanum, 1991.

———. "Dos corrientes de reforma en el Carmelo español del siglo XVI: La observancia y la descalcez, frente a la 'Reforma del rey.'" In *Aspectos históricos de San Juan de la Cruz*, edited by Teófanes Egido, 117–42. Ávila, Spain: Institución Gran Duque de Alba de la Diputación Provincial de Ávila, 1990.

———. *La reforma del Carmelo español: La visita canónica del General Rubeo y su encuentro con Santa Teresa (1566–1567)*. 2nd exp. ed. Ávila, Spain: Institución Gran Duque de Alba de la Diputación Provincial de Ávila, 1993.

Tapia, Serafín de. "La alfabetización de la población urbana castellana en el Siglo de Oro." *Historia de la Educación* 12–13 (1993–94), 275–307.

———. "El entorno morisco de san Juan de la Cruz en tierras castellanas." In *Aspectos históricos de San Juan de la Cruz*, edited by Teófanes Egido, 43–76. Ávila, Spain: Institución Gran Duque de Alba de la Diputación Provincial de Ávila, 1990.

———. "Estructura ocupacional de Ávila en el siglo XVI." In *El pasado histórico de Castilla y León*, 2:201–23. 3 vols. Burgos, Spain: Consejería de Cultura y Turismo de la Junta de Castilla y León, 1983.

———. "La sociedad abulense en el siglo XVI." In *Vivir en Ávila cuando Santa Teresa escribe el libro de su "Vida,"* edited by Rómulo Cuartas Lodoño and Francisco Javier Sancho Fermín, 69–133. Burgos, Spain: Editorial Monte Carmelo, 2011.

———. "Las primeras letras y el analfabetismo en Castilla. Siglo XVI." In *Historia*, edited by Teófanes Egido, 185–220. Vol. 2 of *Actas del*

Congreso Internaticional Sanjuanista. Valladolid, Spain: Consejería de Cultura y Turismo de la Junta de Castilla y León, 1993.

Tomé Martín, Pedro. *Los Hermanos de Teresa de Ávila en América*. Ávila, Spain: Institución Gran Duque de Alba de la Diputación Provincial de Ávila, 2015.

Ubarri, Miguel Norbert. *Jan Van Ruusbroec y Juan de la Cruz: la mística en diálogo*. Madrid: Editorial de Espiritualidad, 2007.

Vázquez de Prada, Valentín. "La economía castellana en la época de Santa Teresa." In *Congreso Internacional Teresiano (4–7 octubre, 1982)*, edited by Teófanes Egido et al., 229–46. Vol. 1. Salamanca, Spain: Universidad de Salamanca, 1983.

Velasco Bayón, Balbino. "Infancia y formación carmelitana de San Juan de la Cruz." In *Historia*, edited Teófanes Egido, 417–26. Vol. 2 of *Actas del Congreso Internaticional Sanjuanista*. Valladolid, Spain: Consejería de Cultura y Turismo de la Junta de Castilla y León, 1993.

———. *San Juan de la Cruz: A las raíces del hombre y del carmelita*. Madrid: Editorial de Espiritualidad, 2009.

Vigil, Mariló. *La vida de las mujeres en los siglos XVI y XVI*. Madrid: Siglo Veintiuno Editores, 1986.

Vizuete Mendoza, J. Carlos. "La prisión de San Juan de la Cruz: El convent del Carmen de Toledo en 1577 y 1578." In *Historia*, edited Teófanes Egido, 427–36. Vol. 2 of *Actas del Congreso Internaticional Sanjuanista*. Valladolid, Spain: Consejería de Cultura y Turismo de la Junta de Castilla y León, 1993.

Wilhelmsen, Elizabeth Christina. *San Juan de la Cruz y su identidad histórica: Los telos del León Yepesino*. Madrid: Fundación Universitaria Española, 2010.

INDEX

A

affective spirituality, 133–134
agriculture, economy and, 8, 51–52
Ahlgren, Gillian, 224, 225
Albert Avogadro, Patriarch of Jerusalem, 78
Albertine Rule, 78–79, 81
Albi, France, 86
Alcalá de Henares, Council of, 66
Alcaraz, Pedro Ruiz de, 160, 161, 162–163
Alonso de la Fuente, 166, 166n41, 221
Alumbrados ("enlightened ones"), 151–171
  beatas and, 152, 168–169, 170
  conversos as, 160, 160n23
  Edict of 1525, 130, 160–163, 161n25
  Edict of 1574, 164–165
  errors of, 129, 135, 137, 141, 156, 161
  Extremadura, 159, 163–166
  Franciscans and, 154–155, 154n7, 162
  general beliefs, 131, 154, 156–159, 157n12, 158n15, 162
  individual groups, 159–167
  Inquisition in Andalusia, 167, 201–202
  Inquisition at Toledo, 160–163, 203
  Inquisition's focus on, 151, 154n7, 170, 183–185, 209
  Inquisition's initial phase, 119, 130
  Inquisition's understanding of Alumbrado beliefs, 153, 154n7, 155, 158n15
  introduction, xix
  John of the Cross's influence on, 167
  shared roots, 154–156
  Toledo, 159, 160–163, 203
  as umbrella term, 152–153
  Upper Andalusia, 159, 167, 201
  women as, 151–152, 164, 167, 219
Alvarez, Catalina (John of the Cross's mother), 49, 50–51
America. *see* New World
Andalusia
  Alumbrados, 159, 167, 201
  beatas, 168
  Calced-Discalced disputes, 95–96, 205–206, 205n55
  Carmelite reform efforts, 88–89, 93, 94–96
  Castile comparisons, 4–5
  closure of Discalced houses, 96
  Inquisition, 167, 201–202

251

Andrés Martín, Melquíades
　on Alumbrados, 154n5, 158, 161n25, 162
　on Jewish and Muslim influences on Spanish mysticism, 126n22
　key characteristics of spirituality of sixteenth-century Spain, 128–137
　on number of spiritual writers in Spain, 126
　on unfolding of Spanish mysticism, 118–120, 118n5, 119n8, 123, 132
anti-Semitism, 175, 175n7, 176–177, 180
Antonio de Jesús, 80
Apogeo de la mística cristiana (Pacho), 118n6
apophatic tradition, 114, 116
Aquinas, Thomas, 60, 68, 69
Aragon
　Albigensian heresy, 175
　books from, 124
　Carmelite history, 87
　Carmelite reform efforts, 93
　as economic powerhouse, 5
　Jeronimites, 66
　Jewish population, 177
The Ascent of Mount Carmel (John of the Cross), 136
Ascent of Mount Sion (*Subida del Monte Sión*) (Laredo), 140, 140n51, 147
asceticism, 136, 140–141
Audet, Nicholas, 87, 88, 91, 93
Augustine, St., 123, 140, 145

Augustinians, 30, 31, 55, 66
austerity, 136–137
autos de fe, 164, 167, 190–191, 191n34
Avignon papacy, 60, 84
Ávila, 24–33. *see also* Monastery of the Incarnation
　Carmelite history, 88
　Church in, 29–32
　city walls, 3, 25
　economy, 26, 28–29
　history, 24–26
　introduction, xviii
　John of the Cross in, 24
　people, 26–28, 27n4
　reform efforts, 31–32
　Teresa in, 24, 25, 28, 32–33
　widows and their children, 52
　women's defense of, 218
Avogadro, Albert, 78

B

Baeza, 168, 209
Báñez, Domingo, 147, 198, 202–203
Barrón, Vicente, 124, 147
Beas, Carmel at, 203
beatas (lay women)
　Alumbrados and, 152, 168–169, 170
　defined, 71
　Guiomar de Ulloa, Doña as, 32, 200, 219
　Inquisition and, 72, 167, 201–204, 206
　John of the Cross and, 72, 167
　McGinn on, 218n5

reform of women's religious
orders and, 70–72
Teresa of Ávila and, 72, 218–219
beaterios, 71, 102–103, 168
Benedictines, 30, 66, 67, 132–133
Bernard of Clairvaux, 115, 116, 140, 146
Bernini, Gian Lorenzo, 166
Bible
   access to, 143
   Alumbrado use of, 158–159
   Castilian translations, 134
   Inquisition's ban on translations, 143, 185
   polyglot Bible, 64
   reading and meditation on, 134
   Teresa of Ávila's knowledge of, 143–144
Bilinkoff, Jodi, 30n8, 31
Black Death, 60, 65, 83–84, 177
"Black Legend," 174
Blázquez, Jimena, 25, 218
Bonaventure, St., 116, 140, 146
Book of Prayer and Meditation (*Libro de la oración y meditación*) (Luis de Granada), 132–133, 146
books
   Castilian language, literacy, and literature, 6, 12–15, 123, 126–127, 134
   censorship and indexes of books, Inquisition, 185–187
   Index of Forbidden Books, 64, 73, 119, 163, 185–187, 200
   John of the Cross's reading, 114–115, 118, 142
   spiritual antecedents of Teresa of Ávila and John of the Cross, 122–128
   Teresa of Ávila's reading, 13, 13n16, 117–118, 142–148
Boscán, Juan, 12
Bruno, St., 76

C

Calced
   conflict with Discalced, 90, 95–96, 205–206, 205n55
   John of the Cross's imprisonment in Toledo, 89–90
   purity of blood statutes, 41n8
   reform in Andalusia, 96–97
Camaldolese, 76
Carmel, Mount, 77, 78
Carlos V. *see* Charles V, Holy Roman Emperor
Carmelite Rule
   first mitigation (1247), 79–82, 79n8, 91–92, 101
   second mitigation (1432), 81, 83–85, 86, 101
Carmelites, 75–99. *see also* Calced; Discalced
   constitutions (1281), 82
   contemplation/outreach tensions, 80–81
   crossed jurisdictions, 89–97
   decline and mitigated rule of 1432, 83–85
   Elijah and, 77, 78, 81–82, 83
   first mitigation (1247), 79–82, 79n8, 91–92, 101
   first monks, 82–83

foundational vision, 83
identity, 81–82
introduction, xviii
Marian devotion, 78, 82, 83, 104
as mendicants, 80
monasteries in urban areas, 80
monastery in Ávila, 30
nuns, establishment of, 86–87, 102
origins, 76–77, 144
Philip's reform efforts, 94–95
purity of blood statutes, 41n8
reform efforts, 5, 67, 85–89, 91–96
reform goals, 75, 86
responsibility for needy, 53
ressourcement (back to the classics), ix
Rule of St. Albert, 78–79
second mitigation (1432), 81, 83–85, 86, 101
state of order, during time of Teresa of Ávila and John of the Cross, 87–89
transfer to Europe and the first mitigation, 79–82, 79n8
Carmelites (Smet), 90n26
Carro de dos vidas (Gómez), 127
Carthusians, 67, 76
Castile
  Andalusia comparisons, 4–5
  Carmelite history, 87–88
  Carmelite reform efforts, 87, 88–89, 93, 95
  castles and fortified cities, 3
  crossed jurisdictions of Carmelites, 95–96
  economy, 7, 10
  Franciscan reform, 66
  Jeronimites, 66
  Jewish population, 177
  name, 3
  "reconquest" (*Reconquista*), 3
  social hierarchy, 38–39
  in unified Spain, 5
Castilian language, literacy, and literature, 6, 12–15, 123, 126–127, 134
Castillo, Hernando del, 202
castle: interior "castle" in Teresa of Ávila's works, 25
Catalina de Cardona, 219
Catalonia, 93
Cátedra, María, 24n1
Catherine of Aragon, 5
"Catholic Kings," 61–62, 182
Cazalla, Agustín, 200
censorship and indexes of books
  Index of Forbidden Books, 64, 73, 119, 163, 185–187, 200
  Teresa of Ávila's books, 223
Century of Gold. *see* Spain, sixteenth century
Cepeda, Alonso Sánchez de (Teresa of Ávila's father)
  finances, 46
  first wife of, 28
  Inquisition and, 192n36
  Jewish heritage, 43
  literacy and, 13, 13n16
  number of children, 35
  social status, 39, 42, 42n11, 43–47, 193
  Teresa's education, 216

Cepeda, Francisco (Teresa of Ávila's uncle), 44–47, 192n36, 193
Cepeda, Inés de (Teresa of Ávila's grandmother), 45
Cepeda, Pedro (Teresa of Ávila's uncle), 44–47, 192n36, 193
Cepeda, Ruy (Teresa of Ávila's uncle), 44–47, 192n36, 193
Cerda, Luisa de la, 110
Chaide, Pedro de, 127
Charles I, King (Spain). *see* Charles V, Holy Roman Emperor
Charles V, Holy Roman Emperor, 5–6, 6n1, 25–26, 62, 122
Christian mysticism. *see* mysticism
Christocentric spirituality, 134–135, 159
Church, in Ávila, 29–32
Cisneros, Cardinal Francisco Jiménez de
    "Catholic Kings" and, 61–62
    promotion of mysticism, 117, 124
    promotion of publishing, 15, 64, 122–123, 124
    reform efforts, 15, 64, 88, 123
    University of Alcalá, founding of, 15, 64
Cisneros, García de, 127, 132
Clement VIII, Pope, 97
clergy
    Ávila population, 27, 27n4
    hierarchy within, 39
    number of, 27
    reform of, 62–63
    tax exemption, 10–11, 27, 39
cloth production, 8–9, 29

The Cloud of Unknowing (anonymous), 115–116, 117, 139
Columbus, Christopher, 2
communications. *see* language, literacy, and literature; letters and mail
Comuneros revolt, 25–26
concubinage, 62–63
Confessions (Augustine), 123, 145
confraternities, 53
The Constitutions (Teresa of Ávila), 61, 144, 146
Contemptus mundi. see The Imitation of Christ (Thomas à Kempis)
conventuals, 65
conversos
    Alumbradism and, 160, 160n23
    Inquisition, 175, 175n7, 176–180, 183–185, 188, 192
    Jewish practices, 177–178, 183
    literacy rate, 13
    separated from Jewish communities, 182
    suspicions concerning, 177–178
    Teresa of Ávila's family background, 34, 36, 43, 172, 192–193
Convivencia ("coexistence"), 176
Córdoba, 167, 201–203
Council of Alcalá de Henares, 66
Council of Lyons (1274), 79n7
Council of Trent
    catechesis concerns, 178
    cloister for nuns mandate, 110
    index of forbidden books, 187
    preaching mandate, 63
    reform mandate, 66, 90, 91, 92–93, 94

Critique (Teresa of Ávila), 196
Crusades, 76–77, 79

D

The Dark Night (John of the Cross), 136
Dávila de Ahumada, Doña Beatriz (Teresa's mother), 13n16, 216
Daza, Gaspar, 31–32
dejados ("abandoned ones"). *see* Alumbrados
De Mistica Theologia (Gerson), 117
descalzos, 65–66
detachment, 136
Devotio Moderna, 61, 132
Díaz, María. *see* Maridíaz
Dionysius the Areopagite, 114
Discalced
    closure of houses in Andalusia, 96
    conflict with Calced, 90, 95–96, 205–206, 205n55
    constitutions (1581), 18–19
    Discalced Congregation, 97
    Discalced Province, 97
    foundation myths, 37
    nuns as, 92
    Order of Discalced Carmelites, 97
    purity of blood statutes, 36, 41n8
    reform and, 67, 95–96, 100
    religious house for women in Ávila, 30
    walking as requirement for friars, 18–19
diseases, 28
Dobhan, Ulrich, 215n1

Dominicans
    conflicts with Franciscans, 130
    human rights and justice, 16
    influence on Teresa of Ávila, 147
    Inquisition and, 69, 175
    methodical mental prayer, 132–133
    monastery in Ávila, 25, 30
    number of, 67
    purity of blood statutes, 41n8
    reform, 68, 69
    reform of other orders, 94, 95, 96
    study of Aquinas, 68, 69
Duruelo, 63, 80

E

Eboli, princess of, 39, 201
Eckhart, Meister, 116, 124
economy
    anti-Semitism and, 176–177
    Ávila, 26, 28–29
    Black Death, 177
    inflow of precious metals and economic decline, 10–12
    John of the Cross's early years, 48–57
    Monastery of the Incarnation and, 108–111
    Teresa of Ávila's early years, 38–47
    wealth and bankruptcy, 6–9
Edict of 1525, 160–163, 161n25
Edict of 1574, 164–165
education and universities, 15–16, 64, 68, 122
Ejercitatorio de la vida espiritual (García de Cisneros), 127

Elijah (prophet), 77, 81–82, 83
epidemics, 28
Erasmus
  humanism, 6, 64, 122
  in Index of Forbidden Books, 185, 186
  view of women, 219
erotic spirituality, 164–165, 167, 169
escolásticos. see learned
espirituales. see spirituals
Eugenius IV, Pope, 85
Exercitatorio de la vida espiritual (The Practice of the Spiritual Life) (García de Cisneros), 132
external works, 135–136, 137
Extremadura, 159, 163–166, 208–209

F

Ferdinand, King
  Ávila palace, 25
  as "Catholic Kings," 61–62, 182
  church reform efforts, 61–62
  as Columbus's patron, 2
  expulsion or forced conversion of Jews, 40, 180–182
  Inquisition, 179
  marriage, 5, 61
  as protector of Jewish communities, 180
  unification of Spain, 5
Fernández, Pedro, 95
Flos sanctorum (Pedro de la Vega), 145n58
Flos Santorum (collections of lives of saints), 144
Fontiveros, 48

Fourth Lateran Council (1215), 78–79
Fourth Spiritual Alphabet (Osuna), 154n7
Francisca de los Apostoles, 203
Franciscans
  Alumbrados and, 154–155, 154n7, 162
  conflicts with Dominicans, 130
  Franciscan Conceptionists, 30
  humility, 227
  influence on Teresa of Ávila, 146–147, 227
  Inquisition, 162
  methodical mental prayer, 132
  monastery in Ávila, 30
  number of, 67
  prayer of recollection, 68, 69, 114, 119, 121, 139, 154–155
  purity of blood statutes, 41n8
  reform, 66, 68, 69, 121

G

García de Toledo, 131, 147
Gerson, Jean, 116, 117
gold, 2, 10
Golden Age. *see* Spain, sixteenth century
Gómez, García, 127
González, Doña Elvira, 103
Gotarrendura, 29
Granada, kingdom of, 2, 5
Granada, Luis de
  influence on Alumbrados of Extremadura, 164
  influences on, 124
  promotion of deep prayer, 69, 127

Teresa of Ávila's recommendation
of, 147
works by, 127, 132–133, 146
"grandees" (social class), 38–39
Gratian, Jerome
accused to Inquisition, 206–207
animosity toward, 205n55
Teresa of Ávila and Inquisition,
205, 206
Teresa of Ávila's Carmel in
Seville, 203
as visitator in Andalusia, 89,
96–97, 97n33
Great Crisis (1525–1560), 119–120
Great Schism, 60, 84
Gregory I (the Great), Pope, 140, 145
Gregory IX, Pope, 79
Gregory XIII, Pope, 96, 97
"ground" (*grunt* or *grund*) of soul,
135
Guigo II, 144
Guiomar de Ulloa, Doña, 32, 200,
219

H
hagiographic lives, 36–37
health and medicine, 28
Henry VIII, King (England), 5
hermit movement, 76–79
hidalgos (social class), 39, 43–47,
46n15
history of Ávila, 24–26
Holy Land: Crusades, 76–77
Holy Roman Empire: extent, 5–6
honor, social class, and poverty, 34–59
hagiographic lives, 36–37
introduction, xviii

John of the Cross's early years,
48–57
John of the Cross's family
background, 49–51
at Monastery of the Incarnation,
30, 42, 107–108
obsession with honor and
lineage, 40–47
pleito de hidalguía, 43–47
poverty in sixteenth-century
Spain, 11–12, 51–57
social hierarchy, 38–39, 42, 69,
107–108
Teresa of Ávila's criticism of, 34,
35, 41–42, 42n11
Teresa of Ávila's early years,
38–47
Honorius III, Pope, 79
Horeb, Mount, 77
Huerga, Alvaro
on Alonso de la Fuente, 166n41
on Alumbrados, 152n1, 153n3,
154n6, 159, 164–165
on Alumbrados' doctrine, 162
on relationship of *beatas* and
Alumbradism, 168
Hugh of Balma, 117, 127, 140
Hugh of St. Victor, 116, 140
humanism, 6, 64, 122
human will, 134
Hundred Years' War (1337–1453), 84

I
Ibañez, Pedro, 131, 147
Ignatius of Loyola, St.
battle wounds, 46
influences on, 132

The Spiritual Exercises, 127, 131, 148, 164, 203
The Imitation of Christ (Thomas à Kempis), 61, 146
Incarnation, Monastery of the. *see* Monastery of the Incarnation
Index of Forbidden Books, 64, 73, 119, 163, 185–187, 200
Innocent IV, Pope, 80
Inquisition, 172–212
   Alumbrados, beliefs of, 153, 154n7, 155, 158n15
   Alumbrados, focus on, 151, 154n7, 170, 183–185, 209
   Alumbrados, initial phase, 119, 130
   Alumbrados of Andalusia, 167, 201–202
   Alumbrados of Toledo, 160–163, 203
   beatas and, 72, 167, 201–204, 206
   Bible translations, ban on, 143, 185
   "Black Legend," 174
   censorship, 64, 73, 119, 163, 185–187, 200
   conversos 175, 175n7, 176–180, 183–185, 188, 192
   from *conversos* to Alumbrados and "Lutherans," 183–185
   deep prayer for the "masses" as dangerous, 129, 130
   doctrinal knowledge of accused, 63
   Dominicans and, 69, 175
   duration, 173
   executions, 183–184, 184n20, 189–191
   expulsion or forced baptism of Jews, 2, 180–183
   fear of, 193–194
   in general, 173–194
   headquarters in Santo Tomás monastery, Ávila, 25
   Index of Forbidden Books, 64, 73, 119, 163, 185–187, 200
   introduction, xix, 172–173
   Jews and, 43, 176–180, 188–189
   John of the Cross and, 209–210
   number of trials, 184n20
   origins, 174–175
   procedure, 187–193
   Protestants and, 73, 153, 184, 185
   punishment, 189–191, 192
   Teresa of Ávila, accused (1570s), 165, 167
   Teresa of Ávila, as person of interest, 172, 194–209
   Teresa of Ávila, Córdoba tribunal, 201–203
   Teresa of Ávila, Seville tribunal (first phase), 203–205
   Teresa of Ávila, Seville tribunal (second phase), 205–208
   Teresa of Ávila's attitude toward, 194–199
   Teresa of Ávila's encounters with, 147, 199–201
   Teresa of Ávila's grandfather and, 29, 43, 45, 47, 190, 191–193, 192n36, 199

Teresa of Ávila's *Life* and, 147,
    195–196, 195n44, 199, 200,
    201, 202, 204, 226
Teresa of Ávila's protection
    against, 70
Teresa of Ávila's works, posthumous inquiries concerning,
    208–209, 210, 220–221
at Toledo, 29, 47, 191–192,
    191n34, 203
torture, 189
women mystics and, 199–200,
    219
Institution of the First Monks (*Liber de institutione primorum monachorum*) (Ribot), 82–83, 144
interior "castle," 25, 137
The Interior Castle (Teresa of Ávila),
    122, 135
interiority, 135
interior prayer ("mental prayer"),
    131–133, 135
Isabel de la Cruz, 160–161
Isabella, Queen
    Ávila palace, 25
    as "Catholic Kings," 61–62, 182
    church reform efforts, 61–62
    as Columbus's patron, 2
    expulsion or forced conversion of
        Jews, 40, 180–182
    Inquisition, 179
    marriage, 5, 61
    as protector of Jewish communities, 180
    as strong, determined leader, 218
    unification of Spain, 5
Islamic forces. *see* Muslims

J

Jerome, St., 145
Jeronimites, 66, 67
Jerusalem, 77. *see also* Patriarch of Jerusalem
Jesuits
    founding, 12, 67
    humility, 227
    influence on Teresa of Ávila, 32,
        147–148, 227
    monastery in Ávila, 30
    purity of blood statutes, 41n8
    reform efforts, 31
    schools, 16, 56, 67
    spread through Spain, 67
Jews. *see also* conversos
    Convivencia ("coexistence"),
        176
    expulsion from Ávila, 27, 103
    expulsion or forced conversion
        of, 2, 4, 40, 180–183
    Inquisition, 43, 176–183,
        188–189
    population in Spain, 181
    protected by Spanish monarchs,
        179
    Spanish mysticism and, 125–126,
        126n22
    taxes, 181
John of Ávila
    as advocate for good religious
        education, 54n31, 63
    Alumbrados, 164, 201
    background, 31–32
    influence on Teresa of Ávila,
        31–32
    Inquisition and, 201

review of *Life* (Teresa of Ávila), 32, 63, 198
works by, 127
John of the Cross. *see also* spiritual antecedents
Alumbradism and, 167
in Ávila, 24
beatas and, 72, 167
beatification process, 210
birth and childhood, 48, 52, 54
Carmelite Order during time of, 87–89
Carthusians and, 76
Christocentric spirituality, 135
as confessor, 105
Discalced mission in Mexico, 3
as Doctor of the Church, xv
education, 12, 15, 16, 55, 56, 93
family background, 8, 9, 34–35, 36–37, 49–51, 209
father (*see* Yepes, Gonzalo de)
finding God within, 135
hagiographic life, 36–37
imprisonment in Toledo by Calced Carmelites, 89–90
Inquisition and, 203, 209–210
insistence on sound spiritual guidance, 170
introduction, xv
as John of St. Matthias, 93
letrados/espirituales and, 70, 130, 220
in Medina del Campo, 12, 16, 48–49, 54–56
methodical mental prayer, 133
ministry, 35, 41, 53, 57, 63, 80
mother (*see* Alvarez, Catalina)
mysticism, 113, 114–115, 118, 137, 148
nada teachings, 136
personal character, 81
poverty in sixteenth-century Spain, 51–57
poverty of his family, 53–54
reading, 114–115, 118, 142
reform efforts, 75, 89
religious influences on, 68, 83, 114–115, 155
religious poverty, embrace of, 35–36
as resident orderly in hospital for the poor, 55–56
short stature, 52
socioeconomic context of early years, 48–57
travel, 16–18
John of the Cross, works by
abbreviations for, xiv
Alumbradism and, 167
The Ascent of Mount Carmel, 136
bibliography of, xvin2
The Dark Night, 136
images and analogies in, 141–142
Inquisition's posthumous inquiries into, 210
letters, 19
poetry, 12, 123, 166
use of terms to avoid appearance of heresy, 163
journey, initiation of, 133
Journey to Carith (Rohrbach), 98
Juan, Prince, 25
Juana, Queen, 5–6

judeoconversos. see conversos
Julián de Ávila, 32
jurisdictional disputes, 89–97, 194

K
Kamen, Henry, 174, 182, 193, 194
Kavanugh, Kieran, 79n8, 98
Kempis, Thomas à, 61, 146
knowledge of God, 134, 137, 141

L
language, literacy, and literature. *see also* books
   Bible translations, 134
   Castilian language, 6, 12–15, 123, 126–127, 134
   letters and mail, 19–21
   literacy, 12–15
   vernacular translations, 64
Laredo, Bernardino de, 117, 127, 139, 140, 140n51, 147
Latin America. *see* New World
learned (*letrados/escolásticos*), 68–70, 129–131, 220
León, Luis de, 14, 127, 220–221
letrados. see learned
Letter 283 (Teresa of Ávila), 207
Letter 284 (Teresa of Ávila), 207
Letter 294 (Teresa of Ávila), 207
letters and mail, 19–21, 206, 207
Liber de institutione primorum monachorum (*Institution of the First Monks*) (Ribot), 82–83, 144
Libro de la oración y meditación (*Book of Prayer and Meditation*) (Luis de Granada), 132–133, 146

Life (Teresa of Ávila)
   influences on, 144, 147
   Inquisition and, 147, 195–196, 195n44, 199, 200, 201, 202, 204, 226
   John of Ávila's review of, 32, 63, 198
   Monastery of the Incarnation in, 93–94, 100
   priest-confessor in, 62
   self-references, 221
   Valdés Index in, 185, 200
   on women, 221–222
limpieza de sangre. see purity of blood
lineage, Spain's obsession with, 40–47
literature. *see* language, literacy, and literature
Llamas Martínez, Enrique, 205n55, 207n57, 209
Llerena. *see* Extremadura
Lonergan, Bernard, x
Lorenzo (Teresa of Ávila's brother)
   in Ecuador, 3
   financial realities, 46–47
   Teresa of Ávila's complaints to, 7
love, knowledge of God and, 134, 137
Ludolph the Carthusian (Ludolph of Saxony), 124, 143–144, 146
Luther, Martin, 186
"Lutherans," Inquisition and, 161, 183–185

M
Madrid, 21, 202
Magdalena de la Cruz, Clare, 199–200

mail. *see* letters and mail
Maldonado, Alonso, 2–3
Mantua, Italy, 86
Marcos, Juan Antonio, 228
María de Jesús, 219
María del Corro, 203–204
María de Olivares, 210
María de Santo Domingo, 199
Marian devotion, 78, 82, 83, 104
Maridíaz (María Díaz), 32, 218–219
Maroto, Daniel de Pablo, 42n11, 145, 146–147
McGinn, Bernard, 128n27, 138n46, 218n5
medicine, 28
Medina del Campo
  confraternities, 53
  hospitals, 56
  Inquisition, 200
  Jesuit school, 56
  John of the Cross in, 12, 16, 48–49, 54–56
  socioeconomics, 11, 48–49, 54
  as trading center, 17
  widows and their children, 52
meditation, 131–133
Mendoza, Alvaro de, 202
men's religious orders, reform of, 64–70
mental prayer, 131–133, 135
Mercedarians, 67, 94
metals, 2, 10–12
methodical mental prayer, 131–133
Mexico, Discalced mission, 3
misogyny, 215–221
missionary zeal, 2–3, 121

mitigation
  first mitigation (1247), 79–82, 79n8, 91–92, 101
  second mitigation (1432), 81, 83–85, 86, 101
monasteries
  in Ávila, 30
  Teresa of Ávila's founding of, 6–7, 11, 19, 42, 80, 137, 200
Monastery of St. Andrew, 87
Monastery of St. Joseph, Ávila, 100, 147
Monastery of the Incarnation, 100–112
  cells, 107
  characteristics, 71
  economy's impact on, 12, 108–111
  founding, 102–103
  funding, 106, 108
  habits, 107–108
  introduction, xviii
  in *Life* (Teresa de Ávila), 93–94, 100
  as little village in itself, 102–104
  Moralia in Job (Gregory I (the Great)), 145
  neither decadent nor scandalous, 93–94, 101, 111
  nuns, 93–94, 100–101, 103, 105–111
  Rubeo's visit, 93–94, 101, 102, 105, 107, 108–109, 111
  social hierarchy, 30, 42, 107–108
  spiritual and liturgical life, 104–107
  Teresa of Ávila as prioress, 105, 106–107, 108

visitors, 110–111
vows, 109
wealthy families, ties to, 30, 103–104, 106–110
monks, first Carmelite monks, 82–83
Moors, expulsion from Ávila, 27
Moralia in Job (Gregory I (the Great)), 145
Mujica, Bárbara, 226, 227, 229
Muslims
  in Ávila, 24–25, 27
  Convivencia ("coexistence"), 176
  Crusades and, 77
  defeat in Iberia (1492), 2, 3–4
  expulsion or forced conversion of, 27, 40
  influences on Spanish culture, 4
  "reconquest" (*Reconquista*), 3–4, 121, 181–182
  Spanish mysticism and, 125–126, 126n22
Mystical Theology (Pseudo-Dionysius), 114–115
Mystical Theology (*Sol de Contemplativos/ Viae Lugent Sion*) (Hugh of Balma), 117, 127, 140
mysticism
  antimystical spirit, 130
  books, 122–128
  Jewish and Muslim influences, 125–126, 126n22
  John of the Cross, 113, 114–115, 118, 137, 148
  Pseudo-Dionysius, 114–118
  Teresa of Ávila, 113, 116, 117–118, 146–148, 166

unfolding of Spanish mysticism, 118–120, 118n5, 119n8, 123, 132
unknowing-affective (deconstructive-affective) tradition, 114–116

N

nada (John of the Cross's teachings), 136
Navarre, kingdom of, 5, 46
Netanyahu, Benzion, 175n7
New World
  Alumbrados, 159
  cost to indigenous peoples, 3
  "discovery" and colonization of, 2
  mail service, 21
  missionaries to, 2–3
  precious metals from, 2, 10–12
  trade with Spain, 9
  "unified" Spain and, 4–6
Nuestra Señora de Gracia, Ávila, 30, 31, 145, 210, 216

O

"observants"
  defined, 64
  personal prayer, 68–69
  reform efforts, 65, 66–67, 101
  spirituality, 119
Order of Discalced Carmelites. *see* Discalced
Ormaneto, Nicolas, 96, 97
Orozco, Alonso de, 127
Osuna, Francisco de
  Alumbrados and, 154n7

Fourth Spiritual Alphabet, 154n7
   influences on, 117, 117n3, 124
   on knowledge of God, 117
   on learned/spirituals tension, 129
   prayer of recollection, 127, 140
   Teresa of Ávila's reading of, 101, 114, 117, 139, 146–147
   Third Spiritual Alphabet, 140, 146–147

P

Pacho, Eulogio, 118, 118n6, 126n22
Palma, Bernabé de, 127, 140, 147
Palma, Luis de, 127
Pantoja, Hernando de, 207
Patriarch of Jerusalem, 78, 82
Paul, St., 220, 220n8
Peers, E. Allison, 126, 128n27
Pérez, Joseph, 42n11, 184n20, 208
"perfection," 133, 158
Peter of Alcántara, 146, 224
Philip II, King
   ban on Spanish students from studying in foreign universities, 186
   conflicts with Rubeo, 97
   Council of Trent's cloister for nuns mandate, 110
   Inquisition and, 73
   Protestants and, 73
   religious reform efforts, 67, 90–92, 94–97
   report on Castilian cities, 26–27
plagues, 28, 60, 65, 83–84, 177

pleito de hidalguía, 43–47
Portugal
   expulsion of Jews, 183
   Jeronimites, 66
postal service. *see* letters and mail
poverty
   in Ávila, 28
   changing views of, 52–53
   in John of the Cross's background, 34–37
   longevity and, 35
   schools for poor children, 54–55
   sixteenth-century Spain, 11–12, 51–57
   in Teresa of Ávila's monasteries, 137
The Practice of the Spiritual Life (*Exercitatorio de la vida espiritual*) (García de Cisneros), 132
prayer
   affective spirituality, 133–134
   contemporary centering prayer practice, 139
   "democratizing" of serious prayer, 129, 154–155, 162–163
   images and analogies, 141–142
   interior prayer ("mental prayer"), 131–133, 135
   methodical mental prayer, 131–133
   misogyny, 217
   personal prayer, 68–69
   requiring quiet and solitude, 136
prayer of recollection
   active recollection, 138–139
   Franciscans, 68, 69, 114, 119, 121, 139, 154–155

passive recollection, 138
promotion of, 138–142
as spiritual antecedent of Teresa of Ávila and John of the Cross, 114, 119, 138–142
Teresa of Ávila and, 68, 138–139, 140n51, 147, 217, 222–223
women and, 217
preaching, 63, 134
precious metals, 2, 10–12
priests, reform efforts aimed at, 62–63
printing press, 14, 64
prostitution, 55
Protestant Reformation, 72–73, 119–120
Protestants, Inquisition and, 73, 153, 184, 185
Pseudo-Dionysius, 114–118, 114n1, 140, 147
publishing. *see* books; language, literacy, and literature
purity of blood (*pureza de sangre*), 36, 40–41, 41n8, 177

Q
quiet and solitude, 136
quietism, 161, 162
Quiroga, Gaspar de, 198, 201, 204

R
Rawlings, Helen, 194
recolectos, 65–66
"reconquest" (*Reconquista*), 3–4, 121, 181–182
reformation. *see* Protestant Reformation

reform of the Church and religious orders, 60–74
Ávila, 31–32
beatas and, 70–72
books, 123
Carmelite efforts, 5, 67, 75, 85–89, 91–96
"Catholic Kings" and Cardinal Cisneros, 61–62
characteristics, 67
clergy reform, 62–63
goals, 75, 101–102
introduction, xviii
jurisdictional conflicts, 90–91
men's orders, 64–70
Philip II's efforts, 67, 90–92, 94–97
Protestant Reformation and, 72–73
universities and the renewal of learning, 64
women's orders, 70–72
religious education, 54n31, 63, 178
religious orders. *see also specific orders*
decline due to Black Death, 65, 83–84
purity of blood statutes, 36, 40–41, 41n8, 177
reform, xviii, 60–74
suppression, 79n7
tax exemption, 39
Renaissance humanism, 122
Ribadeneyra, Pedro de, 127
Ribot, Philip, 82–83, 144
road conditions, 16–19, 20–21
Robles, Bernardo, 106–107
Rohrbach, Peter-Thomas, 79n8, 98

Rome
  censorship, 187
  Inquisition, 175
Romuald, St., 76
Rubeo (Giovanni Battista Rossi)
  appointment of Tostado, 97
  conflicts with King Philip, 97
  correspondence with Teresa of Ávila, 21
  Monastery of the Incarnation visit, 93–94, 101, 102, 105, 107, 108–109, 111
  reform efforts, 88–89, 91–96, 101
Rule of 1247. *see* Carmelite Rule
Rule of St. Albert, 78–79, 81

S
St. Joseph, Ávila, 100, 147
Salamanca, 12, 93–94, 123
Salcedo, Francisco de, 31–32, 196
Sánchez, Juan (Teresa of Ávila's paternal grandfather)
  Inquisition, 29, 43, 45, 47, 190, 191–193, 192n36, 199
  Jewish heritage, 43, 191
  marriage, 45
  pleito de hidalguía, 45n14
San José, Ávila, 26, 30, 32
San Pablo de la Moraleja, 88
Santa María de Gracia, Ávila, 30, 31, 145, 210, 216
Un santo para una ciudad (Cátedra), 24n1
Santo Tomás monastery, Ávila, 25
Savonarola, Girolamo, 124
Scholasticism, 69

schools of doctrine, 54–55
Sega, Philip, 97
self-flagellation, 105
self-knowledge, 135, 141, 227–228
Selke, Angela, 160n23
sensual pseudo-mysticism, 164–165, 167, 169
Seville
  Alumbrados, 159
  clergy reform efforts, 62–63
  Inquisition, 203–208
  mail service, 21
  printing press, 122
  Protestants in, 73, 185
  trade, 17
sexual behaviors
  Inquisition's concerns, 206
  spirituality and, 164–165, 167, 169
Siglo de Oro (Century of Gold). *see* Spain, sixteenth century
silver, 2, 10
simplicity, 136–137
Sinai, Mount, 77
sixteenth-century Spain. *see* Spain, sixteenth century
Sixtus IV, Pope, 173
Sixtus V, Pope, 97
Smet, Joachim, 85, 90n26, 97n33
social hierarchy. *see* honor, social class, and poverty
socioeconomics. *see also* poverty
  hierarchical society, 38–39
  honor and lineage, 40–47
  John of the Cross's early years, 48–57
  pleito de hidalguía, 43–47

Teresa of Ávila's early years, 38–47
Sol de Contemplativos (*Viae Lugent Sion/Mystical Theology*) (Hugh of Balma), 117, 127, 140
solitude, 136
Song of Songs, 164
Soreth, John, 86–87, 88
Soto y Salazar, Francisco de, 198
soul, 135, 141
South America. *see* New World
Spain, sixteenth century, 1–23
   1492, 2–4, 180
   Castilian language, literacy, and literature, 12–15
   economy, 6–12
   education and universities, 15–16
   expulsion or forced conversion of Jews, 2, 4, 40, 180–183
   hierarchical society, 38–39
   inflow of precious metals and economic decline, 10–12
   international outlook, 121–122
   introduction, xviii
   letters and mail, 19–21
   misogyny, 215–221
   obsession with honor and lineage, 40–47
   poverty, 51–57
   Protestant Reformation and, 72–73
   Teresa of Ávila as woman of, 213–232
   traveling and road conditions, 16–19
   world trade, 4–6

Spanish Inquisition. *see* Inquisition
spiritual antecedents of Teresa of Ávila and John of the Cross, 113–150
   books, 122–128
   convergence of elements, 121–122
   general characteristics, 128–138
   introduction, xviii–xix
   "prayer of recollection" promotion, 138–142
   Pseudo-Dionysius, 114–118
   Spanish mysticism, 118–120, 123
   Teresa of Ávila's reading, 142–148
The Spiritual Exercises (Ignatius of Loyola), 127, 131, 148, 164, 203
spirituality
   affective spirituality, 133–134
   Christocentric, 134–135
spirituals (*espirituales*), 68, 69, 129–131, 220
Spiritual Testimony 53 (Teresa of Ávila), 205
Spiritual Testimony 58 (Teresa of Ávila), 205
Subida del Monte Sión (*Ascent of Mount Sion*) (Laredo), 140, 140n51, 147

T

Tapia, Serafín de, 27n4
taxes
   burden on middle class and poor, 10–11
   exemption for clergy, 10–11, 27

exemption for nobility, 10–11, 27, 39, 44, 45
from Jewish sources, 181
Teología mística (*Sol de Contemplativos/ Viae Lugent Sion*) (Hugh of Balma), 117, 127, 140
Teresa of Ávila. *see also* spiritual antecedents of Teresa of Ávila and John of the Cross
Albertine Rule and, 71
Augustine and, 145
in Augustinian monastery of women, 55, 145
in Ávila, 24, 25, 28, 32–33
beatas and, 72, 218–219
beatification and canonization, 147, 217–218
birthplace, 29
books read by, 83, 123, 142–148
Christocentric spirituality, 134
Communion, 104–105
confessor, 124, 147
contemplation/outreach tensions, 80–81
critics of, 219–220
decision to enter monastery, 145
devotion, 61
as Doctor of the Church, xv
Dominicans and, 124, 147, 202–203
education, 30, 31, 216
family background, as *conversos*, 34, 36, 43, 172, 192–193
family background, noble status, 11, 34, 36
family background, wealth, 6–7, 8, 28, 29, 34

father (*see* Cepeda, Alonso Sánchez de)
as feminist, 229
financial acumen, 7, 216
founding Carmel at Beas, 203
founding monasteries, 6–7, 11, 19, 42, 80, 137, 200
Franciscan influence on, 146–147, 227
Gratian and, 206–207
hagiographic life, 36–37
health, 145
hierarchical society and, 38–39
Index of Forbidden Books and, 163
Inquisition and, posthumous inquiries concerning Teresa's works, 208–209, 210, 220–221
Inquisition and, Seville tribunal (first phase), 203–205
Inquisition and, Seville tribunal (second phase), 205–208
Inquisition and, Teresa accused (1570s), 165, 167
Inquisition and, Teresa as person of interest, 172, 194–209
Inquisition and, Teresa's attitude toward, 194–199
Inquisition and, Teresa's encounters with, 147, 199–201
Inquisition and, Teresa's *Life*, 147, 195–196, 195n44, 199, 200, 201, 202, 204, 226
Inquisition and, Teresa's protection against, 70
insistence on sound spiritual guidance, 170

introduction, xv
Jesuits and, 16, 31–32, 147–148, 227
John of Ávila as influence on, 31–32
knowledge of biblical stories, 143–144
Laredo as influence on, 139, 140n51
"learned men" as influence on, 169–170, 220
letrados/espirituales and, 70, 130–131
literacy, 13–15
misogyny and, 215–221
missionary work and, 2–3
mitigated rule (1247) and, 71, 91–92, 101–102
mitigated rule (1432) and, 85
at Monastery of the Incarnation, 30, 100–108, 110, 111
mother of, 13n16, 216
mystical texts, reading of, 117–118, 146–148
mysticism, 113, 116, 148, 166
on necessary virtues, 136
observants, 101
opposition experienced by, 138
Osuna as influence on, 101, 114, 117, 139, 146–147
paternal grandfather (*see* Sánchez, Juan)
personal character, 41, 81, 227–228
on Philip II's reform efforts, 67
pleito de hidalguía, 43–47
prayer, deep prayer and, 129, 131

prayer, teachings on, 133
prayer of recollection, 68, 138–139, 140n51, 147, 217, 222–223
Protestants and, 72–73
purity of blood concerns, opposition to, 177
reading, 13, 13n16, 117–118, 142–148
reform efforts, 71, 72–73, 75, 89, 91–92, 100–102, 111
religious poverty, embrace of, 35–36
social expectations, criticism of, 34, 35, 41–42, 42n11
socioeconomic context of early years, 38–47
Spain's obsession with honor and lineage, 40–47
"spirituals"/"learned" tensions, 70, 130–131
state of Carmelite Order during time of, 87–89
statue of, 166
supporters, 197–198, 202–203, 204, 220–221
teachings, 42, 133, 137, 220n8
theological formation, 155
travel, 16–19
view of women, response to, 221–224
as woman of sixteenth-century Spain, 213–232
Teresa of Ávila, works by. *see also Life*
abbreviations for, xiii–xiv
bibliography of, xvin2
Calced-Discalced conflict in, 90

on Carmelite friars at Duruelo, 80
censorship of, 223
The Constitutions, 61, 144, 146
Critique, 196
on humility, 227
images and analogies in, 141–142
Inquisition and, 194–199, 195n44, 208–209, 210
The Interior Castle, 122, 135
interior "castle" in, 25
letters, 19, 20–21, 207, 226
posthumous inquiries concerning, 208–209, 210, 220–221
posthumous publication, 166, 166n41
rhetorical strategy, 214, 222, 224–229
self-knowledge in, 227–228
Spiritual Testimony 53, 205
Spiritual Testimony 58, 205
use of terms to avoid appearance of heresy, 163
vernacular language, 123
water images in, 26
The Way of Perfection, 133, 218, 222–223, 227
women in, 221–224
writing style, 13–14, 123, 224–225, 226, 228
Teresa of Jesus. *see* Teresa of Ávila
textile industry. *see* cloth production
Third Spiritual Alphabet (Osuna), 140, 146–147
Thomas à Kempis, 61, 146
Thomas Aquinas, St., 60, 68, 69

Toledo
Alumbrados, 159, 160–163, 203
Carmelite history, 88
Edict of 1525, 160–163
Inquisition, 29, 47, 191–192, 191n34, 203
John of the Cross's imprisonment, 89–90
poverty ordinances, 12
Teresa of Ávila's effort to found monastery, 42
Tostado, Jerome, 97
traveling and road conditions, 16–19, 20–21
Trent. *see* Council of Trent
Trinitarians, 67, 94
Tyler, Peter, 114, 114n1, 115, 116, 128n29

U

union with God, 157–159, 162, 164, 165
universal call to holiness, 129
universities, 15–16, 64, 68, 122
University of Alcalá, 15–16, 64
University of Salamanca, 15–16, 87
Upper Andalusia, Alumbrados in, 159, 167
urbanization, 8–9

V

Valdés Index. *see* Index of Forbidden Books
Valladolid
Benedictine reform, 66
government archives, 43
Inquisition, 200, 202

mail service, 21
poverty ordinances, 12
printing press, 123
Protestants in, 73, 185
widows and their children, 52
Vargas, Francisco, 95–96
Vega, Garcilaso de la, 12
Vega, Pedro de la, 145n58
Viae Lugent Sion (*Sol de Contemplativos/ Mystical Theology*) (Hugh of Balma), 117, 127, 140
Via spiritus (Bernabé de Palma), 140
Victorines, 116
Vita Christi (Ludolph the Carthusian), 143–144, 146

W

The Way of Perfection (Teresa of Ávila), 133, 218, 222–223, 227
Weber, Alison, 224, 225
women, sixteenth-century Spain, 213–232. *see also* beatas
  as Alumbrados, 151–152, 164, 167, 219
  Inquisition and, 199–200, 219
  introduction, xix
  low esteem of, 30
  misogyny and, 215–221
  Teresa of Ávila's response to views of, 221–224
  Teresa of Ávila's rhetorical strategy, 224–229
women's religious orders
  Carmelite nuns, 86–87, 102
  as centers for noble women, 70
  contemplation/outreach tensions, 80–81
  houses in Ávila, 30, 31
  reasons for entering, 65, 70, 103–104
  reform of, 70–72
wool industry, 8, 29

Y

Yepes, Francisco de (John of the Cross's brother), 50, 54, 57
Yepes, Gonzalo de (John of the Cross's father), 49, 50–51
Yepes, John de. *see* John of the Cross
Yepes, Luis de (John of the Cross's brother), 52

Other Books by Mark O'Keefe, O.S.B.

*Virtues Abounding: St. Thomas Aquinas
on the Cardinal and Related Virtues for Today*
Cascade Books, 2019

*The Way of Transformation: Saint Teresa of Avila
on the Foundation and Fruit of Prayer*
ICS Publications, 2016

Love Awakened by Love: The Liberating Ascent of Saint John of the Cross
ICS Publications, 2014

Deciding to Be Christian: A Daily Commitment
Liguori, 2012

Priestly Wisdom: Insights from St. Benedict
Abbey Press, 2004

Priestly Prayer: Reflections on Prayer in the Life of the Priest
Abbey Press, 2002

Priestly Virtues: Reflections on the Moral Virtues in the Life of the Priest
Abbey Press, 2000

*The Ordination of a Priest: Reflections on the Priesthood
in the Rite of Ordination*
Abbey Press, 1999

In Persona Christi: Reflections on Priestly Identity and Holiness
Abbey Press, 1998

*Becoming Good, Becoming Holy:
On the Relationship of Christian Ethics and Spirituality*
Paulist Press, 1995; St. Pauls/India, 1997; St. Pauls/Philippines, 1997

What Are They Saying About Social Sin?
Paulist Press, 1990

About Us

ICS Publications, based in Washington, D.C., is the publishing house of the Institute of Carmelite Studies (ICS) and a ministry of the Discalced Carmelite Friars of the Washington Province (U.S.A.). The Institute of Carmelite Studies promotes research and publication in the field of Carmelite spirituality, especially about Carmelite saints and related topics. Its members are friars of the Washington Province.

Discalced Carmelites are a worldwide Roman Catholic religious order comprised of friars, nuns, and laity—men and women who are heirs to the teaching and way of life of Teresa of Ávila and John of the Cross, dedicated to contemplation and to ministry in the church and the world.

Information about their way of life is available through local diocesan vocation offices, or from the Discalced Carmelite Friars vocation directors at the following addresses:

Washington Province:
1525 Carmel Road, Hubertus, WI 53033

California-Arizona Province:
P.O. Box 3420, San Jose, CA 95156

Oklahoma Province:
5151 Marylake Drive, Little Rock, AR 72206

Visit our websites at:

www.icspublications.org and *http://ocdfriarsvocation.org*